Religion and Modernization in Southeast Asia

Religion and Modernization in Southeast Asia

FRED R. VON DER MEHDEN

SYRACUSE UNIVERSITY PRESS   1986

The paper used in this publication meets the minimum requirements of American National Standard for Information Sciences—Permanence of Paper for Printed Library Materials, ANSI Z39.48–1984. ∞

Library of Congress Cataloging-in-Publication Data

Von der Mehden, Fred R.
Religion and modernization in Southeast Asia.

Bibliography: p.
Includes index.
1. Asia, Southeastern—Religion. 2. Technology—
Religious aspects. 3. Economic development—Religious
aspects. 4. Religion and civilization. I. Title.
BL2050.V66   1986   306'.6'0959   86-3709
ISBN 0-8156-2360-7 (alk. paper)
ISBN 0-8156-2361-5 (pbk. : alk. paper)

Manufactured in the United States of America

To Jennifer Lee
The New Generation

Fred R. von der Mehden was born and educated in California. His first academic post was at the University of Wisconsin-Madison where he was professor of political science and chairman of East Asian Studies. Since 1968 he has been Albert Thomas Professor of Political Science at Rice University, where he is also editor of Rice University Press. The author has studied Southeast Asia since the late 1940s and lived in most of the countries covered in this book. During those years he has been an advisor to Southeast Asian and United States agencies involved in economic and social development programs, lectured throughout the region on development, politics, and religion and written widely on those subjects. Books he has written closely related to this volume include *Religion and Nationalism in Southeast Asia* and *Southeast Asia 1930–1970*.

Preface

This volume is a result of efforts to understand the nature of the interrelationship of religion and modernization in Southeast Asia in the light of the theoretical assumptions presented by postwar social scientists. Thus, whereas religion in that region has acted both as an inhibitor and agent of change, the social science literature spoke primarily to the negative role of religion in modernization. There has also been a resurgence of Islam and Buddhism in countries such as Malaysia and Thailand although we were told that modernization almost inevitably leads to secularism. In fact, the very complexity of the process of change defies most efforts to formulate over-arching theories that integrate religion and modernization. Rather, it demands well-defined concepts within which we can compare across varying political and religious cultures. Southeast Asia provides an excellent laboratory in which to make such comparisons, given the sizable representation of all the major world religions within an environment going through obvious political and technological change.

This book reflects many years of research and travel in Southeast Asia and, as such, owes its existence to a multitude of individuals both in that region and the United States. In Southeast Asia there have simply been too many people who have given of themselves to expand my understanding of their cultures to mention any single one. In the United States I am particularly grateful to the libraries at Stanford, the University of California at Berkeley, and Cornell for the use of their facilities and to Rice University for providing me the time and funds for my research. At Rice I wish to acknowledge the help of John Ambler in reading parts of the manuscript and to Margaret Greenwood and Alice Olson for their patience in typing the original and revisions of most of the chapters. Special thanks go to my wife, Audrey, for having to listen to my at-times inchoate efforts to put this book together.

Houston, Texas   FRvᴅM
Fall 1985

Contents

LIST OF TABLES

FIGURE

Religion and Modernization in Southeast Asia

1

Religion and Modernization

During the first decades after World War II, social scientists experienced the heady rise of interest in concepts of change in the Third World, only to be followed in recent years by a waning of enthusiasm. Through the 1950s and 1960s, an increasing number of scholars wrestled with issues of modernization, Westernization, political development, and their differences and permutations as they sought to formulate conceptual frameworks to explain the character of the changes they perceived to be taking place in Afro-Asia and Latin America. While some scholars are still concerned with these issues, those who remain intrigued with the Third World tend to concentrate their efforts on more narrow empirical analyses.

This decline in interest in broader conceptual questions may be attributed to a variety of factors including difficulties in operationalizing many of the concepts, a lack of consensus on definitions, the very complexity of the development process, and a general disengagement from our previous fascination with broad gauge theory. What follows is not intended to be a review, critical analysis, or new presentation of development theory as a whole. Rather, it seeks to critically analyze one aspect of that often rich literature, that dealing with the relationship of religion to modernization. It is the contention here that the often simplistic and data-free treatment of this issue encapsulated many of the deficiencies of modernization theory.

Ideas developed in this book were conceived over thirty years of studying Southeast Asia in terms of the role of religion and ideology in a changing environment. They came from a certain sense of frustration and dissatisfaction with models of modernization and development formulated by social scientists that did not appear to correspond to realities unfolding in the field. Both the interrelationship of religion to modernization and the people involved in the process were far more complex than they were portrayed to be in much of the academic literature. These earlier analyses have led to this attempt to assess the kinds of conceptual frameworks that have been proposed and then to consider their usefulness in explaining processes of change in Southeast Asia.

The first part of this volume analyzes efforts to treat the place of religion in the modernization process. Rather than reviewing the wide range of literature on modernization and development, it concentrates on how social scientists have assessed the role of religion in a limited delineation of what we characterize as the major elements of modernization. In order to understand how various models arose, this section also addresses the impact of the intellectual climate of the period on scholars of development. This is done by analyzing both influences on contemporary social scientists and the manner in which earlier European and American academics, missionaries, journalists, civil servants, and travelers dealt with the relationship of religion and modernization. In order to illustrate the latter, the way in which religion and modernization were described in pre-World War II Southeast Asia is reviewed.

The second major part of this volume is an in-depth analysis of the complex nature of the impact of the various religions of Southeast Asia on the modernization process. Concentrating on Burma. Thailand, Malaysia, Indonesia, and the Philippines, an attempt is made to break down the concepts of both religion and modernization in order to delineate more clearly the relationship between the two.

MEANINGS OF MODERNIZATION

The term "modernization" has been employed in a wide range of fields and contexts, from art to politics and agriculture to religion.[1] Questions dealing with modernity, change, and development have been considered over the centuries by the West's intellectual elite including Aristotle, Kant, Rousseau, Weber, Condorcet, Bacon, Fontenelle, Voltaire, Durkheim, Hegel, Marx, and others.[2] Even when confined to the concepts of modernization as formulated by twentieth century social scientists dealing with the Third World, the myriad of definitions and theories can boggle the mind. During the last three decades alone, many of the brightest minds in the discipline have attempted to contend with meanings of modernization, Westernization, and development including G. Almond, D. Apter, L. Binder, C. Black, J. Coleman, S. Eisenstadt, A. Diamant, K. Deutsch, S. Huntington, A. W. Ilchman, A. Inkeles, J. LaPalombara, D. Lerner, D. McClelland, T. Parsons, W. Rostow, D. Rustow, E. Shils, and many, many others.[3]

Modernization, as differentiated from other aspects of change theory, has been variously defined by social scientists. Lerner first wrote in his influential book, *The Passing of Traditional Society*, that concomitants to modernization were empathy, urbanization, media and political participation, and literacy.[4] A decade later, in a 1968 article on "Modernization" in the *International Encyclopedia of the Social Sciences*, he defined his topic as "the social change whereby less developed societies acquire characteristics common to more developed societies."[5] Marion Levy analyzed the concept in more technological terms stating: "The greater the ratio of inanimate to animate sources of power and the greater the multiplication of effort as the effect of application of tools, the greater the degree of modernization."[6] Both D. Rustow and C. Black saw modernization as the process by which man has become able to control nature, in part through his use of modern technology.[7] J. Scarritt followed in the same vein, but added the impact of technological change, writing in 1972, "We shall use the terms "modernization" to refer to the general social consequences of the adoption of advanced technology." [8] Z. Suda, following Rustow's paradigm, with adjustments, saw economic growth (in most cases industrialization) as an essential element in modernization along with the institutionalization of morality.[9] McClelland, Inkeles, and Smith sought to assess the attributes of individual modernity.[10] Meanwhile, most anthropologists found these efforts, and particularly the tendency to dichotomize tradition and modernity, to be outside their intellectual repertoire.[11]

Political development, which over time became intertwined with the concept of modernization, suffered from an even greater lack of consensus. When L. Pye delineated ten different definitions of political development,[12] D. Rustow commented that this was "obviously at least nine too many"[13] and S. Huntington argued that "if there are ten definitions of political development, there are ten too many, and the concept is, in all likelihood, superfluous and dysfunctional."[14] Among these varying meanings were J. Coleman's view that political development is an "open-ended increase in the capacity of political man to initiate and institutionalize new structures, and supporting cultures, to cope with or resolve problems, to absorb and adapt to continuous change, and to strive purposively and creatively for the attainment of new social goals."[15] G. Almond and G. Powell defined political development as "the increased differentiation and specialization of political structures and the increased secularization of political culture."[16] A. Diamant called political development "a process by which a political system acquires an increased capacity to sustain successful and continuously new types of goals and demands and the creation of new types of organizations."[17] S. Huntington's strong support for the role of institutions can be found in his definition. "Political development involves the creation of political institutions sufficiently adaptable, complex, autonomous, and coherent to absorb and order the participation of these new groups and to promote social and economic change in the society."[18] Some scholars, numerous jounalists, and the general public in the United States have appeared to define political development as the achievement of liberal democracy while, hardly less simplistically, Marxists have conceptualized the process through the dialectic. Finally, D. Rustow and R. Ward have provided a list of characteristics that include many of the attributes covered by other authors:

1. a highly differentiated and functionally specific system of governmental organization;

2. a high degree of integration within this governmental structure;

3. the prevalence of rational and secular procedures for the making of political decisions;

4. the large volume, wide range, and high efficiency of its political and administrative decisions;

5. a widespread and effective sense of popular identification with the history, territory, and national identity of the state;

6. widespread popular interest and involvement in the political system, though not necessarily in the decision-making aspects thereof;

7. the allocation of political roles by achievement rather than ascription; and

8. judicial and regulatory techniques based upon a predominately secular and impersonal system of law.[19]

It would be possible to enter into an extensive disquisition on the strengths and weaknesses of positions that we have only briefly noted. However, not only has this been done well by previous authors,[20] but for our needs we seek to address only two tasks: to summarize the degree of consensus that has appeared regarding modernization, and then to turn our attention more specifically to how the relationship between religion and modernization has been perceived by contemporary social scientists.

Two useful efforts to seek order within the seeming chaos of definitions have been made by Lerner and by J. Bill and R. Hardgrave. In his article on "modernization" Lerner saw general agreement on five indicators of modernization: (1) self-sustaining economic growth, (2) political participation, (3) the diffusion of secular norms, (4) a high degree of geographical and social mobility, and (5) personality transformation.[21] For their part, Bill and Hardgrave view modernization as part of the increasing control of his environment by man and see the literature assessing this process along three dimensions: technological, organizational, and attitudinal. They define these as: "The technological dimension involves preeminently industrialization and embodies the contrast between pre-industrial and industrial societies. The organizational dimension reflects the degree of differentiation and specialization and embodies the contrast between simple and complex societies. The attitudinal dimension is that of rationality and secularization and contrasts the scientific versus the religious-magical perspective."[22] In a later section, we will return to aspects of these definitions in an effort to establish the basis for analyzing the interrelationships between religion and modernization.

RELIGION AND MODERNIZATION

Within the wide ranging literature that encompasses modernization, not all authors considered religion in their analyses. Economists and political scientists in particular have given scant attention to the subject. However, the general tendency among American social scientists assessing the process of modernization in the Third World has been to view religion as a negative factor. This has obviously not been a universal judgment as evidenced by the works of Weber and those who have argued that the Weberian thesis regarding Protestantism and the rise of capitalism could be projected into other societies.[23] However, contemporary social scientists have tended to see religion as an obstacle to the achievement of modernization, or its decline as a necessary attribute to that process.

There is a long heritage of viewing non-Western religions as hindrances to progress. To Comte, Spencer, Marx and other intellectual giants of the nineteenth century, religion in general was the problem, while to many in academia, the Christian church, and the general public, "progress" was being retarded by "backward" and "superstitious" faiths such as Islam, Buddhism, and Hinduism.[24] In the next chapter we will review some of these sectarian stereotypes as they were employed to describe Southeast Asia, while Chapter three through eight will analyze in detail the accuracy of postwar observations by social scientists regarding the impact of religion on modernization. At this point, five contemporary accusations made against religion in the Third World are briefly described:

1. The general tenets of Hinduism, Buddhism, and Islam hinder modernization by instilling concepts such as "otherworldliness" or "fatalism" within their adherents. These attitudes weaken the resolve of the population to strive and innovate. Other tenets perceived as fundamental to these religions under attack have been caste in India, usury in Islam, and the role of merit in Theravada Buddhism.

2. The practices that have developed over the centuries divert the faithful from more productive endeavors. For example, feasts, religious ceremonies, gifts to temples, churches, and sectarian organizations or their personnel, and the purchase of religious artifacts are taken from limited expendable income that could be better used for education, housing, or new tools of production.

3. Religious personnel are at best not economically useful members of the community and at worst serious obstacles to change. In the first instance, Marxists in particular have charged Buddhist monks, Catholic priests, and local Muslim religious leaders as being parasites who not only do not perform useful productive labor but receive from the faithful their surplus income or even funds necessary for their livelihood. Second, the clergy are charged with being conservative and traditional, in many cases based upon their fear of loss of their own status or wealth.

4. Religion is a divisive force in society. Deep-rooted religious convictions, reinforced by sectarian leadership, have been seen as contributing to intolerance and political instability. National integration, social mobility, and communications and collective action have been viewed as impeded by communal differences over religion, race, language, and the like.

5. Religion is part of a pattern of attitudes and practices that compose traditional society. In this dichotomized view of the world, traditionalism is perceived as clearly distinct and in opposition to modernity. Often using ideal models, religion is placed alongside other economic, social, cultural, political, attitudinal, and behavioral elements that oppose the challenge of modernity.[25]

These criticisms were summed up by P. Hauser, in a 1959 article in which he reviewed the religiocultural system of Hinduism, Islam, and Buddhism in South and Southeast Asia.

The ingredients of the value systems are in apparent conflict with the new national aspirations for economic advancement. For example, some of the cultural elements which appear to be in conflict with technological development and the attainment of higher levels of living are: the emphasis on spritual rather than material values; the stress laid on the importance of after-life or future existences, as compared with the present existence; the pressure of conformance with, and often intolerance with deviations from, traditional patterns of thought and action; the relatively rigid definitions of roles of members of the family, the village, and the social order at large; the parochialism of the diverse racial, ethnic, linguistic, and territorial groups; the familistic orientation; the tendency to place savings in traditional channels of investments, including non-productive invest-ments like jewels and the relatively large amounts of life-space and energy to traditional cultural and religious rituals, ceremonies, and festivals.

The traditional value systems do not provide the population with incentive for material gain or expectations of advancement based on merit and application. The prestige vocations and occupations tend to be those in government, religion, and agriculture—not the types of occupations identified with economic development. That is, occupations in commerce, industry, and many of the professions and the services have yet to achieve prestige and attract competent people. Moreover, the traditional value systems do not provide the person with general orientation of the type necessary in a monetary, as distinguished from a subsistence, economy, including conceptions of work as a segmental area of activity requiring fixed time, place, and an employer-employee nexus.[26]

A somewhat factually inaccurate Marxist interpretation from the Soviet Youth organ, Komsomolskaya Pravda, went along similar lines:

"One of the most harmful and persistent survivals is religion. It justifies the capitalist order of things, instills into the faithful the feeling of fatality, passivity, and submission to fate, and attempts to bolster up primitive superstition about the development of nature and society. . . . The Buddhist religion divides people into castes of pariahs (the lowest) and Brahmins (the highest)."[27]

The second major theme in the modernization literature grows naturally from these criticisms, although the relationship has been rarely articulated. These aforementioned attributes can be defined as examples of irrational behavior. "Otherworldliness," dependence on the scriptures for guidance, unproductive religious expenditures and personnel, religious intolerance, and so forth are not in the model of the modern scientific man. Progress would mean an end to such dangers to man. In J. B. Bury's famous hymn to progress, he ended the last chapter with: "Looking back on the course of the inquiry, we note how the history of the idea has been connected with the growth of modern science, with the growth of rationalism, and the struggle for political and religious liberty. . . . There began a slow but steady reinstatement of the Kingdom of this world. The otherworldly dreams of theologians *ceux qui renaient la terre pour patrie* which had ruled so long lost their power, and men's earthly home again insinuated itself into their affections, but with new hope of its becoming a place fit for reasonable beings to live in."[28]

The newer social scientists spoke of modernization, rather than progress, although both were fraught with too often unspoken values. To many of these contemporary writers, modernization included, among their essential attributes, an increase in rationalism and secularism.

There is some confusion, or at least inconsistency, as to what is meant by these two concepts. Certainly, if one reviews the leading discussions outside contemporary modernization literature, the task of definition becomes enormous and complex. Thus, D. Apter summed up one aspect of the sociological work on secular norms as follows:

> At its broadest, development is the process by which secular norms of conduct are universalized. These secular norms can be thought of in terms of the distinctions introduced by Maine (between status and contract); Durkheim (between mechanical and organic solidarity; sacred and secular beliefs); Weber (between instrumental and consummatory ends; traditional and legal-rational authority); and Tönnies (between *Gemeinshaft* and *Gesellschaft*). They have been elaborated by Parsons in his pattern variables and by Levy in his analytical structures of aspects of relationships (both of which have

been modified by Moore by his corrective emphasis on the dynamic properties exhibited by social systems at all stages of the developmental process).[29]

For his part L. Shiner has provided six religious concepts of secularization:

> 1) The previously accepted symbols, doctrines and situations lose their prestige and influence; 2) The religious group or religiously informed society turns its attention from the supernatural and becomes more and more interested in "this world"; 3) Society separates itself from the religious understanding which has previously informed it in order to constitute itself an autonomous reality and consequently to limit religion to the sphere of private life; 4) Knowledge, patterns of behavior, and institutional arrangements which were once understood as grounded in divine power are transformed into phenomena of purely human creation and responsibility; 5) The world is gradually deprived of its sacral character as man and nature become the object of rational causal explanation and manipulation; and 6) The culmination of secularization would be a society in which all decisions are based on rational and utilitarian considerations and there is a complete acceptance of change.[30]

Of course, the religious and philosophical literature on rationalism is equally comples, and we do not intend concentrating on either of these two concepts. Rather, the more general view of secularism and rationalism in the post-war modernization field will be presented. However, even this is not as clear as would be desired, given a lack of consensus and often insufficient explanation in employing these concepts. To oversimplify a somewhat turgid topic, we find social scientists dealing with modernization using rationalism and secularism in four broad ways: (1) simple reference to the terms with little or no further explanation; (2) secularism as a decline in religion in its various phases; (3) rationalism; and (4) rationalism and secularism clearly interconnected.

Simple References

In many cases there is simply the statement that rationalism and/or secularism are part of the pattern of modernization. There is little further explanation, although by implication or reference, the conceptual foundation of the employment of these terms may be noted. Thus, Rustow and

Ward listed among other characteristics of political development, "The prevalence of rational and secular procedures for making political decisions"[31]; Lerner included within his indicators of modernization, "a diffusion of secular-rational norms in the culture understood approximately in Weberian-Parsonian terms"[32]; and G. Almond and J. Coleman argued in their *Politics of the Developing Areas* that wherever the modernization process has had its impact, it has culminated in secularization.[33]

These terms, or their equivalents, have also been used by those formulating dichotomized models, such as Palmer, Parsons, and Macridis. For example, R. Macridis and B. Brown divide traditional from modern societies as follows:

> *Traditional* societies are characterized by: subsistence economies; face-to-face social structures in which the family predominates; cultural systems that emphasize heredity, devotion and mystery; and a highly personalized political system that is virtually an extension of the joint family.

> *Modern* societies are the exact opposite in all these respects. They are characterized by industrialized economies; complex and impersonal social structures; a culture that emphasizes the values of science, knowledge and achievement; and a highly bureaucratized political system legitimized through rational processes, like elections.[34]

Secularism as a Decline in Religion

Simpler and clearer has been the presentation of modernization as resulting in the decline in religion in its various aspects. It is argued that the course of modernization, accompanied by urbanization, social mobility, secular education, and industrialization, will ultimately lead to a weakening of religion, magic, and superstition.[35] Some view development as a natural and desirable part of "progress," while others consider the change inevitable, but not necessarily a clear good. For example, C. Black stated that "It has destroyed traditional patterns of life which through the centuries had evolved many humane values" and undermined age-old principles often leading to a glorification of the transitory.[36]

However, a significant number of religious writers, such as S. Snouck Hurgronje and R. Bellah have held that while modernization may have changed religion, it remains an important element of the new societies. Thus, S. Snouck Hurgronje asserted that every major religion has found it necessary to change if it was to continue.[37] In an early article, R. Bellah made the same point: "In conclusion, it seems worthwhile to stress that the process of secularization, which is part of what the transition from prescriptive to principial society is, does not mean that religion disappears. The function of religion in a principial society is different from that in a prescriptive society, but it is not necessarily less important. Moreover, in the very process of transition religion may appear in many new guises. Perhaps what makes the situation so unclear is its very fluidity."[38]

Rationalism

In the literature on modernization, rationalism has also come to be defined in a variety of ways. It has been employed in the bureaucracy literature to refer to modern means of organization and decision making, reflecting Weberian influences. Others have considered the term in a means-ends schema to characterize what is considered to be planned, goal-oriented action. Thus, one author on modernization theory quoted approvingly a working definition used in an effort to establish a "rationality index" among North Carolina farmers; "Rationality involves the use of deliberation, planning, and the best available sources of information and advice in arriving at decisions as a means of achieving maximum economic ends."[39] Generally, writers on modernization have considered rationality in terms of goal-oriented behavior, the use of human reason, a belief in science, pragmatic reasoning, and utilitarianism as against dependence on scriptures, magic, and traditional forms of legitimization based upon ascriptive, familistic, and "prescientific" considerations.

The Interconnection of Rationalism and Religion

Not all observers of rationalism and modernization related the concept to secularism and many that did were not wont to further amplify the connection. Some simply contended that the advance of rationalism meant a decline in religion or increase in secularism. Thus, Lerner could approvingly quote the Islamicist G. von Grunebaum's assertion that "Whether from East or West, modernization poses the same basic challenge in the infusion of 'a rationalist and positivist spirit' against which scholars seem agreed, Islam is absolutely defenseless."[40]

More detailed in his acceptance of the impact of rationalism on religion is A. Desai, who wrote that "the rational attitude is the core process of modernization" and that logically following rationalization is secularization. He sees the end result as a nonacceptance of anything on faith, and under logical scrutiny, the formation of a change-oriented rather than a change-resistant society.[41] To most secular-oriented social scientists of the period, modernization appeared to be a logical, evolutionary process from traditional, religiously based foundations of reasoning to a modern, more scientific, and "rational" way of making decisions.

In sum, then, modernization literature, particularly in the 1950s and 1960s, pictured a decline in religious values, attitudes and practices, and legitimacy as modernization proceeded in its inevitable forward progress. With this would come a weakening of the traditional, irrational, unscientific, or prescientific attitudes and behavior that had permeated premodern society and the acceptance of "modern" foundations of reasoning. While many authors failed to provide extensive explanations for their presentations, the general pattern of expectations and descriptions fit an evolutionary developmental model patterned after what was perceived to be the character of the predominantly secular Western world. In the process, what was implicitly or explicitly condemned was the picture painted of the religious environment of Asia by Weber in his *The Sociology of Religion:*

> ...for the various popular religions of Asia, in contrast to ascetic Protestantism, the world remained a great enchanted garden in which the practical way to orient oneself or to find security in this world or the next, was to revere or coerce spirits and seek salvation through ritualistic, idolatrous, or sacramental procedures. No path led from the magical religiosity of the non–intellectual classes of Asia to a rational methodical control of life. Nor did any path lead to that methodical control from the world-accommodation of Confucianism, from the world-rejection of Buddhism, from the world-conquest of Islam, or from the messianic expectations and economic pariah law of Judaism.[42]

We shall return to these issues in a later section.

A better understanding of the negative views of contemporary social scientists toward the role of religion in the modernization process may be found in seeking to assess some of the less obvious reasons for their analyses. Certainly their own investigation of the available data was of paramount importance, but there were also elements in the intellectual climate of the day that were conducive to the judgments that were made.

A viewpoint that will run through much of this volume is that problems of conceptualization, tendencies to oversimplify, and gaps in analysis have often resulted from insufficient empirical research, the intellectual environment in which the investigator has worked, and a paucity of relevant data. What follows is not a general indictment of the field of modernization, nor of the seminal literature which preceded it. It is more a cautionary note which suggests reasons why so much of the conceptual literature written about modernization has not met the test of time.

The high point of the modernization and development field in the United States lasted about two decades from the early 1950s to the early 1970s. It began with the social sciences accepting most of R. Nisbet's premises regarding social evolution: that change is natural, directional, imminent, continuous, necessary, and proceeds from uniform causes, and that "one could categorize non-Western peoples as not simply exotic or difficult but as reflecting lower stages of an evolutionary advancement that was thought to be universal."[43] This picture changed over the years as the process of development was found to be more complex, but the portrayal of religion as at the very least not conducive to modernization continued to be far less challenged in the general conceptual literature than it was in particularistic empirical studies. Several factors pertaining to the social sciences themselves were in part responsible.

"ACADEMIC SCHOLASTICISM"

Modernization literature has long been plagued by an amazingly high level of what might be termed "academic scholasticism"—theory and analysis written in the studies of professors in Europe and America without the benefit of actual research in that field. European sociologists who were to produce much of the seminal literature in this area such as Weber and Durkheim were but the first of a long line of scholars in their profession who eschewed efforts to verify their theories in the field.

If we survey the most influential post–World War II social scientists formulating the conceptual paradigms in the area of modernization and development, we again find a surprisingly high percentage of scholars who had not completed any extensive research in the Third World prior to their major contributions. In fact, the general pattern was initial scholarship in another subject; an intensification of interest during the height of the social science's fascination with the Third World; and then a turning away from modernization topics as general interest in such issues waned. For many, these questions appeared to be only a momentary side-track in their overall professional careers.

Examples abound. G. Almond was known for his work in American foreign policy and the appeals of communism in Italy prior to the publication in 1960 of his groundbreaking edited book, *Politics of the Developing Areas*.[44] He later was to list as his first interest contemporary political systems of Europe. K. Deutsch's article, "Social Mobilization and Political Development"[45] is much quoted, yet his early work was on social communications and he later declared his principal fields to be contemporary political systems of Western Europe and international relations. S. Huntington's *Political Order in Changing Societies*, was much acclaimed after its initial publication in 1968,[46] but his previous books were on United States military and defense issues, and by the 1970s he had turned to other questions such as political participation. J. LaPalombara's original scholarship centered on Italian politics, ideology, and general comparative politics. After his edited books on bureaucracy, political parties, and political development in developing nations, he returned to his earlier interests.[47] D. Lerner, perhaps best known for his *The Passing of Traditional Society*, and later author of the article on social modernization in the *International Encyclopedia of the Social Sciences*,[48] had earlier written on psychological warfare, elites, and political symbols. A. Organski's *Stages of Political Development*, published in 1965,[49] had been preceded by books on population and world politics and followed by a primary interest in the contemporary politics of Western Europe. S. Verba, who with L. Pye edited *Political Culture and Political Development*[50] in 1965, earlier made his reputation in the fields of political behavior and political culture and later wrote little on the Third World. S. Eisenstadt's *From Generation to Generation*, on age groups and social structure, was followed by several influential books on various aspects of modernization.[51] He later turned more to other questions dealing with political sociology and social stratification.

Obviously, there were also social scientists who combined strong first-hand training and field experience in the Third World with interest in conceptual issues in modernization and political development. These included D. Rustow, L. Pye, D. Apter, E. Shils, J. Coleman, and M. Weiner. However, it is somewhat frustrating to find many of their conceptual contributions to the general modernization literature, such as those by Pye and Shils, so data-free and lacking in concrete illustrations from the authors' experience in the field.

Finally, with the exception of Almond, all of the aforementioned authors, and the bulk of the American social scientists involved in the study of modernization in the Third World, received their doctorates in the decade or so after 1947–48. This was the era of great expectations in the social sciences regarding the direction of change taking place throughout the world. There was the overriding belief that the developing world would become more and more like the modern world of the West, which was perceived to be increasingly industrial, democratic and secular. Social evolution, although discounted by many sociologists and anthropologists in the prewar period, remained the sometimes unstated and often openly articulated basis to understanding what was taking place in the Third World. It was not only the Marxists who saw the inevitability of change and with it the secularization of society.[52]

Second, as will be illustrated in the next chapter, much of the literature on the Third World available to these scholars presented a stereotyped, often inaccurate picture of indigenous religions and their adherents, portraying both as obstacles to "progress." Without experience in the field themselves, many social scientists had to depend on this faulty foundation. At any rate, Afro-Asia tended to be a terra incognita to American social scientists, and Latin America was perceived to be the domain of an unholy alliance of the church, military, and landowners which was hindering democracy and progress. Thus, their perceptions of the real world, as substantiated by much of what they read and what little they saw, was one which reinforced the negative view of religion.

A third intellectual current of the period was the strong influence of earlier prominent sociologists such as Weber and Durkheim. These men offered tantalizing insights and hypotheses that have become almost de rigueur in any conceptual analysis of the relation of religion and modernization. However, we also need to recognize difficulties in employing these seminal works when assessing many parts of the Third World. First, it is a long jump from Durkheim's study of primitive societies[53] or Weber's work of factors leading to the independent rise of capitalism in Western Europe [54] to the transitional systems of Afro-Asia in the twentieth century. If nothing else, the greatly increased diffusion of ideas and economic interdependence of our world have made the interaction between religion and political, economic, and social action far more complex. Second, the authors of these works did not analyze the impact of either Islam or Theravada Buddhism, the faiths of over a billion Afro-Asians, in any detail. Weber's monumental work did not assess these religions thoroughly, and it was only in the postwar years that men like R. Bellah, M. Rodinson, and R. Bocock turned to ask similar questions as did Weber, but with different answers. Third, much of this early conceptual work was being written just as much was changing in Afro-Asia, and the comments made regarding these conditions often did not note these developments, perhaps in part due to the author's need to depend on secondary literature. For example, as T. O. Ling commented:

> From the point of view of Weber's verdict on India the unkindest twist of fate was that in 1911, the first really notable large scale example of all-Indian industrial capitalism, the Tata Iron & Steel Company, began production. . . . The capital needed for the construction of the plant was £1¾ million. A prospectus was issued by Tata in August 1907. Nationalist fervour was at its height and the leaders of the movement were urging all Indians to join in and support the Swadeshi movement—to support Indian-owned production of every kind, and to boycott British goods. The result was that from early morning till late at night the Tata offices in Bombay were beseiged by an eager crowd of native investors, old and young. . . . at the end of three weeks, the entire capital for the construction requirement was secured, every penny contributed by some 8,000 Indians. The construction of the plant was begun in 1909. In 1911, when Weber was writing his Hinduismus and Buddhismus, the first iron was being produced by an Indian company.[55]

Finally, contemporary Islam, Buddhism, and Christianity in Afro-Asia are complex syncretic belief systems that vary over time and space. In these environments differences in indigenous beliefs and practices need to be considered when assessing the interaction of religion and modernization. The most striking illustration of this that runs against earlier conceptions can be found in immigrant Hindu, Muslim, and Confucian communities that have become the dominant capitalist elements in many Afro-Asian polities.

SECULARISM AND THE SOCIAL SCIENCES

Weber once commented that he and other social scientists had little "ear" for religion in terms of being believers in the organized faiths of the day. Certainly early influential writers such as Weber, Marx, and Comte were either ambivalent or antagonistic toward religion although

Weber, Durkheim, Simmel, and others saw its great importance in understanding the political, economic, and social process. It remains true that the academy in general and social sciences in particular have existed in a contemporary environment of religious skepticism. Thus, B. Loomer in his paper "Religion and the Mind of the University,"[56] noted that one element of the faculty sees religion as a positive threat to its most precious rights. "For these people religion is not only the opiate of the people, but it is also the great barrier to creative and independent intellectual effort." K. Boulding commented that, "Many social scientists, indeed, are refugees from the Sunday School and are personally quite hostile or at least ambivalent towards organized religions.":[57] R. Bellah wrote in his "Between Religion and Social Sciences" that "it is notable that the best minds in social science by the third decade of the twentieth century were deeply alienated from the Western religious tradition."[58] There is actually some empirical data to lend credence to these generalizations. A survey in 1913–14 and again in 1933 found that distinguished professors in both the social and natural sciences were much more irreligious than their less eminent colleagues.[59] Only 2 percent of high ranking psychologists expressed belief in God and only 5 percent of the most eminent sociologists had similar views. In Europe, where Marxism has tended to be considerably more influential in the social sciences than in the United States, intellectual secularism has remained strong in spite of recent challenges.

Of course, this leaves open the question as to whether personal values have affected scholarly pursuits. Certainly, spokesmen for the believers have been skeptical about the ability of nonbelievers to fully understand their faiths. For example, in the late 1960s, a high percentage of Protestant ministers agreed with the statement, "It is impossible for the sociologist to fully comprehend the meaning and significance of religion unless he himself is a member of the faith."[60] This position has been constantly reiterated by Islamic, Buddhist, and Hindu writers against Western commentators, in general, and it would appear that at least one group of sociologists gave some support to these conditions. In 1964 a poll of sociologists found 73 percent of them agreeing with the statement, "Most sociologists pay lip service to the idea of being value free in their work and are not value free."[61] Given the general environment of the scholar's profession, department, and university, it is at least legitimate to ask if it did not influence his assessment of religion and modernization.

THE PERCEIVED WORLD

Again, it should be underscored that this was an era in which "progress" and modernization were viewed as inevitable and positive forces for good. Modernization not only meant technological change, but a continuation of the march toward democracy and equity. In this process, religion was perceived to be both an obstacle to be overcome and a movement in decline.

As will be illustrated in the next chapter, a considerable body of literature pictured religion as a negative force in the non-Western world. It was viewed as tradition bound, an obstacle to innovation, divisive, and a handmaiden to ignorance. When the social scientist looked about him, he also perceived examples of where modernization including democracy went along with secularization (and one of the aforementioned surveys found that a lack of religious belief was accompanied with liberalism). In Turkey the efforts of Attaturk to modernize and democratize his country contained a campaign of secularization, and revolutionary Mexico appeared to display a similar process. As well, many of the postwar popular nationalists originally articulated support for a secular, democratic, and technologically advanced state, such as Nehru, Sukarno, Castro, and Kenyatta. In contrast, seemingly more traditional religiously oriented leaders were less admired in the West such as Jinnah of Pakistan, Arab nationalists in the Middle East, and conservative elements of the Catholic hierarchy in Latin America.

In the West there also seemed to be a decline in support for various aspects of religious belief and practice. Both in Western Europe and the United States, the first half of the twentieth century was perceived as a steady triumph of secularism. For the Marxists, the Soviet Union, with its militant antireligious stance, was the wave of the future. Thus, looking about him, the scholar saw primarily a reaffirmation of his personal and professional values. It would be unfair to criticize the early post–World War II writers on modernization for not fully understanding events and attitudes which had been given little notice in the literature or had only begun to evolve. The active prewar religious nationalist movement of Afro-Asia had been downplayed by the colonial powers and largely ignored by their scholars. These religionationalist leaders had been characterized as "fanatics" or "traditionalists" when many sought technological and social change within a religious context. As well, few were prescient enough to foresee the dramatic resurgence of Islam, the rise of Protestant fundamentalism in the United States, or the activities of liberal Catholic clergy in the Philippines and Latin America. But these were not part of the perceived world of the 1950s and 1960s.

2

The Inheritance

"There is no such thing as an Oriental mind. It is only an excuse for Occidental dullness."—H. Fielding Hall

Perhaps part of the reason for later misinterpretations of the relation between religion and modernization was the intellectual and popular environment that existed in the pre–World War II era. In this chapter we will be concentrating upon Southeast Asia in order to delineate the host of factors that conspired to enhance popular and academic ignorance and stereotypes. It is the author's contention that the development of modernization theory arose within an environment dominated by intellectual ignorance, often biased reporting, and popular attitudes which were reinforced by the media.

THE AMERICAN ENVIRONMENT

Edward Said, in his provocative book, *Orientalism*, raised the spectre of intellectual bias regarding the Oriental world in general and Islam in particular.[1] He vigorously propounded the view that observers helped to fashion a pattern of inaccurate perceptions of the world they were purportedly explaining. When it comes to Southeast Asia, it is important to underscore the lacunae of knowledge among American social scientists, combined with often biased interpretations of the region. Thus the early postwar formateurs of much of the conceptual bases for models of religion and modernization had to depend upon often suspect secondary sources with comparatively little reinforcement by knowledgeable colleagues.

Let us first explore the American academic and popular environment prior to analyzing pre–World War II literature on Southeast Asia.

Fundamentally, Southeast Asia was an intellectual backwater to the vast majority of the general public, as well as to social scientists during the prewar years. Harold Isaacs, in his often illuminating book on our knowledge of Asia, properly titled *Scratches on Our Minds*, noted a 1942 Gallup poll that found that 60 percent of a national sample of Americans could not locate Japan and China on a map, and followed with the comment that "vagueness about Asia has been until now the natural condition even of the educated American."[2] His own survey of 181 members of the American elite in 1954 found that "much of what turned up was actually familiar, but as old furniture is familiar, inconstant use but unnoticed—stereotyped notions, unexamined generalizations, and, in some cases, hitherto unacknowledged or unspoken prejudices."[3] Certainly if our knowledge of Japan and China were "scratches on our minds," prewar views of Southeast Asia were even more superficial.

The United States had only one colony in the region, the Philippines, and the majority of academic activity dealing with Southeast Asia centered on that area. In fact two-thirds of the dissertations in American universities dealing with the anthropology, religion, sociology, history, geography, and politics of Southeast Asia prior to 1950 dealt with the Philippines. Comparatively little was done elsewhere. D. and B. Sardesai, in their *Theses and Dissertations on Southeast Asia*,[4] list some 200 items, of which only 73 were dissertations written prior to 1950 in the aforementioned disciplines. Prior to 1948 they list only one Ph.D. taken at an American institution in political science on a topic dealing with Burma, Indonesia, Indochina, Malaysia, Singapore, or Thailand.

Of course, this meant that postwar specialists at first found it difficult to obtain formal training in the area. As late as 1962, a survey of ninety Southeast Asian specialists found that less than two-thirds had taken a formal course on a Southeast Asian subject.[5] For those over forty years of age the percentage dropped below 50 percent and for those over sixty to 22.2 percent. It was not until the late 1950s that the major area programs dealing with Southeast Asia really began to develop.

Nor were we very much illuminated by literature and the media. We were certainly ignorant of early indigenous literary efforts such as those of Ahmad bin Abdul Rashid, Malaysia's first novelist, former Burmese Prime Minister U Nu's early works, Thailand's first novel, *Yellow Race, White Race,* by Prince Akat Damkoeng, or the writings of Indonesia's Marah Rusli.[6] Even if Americans had read more broadly, they would have found that much of the local literature of this period which was available in translation was derivative or of such quality that U Nu could comment that he was "ashamed to have other people judge Burmese literature by these trashy works."[7] There were magnificent exceptions, translated into English, but little read, such as J. Rizal's *Noli Me Tangere* and *El Filibusterismo*, that would have given real insight into local values and problems, if they had been widely read in the West.

Novels by Europeans were usually either untranslated, thus reaching a very small American audience, or dealt with European problems in a colonial setting. Thus, few Americans would have read works by two of Holland's finest colonial products, William Walraven or Edgar Du Perron, while the works of men such as Somerset Maugham and Joseph Conrad only employed their tropical setting as backdrops for more universal questions.[8] There were exceptions such as George Orwell, whose *Burmese Days* provides a wonderful picture of the interplay of colonial and local forces.

Nonfictional periodical literature was not particularly illuminating either. A perusal of the *Reader's Guide to Periodical Literature* from 1925 to the outbreak of World War II in June 1939 shows a total of some 250 articles on Burma, Malaya, the Netherlands Indies, and Thailand (Siam). The majority of these dealt with travel (with considerable representation of Bali and other exotica), international issues, and missionary activities (primarily from the *Missionary Review*). In the last four years prior to the war about 40 percent of all articles came from one journal, *Asia*. In general this literature tended to be superficial and light in content.

As for the motion pictures, we were almost overwhelmed by stereotypes. One had the choice of Gary Cooper saving the grateful Filipinos from the fanatical Moros, intrepid explorers in the jungles of Borneo, a variety of travel films, or Hope and Crosby on the "Road to Bali." If our picture of the Southeast Asian was one of a somewhat backward, perhaps dangerous, certainly exotic, and fanatical individual living in an indolent tropical atmosphere, the media helped to foster that view. However, as we will now see, this was a stereotype heavily reinforced by nineteenth and twentieth century observers of the region.

EARLY OBSERVATIONS

Those who were to inform us of the complexities of Southeast Asia through books, articles, journals, and lectures were generally from four groups: government officials, journalists and travelers, missionaries, and academics. Some of our first glimpses of the region came from official missions to the royal courts of Burma, Thailand, and what is now Vietnam.[9] Often spending extensive periods of time in the country, they presented us with lengthy descriptions of life in the court and capital. Later other resident government officials were to add their observations. Some were attached to independent entities as advisors, such as J. G. D. Campbell[10] and H. Warrington Smyth[11] in Thailand. Others were attached elsewhere and wrote of their visits to other colonies, as did Sir John Bowring, former Governor of Hong Kong, after his visit to the Philippines in the 1850s[12] and Sinibaldo de Mas, sent by the Spanish government to report on its Eastern colonies.[13] However, the most experienced and prolific writers were generally the colonial administrators themselves, ranging from Singapore's founder, Stamford Raffles,[14] Sir Frank Swettenham,[15] Governor of the Straits Colony and High Commissioner of the Federated Malay States, Governor General J. Siberg of the Dutch East Indies,[16] and early American administrators such as Senior Justice on the Philippine Supreme Court, G. A. Malcolm,[17] and D. C. Worcester,[18] to more recent commentators such as J. S. Furnivall,[19] George Orwell,[20] and H. Van Mook.[21] Their work varied from careful descriptions of flora and fauna or administrative rules to apologias for their own policies. As we shall see, often such descriptions were either guises for policy positions or reflections of unconscious bias.

The second group of observers were journalists and travelers. Their products ranged from the detailed and often extremely perceptive writings of resident journalists to the emotionally patriotic pieces of American reporters during the "Philippine Insurrection," and rather picturesque travel books and articles. Without the language or training, these journalistic and travelers' tales tended toward the superficial. Early journalists in particular were likely to have biases that they brought with them from the field. This was exemplified by the work of J. M. Brown[20] on the Dutch East Indies, which he employed as a vehicle for his views on colonial policy, and the post–Spanish-American war reports of American correspondents who were writing to suport their home papers' positions on annexation. The height of this kind of journalism came during World War II when nationalist movements that cooperated with Japan received less than objective reporting. As to the typical travel book, only rarely did it provide useful insights into the political and social values and problems of the indigenous population.

Third, there were the almost ubiquitous missionaries. American missionary groups were to be found in the Philippines, East Indies, Thailand, and Burma, and with their counterparts in China, they were a major prewar window to Asia. The strong evangelical strains of

Protestantism during this period, combined with the necessity of missionary tours of the United States to obtain funds for their overseas activities, had a considerable impact on those who were to be our political and academic leaders in the postwar years. Thus, Isaac's survey of members of the American elite showed the strong and permanent impact of these returning missionaries.

> Visiting missionaries back from China appeared quite frequently to tell about their work, ministers and Sunday school teachers spurred their flocks week after week to help in the cause. Pennies, nickles, dimes and dollars, heaping into the millions, were folded carefully into envelopes or dropped into collection plates or baskets by children and adults week in and week out, year after year. Here is where young minds were scratched most meaningfully and most permanently.
>
> There was impressive evidence of this among the panel's 137 Protestants and 13 Catholics. When they were asked to recall their earliest associations connected with Asia, 123 of these individuals quickly mentioned "missionaries"—missionaries seen or heard or heard about, mission committees that would meet in their homes, mission publications on the table in the parlor, an essential part of the good Christian life, in support of which, from the earliest years, they yielded up weekly their cherished coins.[23]

A further product of the missionary experience has been the number of scholars of Southeast Asia who either had missionary backgrounds or were the children of missionaries including John Cady, Lucian Pye, and Kenneth Landon.

The missionary obviously had a closer relationship to the local population than other members of the European-American population. It was a necessity to learn the language and personal contact was essential. This did not prevent early missionaries from holding highly prejudicial views of the native and his religion. Later they were to become involved in local religiopolitical issues, often in support of their converts against the nationalist movements of Burma, Indochina, and Indonesia.

Finally, there was the increasing number of academics concentrating on Southeast Asia. There had long been an interest in the region among botanists, zoologists, and other members of the "hard" sciences, but their counterparts in the social sciences were far rarer. Historians and anthropologists were the first, with the economists, sociologists, and political scientists coming later. Many of these academics were attached in one way or another to the various colonial governments. With the coming of World War II, the American contingent was brought into wartime intelligence and information efforts. Many of these colonial servants, cum academicians, did first-rate work, not always in accordance with colonial policy. Yet, the number of independent scholars on Southeast Asia remained small in the prewar years, with the exceptions of a sizable American contingent interested in the Philippines and an extremely well-versed Dutch group concentrating on the East Indies.

If, as we commented in the last chapter, the secularist tendencies of later social scientists were influenced by their intellectual environments, what forces molded these earlier observers? Four factors would appear to have been paramount:

1. ignorance
2. a sense of racial superiority
3. religion
4. government policies

Ignorance

Certainly a significant number of the travelers and journalists who wrote about Southeast Asia were not experts on the area and their comments were made on the basis of short visits and no particular linguistic or academic background. As well, books were sold on the basis of the exotic nature of the region and played to the popular biases of the day. Only a somewhat diminished charge of ignorance can be made against many of the colonial civil servants and businessmen who interpreted the region to the world. Often residing in urban centers, interacting primarily with other Europeans, and carrying the intellectual baggage of their day, they usually knew little of the rural population, their beliefs, social patterns, and daily activities. As well, the Asians with whom they tended to have the most contact were not part of the traditional rural folk, but were the industrious overseas Asians or Indians and members of the indigenous elite. The more knowledgeable assessments of men such as Swettenham, Snouck Hurgronje, and Foreman were often overshadowed in the popular media by more sensational reporting.

Racial Inequality

These were the years of the "white man's burden," backward races, and hereditary foundations to racial inequality. While the secular social scientists mentioned in the last chapter may have expounded the belief that religion and other environmental forces inhibited the development of the people, they did not publicly accept the views of their forerunners that these people were naturally inferior. Explanations for racial differences in the prewar years were often based upon the long-term impact of disease and poor climate, "natural laws," or races in their "infancy" in need of the helping hand of the white civilized and Christian world. This popular assumption of the inferiority of nonwhite races permeated the media and even academic literature in this era. During the debates on the annexation of the Philippines, the Halls of Congress reverberated with calls for Americans to take up the mission of saving a race incapable of self-government. While blunt racial pronouncements became less frequent in the interwar years, they could still be found during the war and in the debates over postwar independence movements.

Religion

Edward Said has argued, along with others, that our historic biases against Islam in the Middle East seriously colored our views of that religion and its people. Similar comments can be made regarding all the major religions of Southeast Asia—Buddhism, Islam, and Roman Catholicism. The profound impact that the missionary movement had on a group of the American elite was noted earlier. Western clergy, missionaries, and church tracts portrayed the Southeast Asian religions as false and their adherents as ignorant, damned, and inhibited on this earth by their tenets and practices. For rejecting Christ the Buddhists and Muslims were roundly condemned and for a considerable number of Protestant ministers the Roman Catholics in the Philippines were little better. While there were authors who noted desirable facets of these religions, the overall tenor of opinion was negative. This was particularly true of two of the four groups described previously, the missionaries and the travelers. While later years found less public support for the view that the Christian faith was obviously superior, there remained antagonism against or strong criticism of the influences of other religions.

Government Policies

It was long argued by Southeast Asian nationalists, and more recently by indigenous academicians, that the portrayal of the people of the region as ignorant and indolent was a useful means of reinforcing colonial policy. While there have been a variety of facets to this argument, two aspects have been the most prominent. First, by characterizing the natives as indolent, colonial administrators and commercial interests could give credence to assertions that forced labor, debt slavery, required planting of export crops, and other efforts to force the native into labor were necessary. If the colonies were to pay and the native was to be led to see his better interests, then he had to be brought out of his traditional lazy ways into the modern world. Second, if these people were ignorant and backward, colonialism was necessary to prepare them to become useful members and contributors to the civilized world. It was only through the benign, disciplined, and virtuous rule of the West that the native could be led out of his depraved state.

Given this environment and the character of these writers, what pictures of Southeast Asia and the relation of religion to modernization did they portray? Looking through the lens of their biases, what would the uninitiated observer see? Professor Syed Alatas of the University of Singapore wrote a book published in 1977 entitled *The Myth of the Lazy Native*,[24] in which he recounts the views of foreign observers of the Malay people of Indonesia, the Philippines, and then Malaya. This "myth" was to be found throughout Southeast Asia and was to become the foundation stone for apologias for colonialism, explanations of native "backwardness," and cries of despair from colonial administrators. Basically, the argument was that the indigenous population was indolent, lazy, and lacking in innovation. The following are some examples of this perception culled from the literature. It should be noted that the open articulation of such attitudes tended to diminish by the 1920s but did not die out altogether, certainly in the minds of many foreign officials and businessmen.

Burma

According to J. Dautremer, once Consul of France in Rangoon, "Thus, with no inclination for work or for regular employment, with a End of take(21-28.OUT) love of nothing but dancing and play-going, and above all for Buddhist meditative langour, he is gradually being supplanted by the Indian worker . . ."[25] On his part, J. Nisbet, a British observer, found the Burmese to be lazy, lacking in mechanical ability and initiative, and impulsive and illogical.[26] H. Fielding Hall, who spent many years in the area, found the Burmese as "primitive" and a race "in its childhood"[27] and, while not very industrious, happy. As he wrote in the latter nineteenth century, "He will never be very rich, very powerful, very advanced in science, perhaps not even in art, though I'm not sure of that,"[28] but he would be happy.

The Dutch East Indies

In the early nineteenth century then Governor General J. Siberg argued that without forced labor the Javanese would be too sluggish to live more than a subsistence living, a position that persisted into the twentieth century when an Australian journalist argued that, "the sterility of all idleness is upon it, and it will be enslaved, or else die out."[29] This author, referring to the "infantile Oriental mind," believed that what these people needed was the benevolent despotism that colonialism could provide. At the same time an American traveler was equally derogatory, stating that: "Of the personal characteristics of the Malays of Menangkabau, as in fact all Malays wherever found, there is little good to be said.'[30] He described them as brave in the manner of fanatic, vicious, underhanded, and hard-working, but all this by necessity rather than choice. Finally, economic historian Clive Day, commenting in 1904, asserted that: "Nothing less than immediate material enjoyment will stir them from their indolent routine." In addition, he noted that: "In practice it has been found impossible to secure the services of the native population by any appeal to an ambition to better themselves and raise their standard."[31]

Malaya

The general view of the Malay was that he was lazy and lacked initiative as, according to Swettenham, "The leading characteristic of the Malay is a disinclination to work."[32] Another British official, Hugh Clifford, noted that "He never works if he can help it, and often will not suffer himself to be induced or tempted into doing so by offers of the most extravagant wages.[33] As late as 1937, in a periodical known for

its liberal and even radical articles, an American wrote an article with
the subtitle "The Malay knows by intuition that work is a curse." He
asserted that, "you search in vain for an adult male doing useful work,"
and "the outstanding characteristic of all Malay people is indolence."[34]
Yet many of these same authors argued that the Malay would work quite
hard if it were for fun, such as hunting, or if the activity interested him.
Still, the Malay continued to be viewed as displaying a certain lassitude
and, as one early twentieth-century author asserted, "even the Malay's
best friends are compelled to admit that he does not take kindly to manual
labor."[35]

The Philippines

Throughout the eighteenth and nineteenth centuries there were
numerous comments about laziness and indolence of the Filipino. Early
European visitors termed them lazy, indolent and lacking in incentive.
According to three late-nineteenth-century observers,

> Compared with the European or American standard of intelligence
> and civilisation, the inhabitants of all these islands that form the great
> Malayan archipelago are but infants alongside a grown man, and to
> treat them otherwise is contrary to common sense, contrary to
> experience, and contrary to the best interests of the subject race.[36]

> The Philippine native, like most Orientals, is a good imitator,but
> has no initiative genius, he is not efficient in anything. . . . The
> native is indolent in the extreme and never tired of sitting still, gazing
> at nothing in particular.[37]

Noting that the Filipinos were lazy, deceitful, and like children, another
author commented that, "What the people of the Philippines really need
is a mild enlightened, but firm despotism, something like that of the
English in India."[38] He further remarked that: "It must be remembered
that one-half of the inhabitants of the Philippines are savages, and the
other half cannot be said to be more than half civilized. . . ."[39]

Thailand

The Thais were similarly described as lazy, apathetic, and lacking
in ambition. In the terms of one British advisor, "The Siamese are not
a people of lofty ideals or noble aspirations,"[40] while a French visitor

to the country when the capital was in Ayudthia remarked on the Thais' "invincible indolence."[41] Again there were statements that much depended on the type of activity. "They are lazy when ordinary work has to be done, but busy enough when preparations have to be made for amusements or holiday processions."[42]

There is always the tendency in making a point to overstate the case, and it is important to note that not all observers viewed the Southeast Asian as indolent and lacking in ability. Some viewed him as inherently hard-working while others, such as Clifford, Winsted, and Swettenham in Malaya, argued that the indigenous people were industrious when it was in their interests or worked in a manner different from the European.[43] However, the overall tone of much of the literature on the area, at least up to the 1920s, caustically, neutrally, or sympathetically gave substance to the charge of native lassitude. And, in turn, this indolence was given as reason for the lack of change and inability to modernize in the fashion of the European. Lazy, apathetic, and lacking in initiative, the indigenous population could not effectively compete with the European, let alone the overseas Indians and Chinese.

NONRELIGIOUS EXPLANATIONS

Yet, if there was a high degree of consensus about the pattern of life of the native, there were a myriad of reasons presented as to why that condition existed. Thus, the hero of Philippine independence, Rizal, could write an article entitled "The Indolence of the Filipino," in which he stated that the "indolence in the Philippines is a chronic, but not a hereditary malady"[44] and "We must confess that there indolence actually and positively exists."[45] However, Rizal had quite different explanations than most Europeans. It is here that we begin to see how religious forces enter the picture. Initially it should be noted that religion was not the only, and often not the major reason forwarded for indolence, but it was a persistent one. As to the nonreligious factors, they fell into four often interrelated categories:

1. climate
2. abundance
3. heredity
4. government and commercial policies

Climate

Climate was often mentioned as a factor in leading to indolence (Rizal, Crawfurd, A. D. Hall, Swettenham, Foreman, Smyth, Brown). Most noted the debilitating nature of tropical conditions, with some such as Rizal and A. D. Hall observing that the climate resulted in similar life-styles for the Europeans in the area. A few argued that under different circumstances the Southeast Asian might act otherwise, as did H. Warrington Smyth, who asserted that the Thais were robbed of their backbones when they moved down to the enervating plains.[46] However, many a colonial administrator would probably repeat, perhaps in less dramatic terms, the comments of J. M. Brown when he wrote, "It needs the hard winter of the temperate zone, the inclemency and uncertainty of the season, and the niggardliness of nature to develop in men the foresight, the self-discipline, and the quickness of the brain that are the requisite foundation of a self-ordered community."[47] However, the ease of life within a warm climate, in which housing, clothing, and food were easily handled, could also weaken the drive of a people. According to one scholar commissioned by the University of Chicago in 1901 to report on Southeast Asia,

> As far as my own observation extends, I should say that the Malay of the Peninsula is the most steadfast loafer on the face of the earth. His characteristics in this respect have been recognized by everyone who has come in contact with him. . . . He builds himself a house of bamboo and attaps, plants enough rice to fill out the menu which stream and forest afford him and for nine-tenths of his waking hours, year in an year out, he sits on a wooden bench in the shade and watches the Chinaman and the Tamil build roads and railways, work the mines, cultivate the soil, raise cattle, and pay the taxes.[48]

Abundance

This leads us to the second interlocking factor: the abundance provided by nature, which weakened the resolve of the native to be industrious. Why should he work for the European in unfamiliar employment if his basic needs were met? The descriptions of life in the tropics were often ones of a happy, lazy paradise in which one simply lay under the tree waiting for the coconut to fall into his lap. As an early nineteenth-century Spanish priest reported of life in the Philippines, fishing fit the local personality. "In this occupation the inhabitants of these islands take more delight than anything else, as it is a pursuit which at once indulges their indolent habits and gratifies their partiality to fish in preference to animal food. Throughout the country are found many other productions contributing to the support of life which, though not so relishing as those enumerated above, are probably better suited to their relaxed habits; and the pith of the palm, shoots of the sugar-cane, green withes, and other succulent productions, serve for food to those who have no desire to labour for their subsistence."[49] Another observer would call this abundance of food "race suicide."[50]

Heredity

To many this combination of abundance and climate over the generations led to laziness as an endemic trait in the populace that could not be changed or, if so, only over a considerable period of time. It was argued that by his very nature, as one writer said, "from the embryo," the native was indolent, weak of intellect and lacking in initiative. This popular attitude of the early years continued in various guises. It was what Raymond Kennedy called international "Jim Crowism" in post–World War II America when many felt that only whites were capable of achieving self-government and democracy. The belief in hereditary incapabilities of the native was certainly part and parcel of the colonial ideology, particularly within the general European population.

Government and Commercial Policies

It was the indigenous intelligentsia who were to raise most articulately the argument that native indolence, both in actuality and perception, was a result of colonial rule. Men such as Rizal and later Alatas were to argue that it was not unreasonable for the Southeast Asian to not wish to work in unfamiliar and undesirable factory, plantation, and mining jobs; that the Europeans blocked upward mobility for those who sought to better themselves; and, that, given the cruelty and injustice of the colonial regimes, there was little reason to strive. Rizal noted that with the Spanish themselves providing a model of indolence and immorality, what was the native to look to as an example, and that the Filipino had been far more industrious prior to the Spanish arrival.[51] Later writers were to assert that most natives were not lazy, but that this portrayal of the indigenous population as lazy, deceitful, and lacking in innovation was part of a conscious and unconscious colonial ideology which sought to denigrate the native and profit from him. While many of these arguments have undeniable merit, it would be emphasized that they were rarely employed by European and American prewar observers with the exception of radical and reform elements writing primarily since the late nineteenth century.

To recapitulate to this point, the prewar American public had little knowledge of Southeast Asia and what it had was largely simplistic and stereotypic. The American social scientist was little better informed. In part the view of the Southeast Asian was derived from the literature extant at the time and that tended to describe the inhabitants of that region as indolent, lacking in initiative and ambition, and basically unable to take on the arduous tasks of modernization. If drive, a willingness to work, and self-motivation were necessary to attain what in the West was meant by modernization, then the views of many observers gave little hope that Southeast Asia would be successful in gaining that goal. In fact, even those who counterargued that the native was not indolent asserted that he was industrious in areas not recognized by Westerners and, by implication, not interested in the kind of employment that would achieve "progress." A number of nonreligious reasons were given to explain these weaknesses in national character, including a debilitating climate, the abundance of nature, heredity, and colonial rule. The rest of this chapter will concentrate upon religious explanations for the inability to modernize, assessing the various arguments forwarded, and the possible repercussions of these contentions on later models of modernization.

RELIGIOUS EXPLANATIONS

Prior to launching into an analysis of perceptions of the role of religion in modernization, a short description of the religious geography of Southeast Asia is in order. This region contains representatives of all the world religions. Buddhism is the major faith of Burma, Thailand, Cambodia, Laos, and Vietnam, with the Theravada Buddhism version followed in all but Vietnam. Islam predominates in Indonesia and Malaysia, with minority elements in the Philippines, Burma, Thailand,

TABLE 2.1

Religious Patterns in Southeast Asia

Country	Former Colonial Power	Percentage of Adherents			
		Buddhist	Christian	Muslim	Other
Burma	United Kingdom	85%	2%	4%	4%
Indonesia	Holland	–	9	90	1
Malaysia	United Kingdom	25	25	53	22
Philippines	Spain and USA	–	93	5	1
Thailand	None	92	1	4	3

and Singapore. Christianity is the religion of most Filipinos and of important minorities in Burma, Vietnam, and Indonesia. Hinduism is to be found on Bali, Indonesia, and among the overseas Indians. Various Chinese religious beliefs are supported within the Chinese overseas community.

Reviewing the literature, it is possible to place the various views of the relation of religion to modernization into three categories; religion as interactive with society; religion as influencing the believer in his attitudes and practices; and religion as having an impact on the external environment. Of course, it should be noted that many writers either did not even discuss religion in terms of the aforementioned characteristics of the Southeast Asian or commented that, given the weak influence of religion and the "back-sliding" nature of the populace, religion was unimportant or irrelevant. The latter view obviously missed the point that the "purity" of the religion did not necessarily affect its influence on acts and perceptions. Others insisted that even if the religion was important and real to the people, it had no impact on change. In the words of the less than unprejudiced J. M. Brown, "nor does the religion bring any Western illumination or morality as Christianity does; it practically leaves the people much as they were but for a prayer mat and a devotion to Mecca."[52]

Religion as Interactive

A number of prewar writers, while accepting the description of the Southeast Asian as in one way or another indolent and lacking in initiative, did not argue that these characteristics were necessarily *caused* by religion. Rather, there was a natural and mutual interaction between a passive or nonvigorous faith and a people displaying similar attributes. It should be noted that these comments were presented primarily in generalities with little if any reference to specific elements of the religion. This interactive theory was particularly prevalent among observers of Thailand and Burma where, it was argued, an easy life went well with a faith which did not demand material advancement and development. A turn of the century British resident of Thailand stated, quite correctly, that "Buddhism has become inextricably intertwined with Siamese habits, customs and character,"[53] but also asserted the less empirically verifiable comment that, "their own apathetic natures have conspired with the thinking of their creed to deaden anything like enthusiasm."[54]

A more well-known and dramatic writer was H. Fielding Hall who believed that not only had Buddhism interacted with Burma's earthly paradise, but had tended to weaken the ability of the people of the country to face the world's problems or counteract British rule. The following lengthy statement reflects his views and the title of the book from which it comes, *A People at School*:

> The world is not a hospital but a battle-field, no garden of the lotus-eaters, but of very stern realities. Necessity is the maker of men. . . . it is the gospel of progress, of knowledge, of happiness. And it is taught not by book and sermon, but by spear and sword, by suffering and misery, by starvation and death; not by sorrow imagined in the future, but very imminent to-day.
>
> This truth, that the world is to those who can best appreciate her and use her, the Burmese had forgotten. In their great valley between the mountain ranges and the sea, secure from all invaders, with a kindly earth yielding food in ample quantities, it had fallen into the second place. . . .
>
> A very beautiful religion, full of great thoughts, full of peace and beauty, it was born to be the helpmeet to the stronger knowledge. It is the softener of life, the sweetener. It gives solace to the fallen, to the weak, a safe asylum for the broken in life. It guards the bays where the storm-driven souls put in to refit. It is the gospel of the sick, the wounded, the dying.
>
> But it is not the leader and guide of men. Its teachings in themselves, as those of other faiths, tend to discontent with the world as it is, to dreams and fancies, to seclusion and idleness, to cowardice and untruth, to neglect of all the world gives . . .

I do not see wherein the Burmese, in so far as they are Buddhists, have matter for complaint that we have conquered them. They had made their leading tenet that war was wrong. They believed or tried to believe that the world is very unhappy. They said there was nothing in it worth having. All was illusion and despair, and release was the best for all. If then we have conquered them, what harm have we done? We have taken from them what they declared they despised. We have relieved them of the functions of government, and government, they said, was one of the great evils. We are developing the wealth of their country for both ourselves and them, but they say that wealth is evil.[55]

Another British observer of the Burmese, W. Harris, described him as "happy by temperament, fortunate in his religion—for Buddhism is eminently suited to his race and character." He went on to say that the Burman sought happiness, not money and that while his nonmaterialist Buddhist faith might not satisfy many, it did him.[56] This harmony of character and faith was also noted among the Malay, but in more pejorative terms. Discussing the impact of Islam, another British writer charged that "It produced the traditional Muslim attitude toward education and science, thus harmonizing with the natural ignorance of the untaught Malay."[57]

A different version of this interactive pattern was presented as late as 1936 by an anthropoligist, Geoffrey Gorer, who saw the lack of drive among the Javanese as related to Islam. As he wrote in his book, *Bali and Angkor*, "I do not find the Javanese very sympathetic: Despite their fertility they give somehow the impression of being a race of old and exhausted people, only half alive. This impression may, I think, be due to their religion, and to the abysmal poverty of the greater number. Poverty, especially uncomplaining involuntary poverty, is numbing and repulsive anywhere; and Mohammedanism is the most deadening of all creeds."[58]

We shall return to assess the validity of such arguments in a later chapter, but at this point it should be noted that observations such as these leave little hope that their subjects would be capable of modernizing. They would be severely hampered in achieving "progress" by a triumvirate of circumstances—according to Hall by a lack of will, an overly "kindly" earth, and a passive religion, while, according to Gorer, the Javanese was plagued by exhaustion, poverty, and a "deadening" faith.

Religion as Causative

A significantly larger group of commentators argued that, rather than there being an interactive pattern, or in addition to such a relationship, religion had a direct causative impact on the faithful, working to weaken or destroy their ability to "progress" and modernize. There were those who linked ignorance and laziness to superstition. Animist beliefs underlying Buddhism, Christianity, and Islam, any non-Christian and even Christians of different sects at times received the appellation "superstition."

In the first instance, by describing the populace as maintaining animist beliefs and practices, the writer established the inferior intellectual base of the community. But, beyond this, particular animist "superstitions" were underscored as inhibiting development. Thus, in the first instance, the author of an article entitled "Malay Psychology" asserted that the "Malay as a race cannot be conceived by any stretch of the imagination a progressive race," but did make good "boys," cooks, gardeners, and chauffeurs."[59] The problem was "like most Orientals, the Malay is remarkably superstitious, and it is extraordinarily difficult to get an idea which has once been introduced to the Malay brain out again." More specific was a writer in *Sociology and Social Research,* whose less than systematic study showed the Malay as having "little or no intellectual curiosity", being extremely indecisive, and having a mind filled with superstition.[60] His lack of intellectual curiosity was attributed to his belief in spirits *(hantu).* Since the spirits could explain everything, there was no need for the individual to burden himself with the effort to think for himself.

Of course, there were also those who considered anyone who did not accept their particular religion as ignorant and superstitious. In a wonderful section that tells more of the author than those she portends to describe, a prolific American writer and world traveler of the late nineteenth century termed the Muslims of Malaya as bigots because they did not accept Christianity, commenting that "as well, they are ignorant and grossly superstitious."[61] This view was regularly reflected in missionary publications and lectures of the period with regard to efforts to convert the Muslims and Buddhists of Southeast Asia. However, it is also to be found in the rhetoric of Protestant churchmen of the turn of the century when describing Catholicism in the Philippines. To many Americans it was, in the words of writers of the time "the duty and manifest destiny of the United States to civilize and Christianize the Filipinos." The Protestant clergy saw it their mission to convert the Moros from "paganism" and the rest from "Romanism."[62]

In either case, there was a persistent view that the Southeast Asian was uncultured, half-civilized, superstitious, and continuing to hold on to incorrect and outmoded religious beliefs. Writers reinforced this view up to World War II with the constant use of such adjectives as "fanatic," "superstitious," "savage." As late as 1939 one of the most widely read journalists in the West, John Gunther, could write in *Inside Asia* that "it is not usually realized that a large number of Muhammaden semi-savages still live under the American flag," referring to the Moros of the Philippines. He later discusses Hindu theology as "staggeringly medieval" and that of the Muslims as not much better.[63]

However, beyond blanket attacks on "superstition" there were frequent more specific criticisms of Buddhism, Catholicism, and Islam as placing obstacles in the way of development. The basic tenets of these religions, at least as defined by these observers, came under fire in various ways. Both Buddhism and Islam were accused of inculcating in their adherents a sense of "otherworldliness" which made them incapable of dealing with the mundane problems of the day. Buddhism was perceived as particularly responsible on two counts. On the one hand the denial of material values and acceptance of his *karma* weakened the Buddhist's interest in working in this life. Or at least it channeled his activities into those religious acts which would gain merit rather than into the kind of labor which would lead to material growth. These misplaced priorities could only be obstacles to the process of modernization.

Beyond this, Buddhism was charged with instilling a mystical "otherworldly" concept of life as a whole which made it difficult to concentrate upon the world as it was. It made its follower a poorer worker lacking in decisiveness and drive. In a book which was the classic description of the life of the late-nineteenth-century Burman, Sir J. G. Scott wrote,

> He cares little for the troubles of the world and the manifold questions of the day which distract the more highly cultured nations. His eyes are fixed uninterruptedly on the dark mysteries which surround our beginning, our end, and every moment of our life.[64]

> . . . the Burmese is content if he has enough to eat and remains a free man, happy if he accumulates sufficient to build a work of merit, or give a free festival to his less fortunate brethren. Who shall say he is not wise?[65]

While the author raised the question as to whether the "happy" Burman was not better off than the money grubbing English and Indians, he certainly did not portray a people willing to labor for change or interested in material advancement.

Buddhism also came under criticism for lacking a sense of social obligation. Arguing that religion was attuned to the attainment of personal merit, it was declared that it inhibited a sense of cooperation and the kind of corporate morality that was necessary to achieve public goals. Thus, one author charged that the high crime rate that characterized much of colonial Burma was but a symptom of bad citizenship, for which Buddhism was partly to blame.[66] Another writer, generally sympathetic to the Burmese, termed Buddhism the noblest of all creeds except that which inculcates a sense of charity and sympathy, but went on to describe the faith as "cold, cynical and thoroughly selfish."[67] Given these attributes some observers could see little in the religion that would lead toward national efforts at development, or even interest in the needs of one's fellow man.

Certain tenets of Islam also came under fire, particularly those that were viewed as the dead hand of religious law, prohibitions against usury, and attitudes toward women. These criticisms tended to be more prevalent in Malaya rather than in Indonesia where the Javanese were seemingly more lax in their religious practices and women appeared less fettered. Thus, one British writer on Malaya could argue that usury prohibitions and the role of women were prime factors "in keeping the Malays from taking a fair share in the material life and control of their opulent land,"[68] while another charged more generally that, "For centuries the stagnation that has overlaid all Muslim lands has received orthodox approval, owing to the doctrine that all knowledge is a religious matter, centering around the contents of the Koran, the multitudenous traditions and the inalterable law."[69]

Beyond what were perceived to be the tenets of the religion itself, a host of practices prevalent in Southeast Asia came under scrutiny with negative reactions. The variety of feasts, festivals, and other religious activities which seemed to fill the people's lives were condemned as wasting their time and precious funds. Since, as many argued, these were the only activities which could bring the native out of his indolent ways to work with any degree of industry, it was even more undesirable that they were for no productive good. It must have been particularly galling to those who believed that these people were practicing heathen superstitions in such an industrious manner.

Coming under particular criticism was the religious leadership of the major religions of the region. The Buddhist monks and their monasteries were seen as contributing little to the material advancement of society and the education they provided was described as outmoded in a modern world. The Islamic leadership and educational system came under even more vituperative invective. Thus one traveler asserted that the resident English in Malaya viewed the *hadjis* (those making the pilgrimage to Mecca) as leading idle lives and living "like leeches in the toil of their fellow man, inciting the people to revolt and run amok."[70] Another Englishman wrote that the young progressive Malay men feared that any undue activity would call out "the fanatical obscurantism that rages against modernists in Muslim theology."[71] As to Islamic education, both its content and those who taught it were often described as overly traditional, having little relation to the needs of the modern industrial world, and opposed to the values and policies of the colonial administrations.

However, for a truly rich literature of invective one must read the charges against the Spanish friars of the Philippines. Accused of ignorance, greed, immorality, laziness, and a multitude of other sins, these men were seen by both Filipino nationalists and many foreign observers as both forces for conservatism in a political sense and obstacles to Filipino social and intellectual development. This is not the place to review the large literature on the alleged perfidies of the friars. The reader is referred to the writings of Rizal and foreign commentators such as A. D. Hall and J. Foreman[72] and the hearings of the Philippines Commission.

Religion and the External Environment

Finally, it was argued that religion limited "progress" by reinforcing conservative secular forces which had their own reasons for wanting to see change forestalled. Thus, numerous authors on the Spanish Philippines argued that Christianity in the colony was an important tool in the hands of the colonial government for the purpose of controlling the economic, political, and social development of the Filipinos. The poorly educated and tradition oriented priest brought from Spain spread the Spanish language and culture, was a conservative economic force, given the extensive land holdings of the religious orders, and gave presence to the colonial administration throughout almost the entire archipelago. While the majority of clerics in the colony were Filipino, the Spanish clergy, with the support of the colonial administration, sought to dominate them and assure that they remain loyal to the crown. It is little wonder that the most articulate nationalists of the era strongly condemned the role of the Catholic clergy in the islands.[73] Nor were the clergy given any more sympathetic treatment by many foreign observers.

In Malaya, on the other hand, it was asserted that Islam had become a tool of the traditional and often venal local royalty. Thus, L. R. Wheeler stated that the influence of Islam was "indissolvably linked with that of royal supremacy."[74] The sultans, reinforced by the blessings of his religion, were viewed by the populace as always correct, weakening efforts to eliminate debt slavery, increasing the passivity of the peasant, and tying the Malay to the old ways. "Still more, it deprived him of the possibility of ever planning or even conceiving any such protection as the middle classes and democracies of Europe gradually achieved." Observers of the period often had a low opinion of these Malay rulers and saw little hope for progress in what they perceived to be an amalgamation of the traditional conservatism and loyalty of the Malay people, a self-centered conservatism among the sultans who were perceived by their people to be the heads of their faith and the "natural" support of Islam for strong monarchical government.

In sum then, religion was characterized as one of the major elements in weakening the resolve of the people of Southeast Asia to modernize themselves. It was not the only factor, but in cooperation with other debilitating forces it was projected in the literature as developing or reinforcing conservatism, tradition, and ignorance. While there were others such as Wheeler and Winsted who disputed the usual portrayal of the native as indolent by nature, there were few foreign observers indeed who were prepared to argue that the major religions of the region were either receptive to or active in the process of modernization.

These pictures of Southeast Asia provided by the literature and mass media have even dimmer counterparts in Black Africa, while Said and others have expounded on the negative stereotypes of the people of the Middle East. It is thus fair to ask how these portrayals must have affected later social scientists attempting to explore the concept of modernization. No doubt the life-styles of these Asian and African peoples were different from the nineteenth- and twentieth-century Europeans, reflecting health, climatic, and cultural factors as well as contrasting priorities. Given the intellectual and popular climate of the day, it is thus not surprising that so many simplistic formulas of modernization were developed, that authors so readily dichotomized modern and traditional societies, and that religion was viewed so negatively. As we noted previously, the majority of the scholars who were seminal in the literature on modernization, men such as Parsons, Weber, Deutch, Almond, and Huntington, had little, if any firsthand knowledge of the Third World. Thus, their conceptual frameworks had to be derived from a flawed literature, the few colleagues who were well-versed in Afro-Asia and/or their own fertile imaginations.

3

Patterns of Analysis

P rior to analyzing the relation of religion to modernization in Southeast Asia, it is necessary to define the limitations and terms of discourse of this study. As previously noted, a fundamental problem of the literature has been the imprecision, lack of consensus, and vagueness that has plagued this field of endeavor. As well, the geographic region under discussion is large and diverse and poses an insurmountable challenge to the single scholar seeking to compare across ten states.

First, the subject of the following analysis is limited in time and space. In terms of time, it focuses on the post–World War II era, although references will be made to forces in the colonial years which shaped later events and attitudes. In part this concentration on the past forty years is the result of the paucity and uneven quality of much of the earlier material and the greater weight given to relevant empirical research and analysis in recent decades. Of particular importance has been the work of anthropologists, and to a lesser extent political scientists and sociologists, in underscoring the role of religion in contemporary Southeast Asia society.

Second, not all the countries of the region will be given equal weight, with the greatest attention being given to Burma, Thailand, Malaysia, the Philippines, and Indonesia. Singapore, as a city-state, simply does not display many of the same characteristics of these more rural polities, while the decision to focus less on Brunei and the Indochinese states of Cambodia, Laos, and Vietnam emanates from the fact that the author has worked in, traveled to, and written about these countries far less than the others. The inability to do research in Indochina since 1975 is obviously a further obstacle.

However, the five countries being assessed offer considerable variation in religious, political, and economic experience. Burma and Thailand are predominately Theravada Buddhist polities. Malaysia and Indonesia are largely Islamic, with the former somewhat more than 50 percent and the latter approximately 90 percent Islamic, while the Philippines is over 90 percent Christian. Each has important religious minorities, with Christians in Burma and Indonesia, the Malay Muslims of southern Thailand, and the Muslim Moros of the southern Philippines, indigeous Hindus on Bali, and followers of Indian and Chinese faiths among immigrants in all five states.

Politically these countries have had different colonial experiences and chose different governmental structures in the postcolonial period. The British administered Burma and Malaysia, the Dutch Indonesia, and the Spanish and the Americans the Philippines, while Thailand remained independent. In the postwar years they all began with relatively democratic regimes, but Burma came under military rule in 1958–60 and again after 1962, as did Indonesia after 1967–68 and Thailand intermittently throughout recent decades. Today Thailand and Malaysia are formally constitutional monarchies with competitive political parties in limited democratic systems; Indonesia is a limited competitive democratic republic dominated by the military; Burma is a one party military dominated state; and the Philippines is slowly moving away from martial law.

Nor have they all been similar in their development policies and their consequences. Postwar Burma has experimented with varieties of socialism, as did Indonesia before the military came to power. Today more liberal, quasi-capitalist economies with heavy official and unofficial government involvement are to be found in all five states but Burma. However, the specifics of development policy vary markedly among the five. Differences in economic well-being are also major, with annual per capita income in Burma approximately $170 and $1,797 in Malaysia, while the other three range from $250 to $815 (Singapore is over $4,000).[1] Although the end of colonialism saw considerable disparity in literacy and education, present literacy tables display greater similarity.

In sum, the five states under scrutiny offer a microcosm of religious, political, and economic experiences. However, diversity in some experiences should not obscure important similarites in others. All came under the strong influence of the West, militarily, economically, and intellectually, during the colonial era. All had to deal with Japanese dominance during World War II. All have anticommunist leadership that has employed military force against insurgents. All have religious minorities as well as communal divisions based upon race, ethnicity, and language and have experienced communal violence. And finally, all have sought to modernize their economies, not always strictly following Western models.

However, major issues that need clarification at this time are how religion and modernization are to be defined so that we can usefully assess the validity of the two central premises of the modernization literature, i.e., that religion has been an obstacle to modernization and that modernization leads to a decline in religion. Given Pye's ten definitions of political development[2] and Shiner's six variations on secularism,[3] the question of definition is absolutely vital. Those aspects of religion and modernization to be emphasized in this study have been chosen upon two bases: their centrality in assessing the interrelationship of the two concepts in the real world, and the availability of data permitting comparative analysis. Both concepts have been broken down into discrete elements, allowing comparison of the elements of religion with those of modernization.

RELIGION

In the chapters that follow, religion will be analyzed in terms of (1) basic tenets, (2) religious institutions, (3) popular beliefs, (4) popular practices, and (5) the manipulation of religious symbols. There are obvious cases where these five elements are intertwined, but insofar as possible an effort will be made to maintain the integrity of these categories. However, at times it may be necessary to collapse two categories, as with popular beliefs and practices. As well, difficulties may arise in categorizing particular actions or beliefs. For example, when is a ritualistic act to be considered a basic tenet and when a popular practice?

Basic Tenets

Basic tenets are those fundamental elements of the religion which have been more or less consistently held across time and sect as the essential dogma of the religion. We do not mean current interpretations or issues which seriously divide adherents to the same faith. Obviously, there may be disagreements about even the most basic elements of the dogma, but we are seeking those beliefs about which there has been general consensus. Thus, in Christianity we would not include conflictual views such as the infallibility of the Pope or contemporary interpretations of the role of religion within the state, but would look rather to the role of Christ and his basic teachings, acceptance of a life hereafter, and an essential monotheism. The core of Buddhism would be the Four Noble Truths and the Eightfold Path, while in Islam the fundamental doctrine would incorporate a strong monotheism and the ritualistic elements of the Five Pillars. However, a constant difficulty in employing this category is maintaining the boundaries as to what is the fundamental doctrine and what is interpretive overlay. We shall adopt a very restricted definition of basic tenets, relegating much to other categories and thereby limiting the importance of this first category.

When we relate basic tenets to modernization we need to examine the extent to which these tenets affect how adherents relate to the world about them, as well as how modernization might change their views of essential dogma. As with other aspects of religion, it is also important to assess support for these beliefs within the society.

Religious Institutions

In each of the religions under discussion there has been some degree of institutionalization of dogma and practice among particular groups of the faithful. Thus, in Christianity there are the doctrines of the various denominations, in Islam the differences among Sunnis and Shiites, plus other schisms, as well as the four schools of jurisprudence, while in Buddhism there are not only the Hinayana and Mahayana schools of thought, but variations in the role of the monk. Within this category particular attention will be given the role and structure of religious hierarchies and the activities and attitudes of ecclesiastical and lay personnel.

Popular Beliefs

Given the heterogeneity of religious faith in Southeast Asia, it is not possible to assess the myriad of religious beliefs in the region. Instead, an effort will be made to concentrate upon those aspects that appear to have an impact upon the process of modernization. Those analyzed here include Buddhist views toward karma and merit, characterizations of the adherents of the region's faiths as "otherworldly," the current religious revival, and contemporary intellectual involvement in questions concerning the role of religion in modernization. These have all been targets of conflicting interpretations which, when combined with often limited empirical data, make analysis difficult.

Popular Practices

The adherents of each of these faiths carry out a host of practices which are popular reinterpretations of basic dogma. In fact, there may be no obvious relationship between popular practices and either fundamental doctrine or accepted theological interpretations. Such practices include special ceremonies for birth, marriage, death, and other life changes; feasts and festivals to propitiate the spirits; particular health or agricultural practices; or activities around important days such as Tet, Easter, Hari Raya, and Thaipusan. Financial expenditures surrounding these practices can be of particular importance in assessing the relationship of religion to modernization, as evidenced by costs attendant to Christiandom's two most sacred holidays, Christmas and Easter.

Symbol Manipulation

Political leadership in Southeast Asia, both at the national and subnational levels, has employed religion as a means of legitimizing governments, encouraging nationalism, formulating or inhibiting programs, unifying or dividing political organizations, and so forth. Depending upon the circumstances, the religion as a whole may become a symbol with little attention to specificity, or a particular aspect may be underscored to implement a single program or project. Obviously such manipulation is not limited to governments and may be attempted by the opposition or private organizations. Examples, which will be expanded upon in later chapters, would include Burmese Prime Minister U Nu's efforts to use Buddhism to foster national development plans, attempts by Malay Muslim leadership in Malaysia to encourage modern development activities among their followers to protect Islam from the challenge of the Chinese, and the undertakings of local and national Thai development officers to employ religious leaders to promote their projects.

MODERNIZATION

Two interdependent factors will be considered core elements of modernization: technological development and the maintenance of a modern nation-state. Each of these subsumes other factors which are necessary for their establishment and continuance. Without doubt, other subcategories could be chosen, but those proposed not only appear to be at the central core of modernization in the twentieth century, but also allow comparative analysis based upon available empirical evidence. What follows is not new, but draws upon the rich literature on modernization formulated over the past three decades.

Technological Change

Following the work of Levy, Black and Rustow, the core of modernization in this era would appear to be relatively rapid technological change in terms of the planning and use of modern industrial and agricultural techniques and equipment. While at one stage this process may resemble Levy's substitution of inanimate for animate sources of power, technological change over time can lead to an even more complex employment of sources and tools. Obviously, this pattern extends to other areas such as transportation, communications, and military hardware. However, if this process is to be successfully developed and maintained, a number of preconditions must be met which are not part of the resource base, financial infrastructure, or other "material" requisites. Among a host of such factors, the two most essential would appear to be education and adaptability to change.

EDUCATION

In the first instance, education conducive to the support of technological change is imperative. It must be of an order that will prepare the individual and society to plan and implement new methods, from basic machinery to complex concepts and techniques. Basic to this is not only preparation in the sciences and engineering, but the ability to analyze and conceptualize. Thus, while traditional religious training, founded upon rote learning and schooling in the scriptural languages, may inculcate a degree of intellectual discipline, it has tended to limit the student's success in the world of technology.

ADAPTABILITY

Obviously, adaptability and education are closely intertwined. Technological change demands a willingness of major sectors of a society to adopt new ways, to modify life-styles and work habits, and to accept an education which will further these divergent patterns. This adaptability does not relate exclusively to the individual worker in the modern sector, for if that person is to accept change then those vital reference groups and persons which shape his attitudes must at least acquiesce to, and hopefully encourage, his activities. This means societal change, or at least an appreciation of the positive elements of change within the social, political, and economic elites.

At this point a number of vital questions related to religion and modernization become important. Are the basic tenets, institutions, or practices of "X" religion antithetical to technological change? Can an individual compartmentalize his attitudes and values so as to maintain a range of religious positions while actively participating in the modern technological sector? Are there particular practices or religious leadership patterns that might inhibit technological change through limiting capital accumulation, discouraging people from entering the modern sector, and the like? What is the role of religious education in preparing students to compete in this new world? Can the government employ and has it employed religious symbols to shape popular attitudes towards the acceptance of change, or have religious leaders attempted to reinforce more conservative interests? These and other questions will be addressed in succeeding chapters.

The Modern State

In the past century the development of a political-administrative entity, the modern nation-state, has been a necessary requisite for the successful maintenance of an environment conducive to technological change. The state has provided the infrastructure favorable to that process in terms of administration, communications, and security. Again, numerous prerequisites could be suggested as necessary for the development and maintenance of such a system. However, if we are to consider variables that can be evaluated with the data now available and which would appear to be important factors in influencing technological change, the list becomes dramatically reduced. For example, if we review the modernization literature, modern political systems have been characterized by such elements as equity, democracy, the allocation of political roles through achievement rather than ascription, and orderly change.[4] It is certainly open to question whether these factors have been necessary for technological change. One need only look to successful technological advances of Hitler's Germany or Stalin's Soviet Union to begin to reconsider whether such factors as democracy are necessary prerequisites.

On the other hand, social scientists have presented us with other attributes of modernization which appear to be quite important, but which are extremely difficult to compare in the real world. For example, two often noted characteristics of a modernized state have been rational decision making[5] and the capacity to handle new demands on a society.[6] What is a "rational" decision? In whose terms? How would we compare a rational decision with an irrational one except at the margins? Questions like these become very important when dealing with religion and modernization. Many authors have equated rational with secular without the care employed by Weber. This can entangle the analyst with such questions as, is it more rational to work toward goals centered on this life or the hereafter? Is it more rational to save your money for the pilgrimage to Mecca or to use it as development capital? Is it irrational to put into positions of authority individuals from your own family, religion, or ethnic group because you trust them and work with them more easily to achieve your common goals (which may include technological change)? As to some of the analyses of capacity to meet demands, many have become almost tautological. Is the proof that a system is capable of meeting demands based upon the fact that it still exists? If a system changes drastically in the face of new demands, does that show success or failure? Are all demands of equal worth?

Rather than wrestle with these and other complex questions, we choose to forward two conditions of a modern nation-state that can be examined cross-nationally. The first is not new and was well articulated by Machiavelli, but is an important factor when considering the impact of religion on the state. There must be sufficient support from those who have the power to influence the state's direction and to maintain the type of stability necessary to develop and sustain technological change. This does not mean democracy or widespread popular support; yet one characteristic of the modern state has been a widened sense of participation and efforts by political elites to foster a belief in mass involvement.

Unless a basic floor is maintained, the state cannot continue to offer the infrastructure of administration, communications, and security vital to technological change. Religion becomes a factor here when religious divisions endanger the viability of the state, as took place at the birth of India and Pakistan, is used to reinforce nationalism, as in Burma and the Netherlands Indies, or when modernization becomes a source of instability in the face of religious opposition.

Second, does the polity have the administrative apparatus that can provide the basic infrastructure necessary to achieve the desired technological change? This is a somewhat limited use of the capacity variable in that we are only attempting to assess administrative capacity in this one area. Here we can ask questions as to whether the demands of religious leadership might weaken the infrastructure, or if particular kinds of religious education or ascriptive requirements might have similar consequences.

In sum, then, modernization is defined in terms of technological change, a process that requires an educated people prepared to adapt to new ways. In the twentieth century this must take place in the administrative-political environment of a nation-state that has the ability to maintain the basic infrastructure necessary to allow for the development and continuation of these changes.

THE IMPACT OF MODERNIZATION ON RELIGION

There has been a second relationship between religion and modernization forwarded in the literature, i.e., the impact of modernization on religion. We cannot say much about assertions in the literature that one element in the definition of modernization is increased secularization, since this is a matter of definition, not causation. Those who have dichotomized traditional and modern societies and placed the sacred in one and the secular in the other have been taken to task sufficiently by Bendix, Gusfield, the Rudolphs, and others.[7] It is a different type of analysis to state that the process of modernization tends to increase secularization, whether it be the loss of power by religious leaders, a decline in loyalty to sacred dogma, or a weakening of religious values. It is not our purpose here to delve into the extensive literature on the attributes of personal, communal, or polity secularization.[8] For the purpose of this study, several elements of secularization have been selected to facilitate an analysis of whether modernization as previously defined has particular consequences for religion. Using Charles Glock's classification,[9] somewhat recast, we will examine the impact of modernization on the degree of attachment to the supernatural, ritual, the religious commitments of the group, general behavior, religious knowledge, and the role of religion in government and political behavior.

Thus, analysis will be made of the impact of religion (segmented into basic tenets, popular beliefs, institutions, popular practices, and the manipulation of symbols) on modernization (interpreted as technological change in a modern nation-state) and, in turn, how modernization has influenced religion (in terms of the categories noted above). The following chapters first examine how each of these aspects of religion has had an impact upon the modernization process in Southeast Asia and then how modernization has affected religion.

4

Basic Tenets and Modernization

Perhaps the elements of religion that have had the least impact on the modernization process in Southeast Asia have been the fundamental tenets of Christianity, Buddhism, and Islam. At the same time, this is a difficult area of analysis given the problems of determining what constitutes the core of any religion, of ethical similarities among religions and of assessing the extent of internationalization of dogma.

In the first instance, both contemporary theologians and the public may differ among themselves and with the other group as to what should be delineated as the basic tenets of the faith. Thus, while Christians may agree on the centrality of Christ and his teachings, a wide range of interpretations as to their meaning and implications are apparent. Similarly, while all Muslims look to the Koran as their foremost religious guide, individual *suras* are interpreted differently and specific policies or acts may be based on different suras. Corollary to this, we do not seek, at this point, to assess the impact of the institutionalized religions which followed or were implanted upon the fundamental dogma. Nor do we wish to delve into the various interpretations of the faith which in many cases enriched and formalized the original tenets. A later chapter will look at aspects of Catholicism in the Philippines, Theravada Buddhism in Burma and Thailand, and variations of Sunni Islam elsewhere in Southeast Asia. This chapter is not intended as an analysis of contemporary religious systems as presented by authors such as Donald Smith.[1] Instead, an effort is made to limit the analysis to the core element of each faith.

Second, all the major world religions proclaim similar ethical codes of brotherhood, rejection of evil, and doing good. Thus, Thray Sithu U

Ba Khin in his *What Buddhism Is* quotes the "Dhammapada" in defining the essence of Buddhism:

> To abstain from evil
> To do good
> To purify the mind
> These are the teaching of all of the Buddhas[2]

Jesus said, "Do unto others as you would that they should do unto you," and a writer on comparative religion said of Islam, "However poorly one may conclude that the music of Islam has been played, the Koranic score itself is perfect. In the area of human relations its ideal is epitomized in the traditional Muslim greeting: "Salam alakum" ("Peace be upon you")."[3]

To the extent that each believer follows those admonitions, little variation is to be expected in the manner in which the religion would affect modernization. At the same time, it would be superficial to argue that these ethical similarities constitute a reason to view all of those faiths as the same, for there remain fundamental differences that cannot be overlooked. Whether these basic variations have any real influence on modernization is another matter.

Melford Spiro points to the danger of easily accepting a causal relationship between dogma and action without fully understanding the extent to which the dogma has been internalized among the faithful. In his excellent work on Burma entitled *Buddhism and Society* he writes:

> . . . it is one thing to assert that religion has a specified influence on one or another of society's social or cultural institutions, and another to demonstrate it; and the ratio of assertion to demonstration in this field has been distressingly high. Students of Asia have been especially prone to interpret many features of society and culture in that part of the world as a consequence of religion: caste, poverty, conservatism, pessimism, spirituality, egalitarianism—these and a host of other real or imputed characteristics of Asia have been variously attributed to the influence of Hinduism or Buddhism. Usually these attributions are less than convincing, relying as many of them do on two types of specious argument.
>
> One type, usually advanced by scholars who assume that the religion of the texts is that of the people, takes its departure from some normative religious doctrine and proceeds to deduce from it a consequent characterological or motivational consequence which, in turn, is postulated as the cause of some observed social variable.

Thus, for example, the conservatism of traditional Buddhist societies has been attributed by some scholars to the pessimism of their populations, which in turn they attribute to such Buddhist doctrines as suffering or karma.

The fallacies in this type of argument are twofold. First, it assumes without proof that the normative religion has been internalized, so that the inferred motivational disposition is in fact present in the population; second, it ignores the fact that in most Asian societies the normative religion is not the only one. As concerns the first fallacy, there is no use in deducing from the normative doctrine of suffering that the Burmese, for example, are a pessimistic people, when (it will be recalled) few Burmese agree with this doctrine. The fact is that the Burmese are not a pessimistic people at all, but if they were, the cause would have to be sought in some other ground than Buddhism. Moreover, as to the second fallacy, most Buddhists have not internalized much of nibbanic Buddhism, while they have internalized much more of that other religion—kammatic Buddhism. And since in some respects these two forms of Buddhism are drastically different, the *actual* influence of the latter form may be entirely unlike the *deduced* influence of the former.[4]

The problem to which Spiro alludes is extremely important, but one that is difficult to handle effectively. There is little systematic, empirical evidence as to the extent to which these religions have been internalized, outside of comparatively limited observations by anthropologists and sociologists. In today's Southeast Asia, social science research is not always easy to do, given decreasing funds and government controls, and while there are an increasing number of anthropologists applying to do field research, they tend to want to concentrate on peoples outside of core population areas. As well, there are any number of methodological pitfalls to surveys formulated to tap religious and ideological attitudes.

This problem is particularly central in Southeast Asia where considerable variation exists in both the doctrine and practice of each religion. Thus, in Islam in Indonesia we find the more orthodox Muslims of Acheh, aptly called the "window of Mecca," the matrilineal Padangers of west Sumatra, the syncretic Javanese with their heavy Hindu and Buddhist influences, and the increasingly secular urban Jakarta population. Even within these communities, there are individuals more knowledgeable of the heritage and theological precepts of Islam while others may practice its obligations only intermittently. Thus, to generalize about the impact of the basic tenets of Islam may be tricky indeed. Even in Malaysia with its more homogeneous Muslim populations and the

Theravada Buddhist communities to the north, considerable variation in levels of internalization exists.

Finally, the fundamental precepts of a religion may be at a plane where there is little obvious connection to modern issues that can be empirically verified. It is difficult to observe direct causal relationships between, say, monotheism, the Trinity or resurrection, and modernization. When combined with the question of internalization of doctrine, this makes efforts to assess the effect of the basic tenets of Christianity, for example, particularly hard.

It is difficult, if not impossible, to empirically verify how fundamental Christian tenets have influenced contemporary modernization in Southeast Asia. This is not to state that Christians have not been active in the process of change, or that education, ideas, and leadership derived from the Christian community have not been important. In fact, the very effort to translate and disseminate the Bible has had important influences on education and literacy in the region. For example, the first major English-Burmese dictionary was by Dr. A. Judson, who after translating the Bible, completed his *Judson's Burmese and English Dictionary* in 1848. Nor does it mean that they are necessarily more secular or less prone to follow the tenets of their faith than followers of other religions. It does mean that if we go to the fundamentals of Christianity as expressed by Christ through his life, death, resurrection, and teachings it is difficult to see how these have systematically had an impact upon the process of modernization. In the basic Christian tenets, one finds neither the ritualistic and particularistic requirements of Islam or institutionalized Christianity, nor the stress on renunciation of this world found in Buddhism. It is particularly necessary to assess how Christians have interpreted the role of Christ and his teachings as they relate to contemporary issues.

Part of the problem then is the great influence of institutionalized Christianity in Southeast Asia and the extent to which the interpretation of basic tenets by the various church organizations have affected the individual. Of course, each church will argue that it reflects the true and fundamental core of Christianity. In a later chapter we will turn to the somewhat easier task of defining the impact of institutionalized Christianity on the modernization process of Southeast Asia.

At the end of this chapter we will return to this issue as we investigate various efforts to show how these basic tenets of the world religions are "modern" as projected by adherents to these faiths. First, we will analyze Islam and Buddhism, giving particular attention to rituals or prohibitions that appear to have consequences for modernization.

Considerable caution has been taken in making any conclusions as to causal relationships between fundamental doctrine and the activities and attitudes of the believers. In the process, considerably more attention is given to religions which emphasize testable ritualistic requirements as part of their original doctrine.

ISLAM

Islam, unlike Christianity, provides the believer with a carefully delineated set of ritualistic obligations. The Koran and the Hadith are specific in terms of what is expected from personal law to ritual. While the Koran speaks eloquently of an almighty, omnipotent God and his relation to man, as a famous Muslim writer noted, it is "a book which emphasizes deed, rather than idea."[5] These deeds or obligations find their core in the "Five Pillars." Islam certainly means considerably more than the Five Pillars, but at the very least there is agreement that they provide an intrinsic element of belief and obligations generally acceptable to all Muslims. The very first and fundamental pillar, "There is no God but Allah, and Muhammad is His Prophet," epitomizes a core which entails much more. As H. A. R. Gibb noted, the Koran stresses "the Oneness of God, the sole divinity in the relations to man, one in his nature, the only Real and Eternal, his unlimited sovereignty over his entire creation, his omniscience and omnipotence, his mercy, forgiveness and beneficence, and the imminence of the Day of Judgement on which God, as Judge, will assign in his sovereign will, mankind to Heaven or Hell, the joys and pains of which are portrayed in vivid imagery."[6] While there have been numerous interpretations as to how the relationship of God to man should relate to the process of modernization, it is difficult to see how this basic creed has influenced that process in the real world of Southeast Asia. As we shall see, some of the institutionalized interpretations may have had more direct impact.

The other four pillars are obligations which all good Muslims should follow and Southeast Asian Muslims do practice to varying degrees. Given the explicit nature of these obligations, it is easier to analyze their relationship to modernization. The second pillar, the performance of daily prayers, cannot be seen as having either a negative or positive effect on modernization as such, but the other three may be more significant in these terms. In each case, we will analyze both the original tenet and how it is dealt with in practice.

Zakat

Often considered as alms in Western literature, *zakat* has historically been a regular assessment, usually 2.5 percent of one's possessions annually. These funds are to be used for aid to the needy and the administration of the collection. Zakat is to be paid on property while *fitrah* is a personal obligation that all are to pay regardless of sex or age, except for the poor. In Southeast Asia, the manner of collection and dispersement of these tithes has varied over time and place. Thus, the exact form of the tithe has differed across the states of Malaysia, although since 1960 efforts have been made to systemize the collection. It has been directly collected by state governments since 1962. In Malaysia there is an official zakat, gathered by an official appointed by the state zakat committee, in the form of one tenth of the farmer's paddy.[7] There is also a village zakat. Urban dwellers pay a tax in lieu of the tithe. At the village level, factors such as landownership and annual production lead to variations in payments and some little allowance is made for hardship cases. In general the poor and indigent are not expected to pay. As well, at the end of the Ramadan, fitrah (alms) are given voluntarily to the poor, religious teachers, and the *immam* (individual in charge of the mosque and prayer leader). In other Southeast Asian countries the collection of zakat is generally left to local or regional organizations. Consequently there has been less consistency and less government involvement. In recent years there have been efforts at cooperation over zakat between the Indonesian government and some Islamic groups.

The amount collected can be quite large. In Malaysia, where better data have been available than in Indonesia, it was estimated in 1968 that $3.5 million was brought in annually, primarily from Malay rice farmers.[8] The percentage of crop varied from state to state. For example, it was 6 percent in Kelantan and 9 percent in Selangor. Given the varied manner of collection elsewhere, it is impossible to obtain a reliable figure. However, the size is such that the use of these funds can become an important question in terms of the economic base for modernization, as it is a major tax on the individual who pays the tithe.

The dispersement of zakat funds is carefully laid out in the Koran to cover aid to the poor and needy, recent converts, those in bondage and debt, stranded travelers, as well as the administration of its collection. In addition zakat has been used for more than these directly sanctioned purposes. In Malaysia funds have gone for religious buildings and education, including education for needy Muslim students. In the 1940s the reformist Masjumi party in Indonesia reportedly used zakat collected by party organizations to benefit farmers and small traders,[9] and in the 1960s President Sukarno urged his people to give zakat, promising it would not be used to pay off the national debt, but rather would be expended on Islamic orphanages and educational institutions.

It would thus appear that in contemporary Southeast Asia zakat has gone primarily for welfare and religious purposes in a manner that stretches but does not break the strictures laid down in the Koran. According to one long-time observer of the Malay scene, this concept of zakat underscores the religion's support for social justice.

> It serves three basic functions, which, if achieved, would create a religious-ethical society consonant with the values of Islam. Morally, the act of *zakat* acts to purify the spirit of the tendency to greed and acquisitiveness. The payment of *zakat* has a social dimension in that a degree of redistribution of wealth is effected whereby the economically advantaged may return some of their wealth to be used for the welfare of the less advantaged. Finally, as a result of redistribution of wealth through payment of *zakat*, the tendency for wealth to be concentrated on a minority is removed.[10]

It is difficult to judge the impact of such measures for social justice and redistribution of wealth on modernization. In the first place, we cannot accurately state what the foregone income going to zakat would be used for. If for feasts, religious building or the *hadj* that's one thing, if for savings, agricultural innovation, and the like, it's another. Second, there is the question of whether this quasi-private means of aiding the poor does not allow the government to redirect its funds into modernizing activities. Finally, some hard-headed technocrats may wish to argue that the financing of religious administration, education, and building is not the optimum use of capital that could be expended in more productive activities. In addition, in Malaysia far too high a percentage of funds collected lies unused in state treasuries collecting no interest.

However, while most zakat funds go for originally intended purposes with some breadth of interpretation, a minority has gone to more obviously modernizing activities. In the previously mentioned case of Masjumi programs, zakat was used to aid in the establishment of consumer and producer cooperatives to free the people from the high interest rates charged by Chinese merchants.[11] These co-ops marketed crops and bought wholesale tools and fertilizer. In 1947, when Sarekat Dagang Islam Indonesia (Indonesian Islamic Consumers Association) was formed under the auspices of Masjumi, zakat was employed to establish the Bank Pembangunan Umat (Bank for the Reconstruction of Society). Its purpose was to advance credit at low rates and minimum security requirements to small merchants and poor persons seeking capital to establish businesses.

More recently, in Malaysia another intriguing use of zakat has taken place. Against limited opposition from local religious leaders, some religious departments have invested zakat receipts in MARA (Majlis Amanah Ra'ayat or Council of the Peoples' Trust). In existence for over two decades, MARA's objectives have been:

1. developing manpower;
2. providing Malays and other indigenous peoples with managerial and technical services;
3. providing Malays and other indigenous people credit facilities for commercial and industrial enterprises;
4. establishing commercial, industrial, transportation, and other projects to expedite Malay entrance into these fields; and
5. providing facilities and services of interest to Malays and other indigenous people in commerce and industry. [12]

Programs of MARA include training, advisory services, providing business premises, creating business projects, loans, and transport projects.

While the use of zakat for such purposes has raised theological questions, as early as 1968 a Malay Congress of Muslim Theologians did agree, among other things, "that *zakat* and *fitrah* funds, including other donations for religious purposes (*wakaf*), can be employed for business and trade that ensure the acquisition of profit."[13] Without going into the problems of administering and implementing either the Masjumi or MARA programs, there can be little doubt that both display important modernization needs and each could be rather broadly interpreted to meet religious goals. While both sought to bring the recipients of their projects into the modern economic sector, they also sought to strengthen the Muslim community against its challengers. In the Indonesian case, the Chinese merchant was a target, while in Malaysia, Muslim political leaders have long sought to increase the abilities of Muslim Malays to compete with the Chinese and Indians. The whole concept of MARA has been to aid the Malay to enter the modern sector succesfully. In a country where Islam and Malay are coterminus, this means helping the Muslim. In these cases it has been possible for religion, social justice, and modernization to reinforce one another.

Ramadan

Every Muslim is expected to fast from sunrise to sunset during the lunar month of the Ramadan. While travelers and those physically unable to fast may be temporarily excused (to be made up later), all able-bodied believers are to abstain totally from food and drink during the prescribed time. Apparent negative effects in tropical Southeast Asia are an obvious slowing of pace during the fasting month, particularly as the day wears on (although in modern urban areas air conditioning is helping). Offices tend to close earlier and there is less activity within the Muslim community. It can be argued that the Ramadan is at least a minor obstacle to technological change in that it weakens the physical and mental capacity of the faithful to work to their fullest, particularly in a tropical climate. It could also be postulated that in pluralist religious societies this long period of fasting reinforces dissension within the nation by publicly displaying differences among the citizenry and impeding the ability of Muslims to compete on an equal footing with members of other faiths.

To this, the Muslim replies that the sacrifices of the month of Ramadan strengthen self-discipline, sensitize the practitioner to the problems of the less fortunate, and sharpen his thinking. These benefits are believed to extend beyond the lunar month of fasting. It must also be said that the public display of religious conviction and possible loss of working time are not unique to Islam, but can be seen in the numerous religious holidays of Burma's Theravada Buddhists or the long Filipino Christmas holidays, although these are not part of the basic tenets of these religions.

The Hadj

If possible, every Muslim should make the pilgrimage (the hadj) to Mecca at least once during his or her life. Historically the hadj has been of considerable importance to the Southeast Asian Muslim community. Perhaps because of living at the seeming periphery of the Islamic world, there has been an especially strong desire to take what was once a most arduous and long journey. The opportunity to interact with fellow pilgrims was taken by large numbers of both men and women. Prior to the depression years of the 1930s, Indonesian pilgrims were so important to the economy of Mecca that they were referred to as the "Rice of the Hejaz" (the area within which Mecca is found). In 1926–27 the total number was 52,412, or 42 percent of all the pilgrims from overseas. In other years, while the total numbers were smaller, the percentages reached as high as 43.7 and 47.4[14] [See Table 4.1]. These figures dropped precipitously in the ensuing years due to war, civil strife, economic problems, government policies, and changing religious practices. It was not until the 1970s that the earlier highs were again achieved, and by the beginning of the 1980s approximately 70,000 Indonesians were making the pilgrimage each year. By that time all but a handful were going by air.

As to the rest of Southeast Asia, numbers have been increasing there as well. Due to the strength of the national economy, a growing sense of Islamic identity and active support by the government, the number of Malaysian pilgrims almost tripled, from 5,229 (of whom 5,011 went by sea) in 1965 to 14,846 (all but six by air) in 1980. At the same time over 7,500 came from Thailand, Singapore, and the Philippines.[15]

Several points have been made regarding the relationship of the hadj to the modernization process. They tend to fall into two categories: the loss of domestic capital which might have enhanced modernization, and the reinforcement of religioeconomic elites. The first argument in its simplest form is that the pilgrim saves, borrows, or uses ready capital for a purpose which has little or no positive developmental role, and possibly major negative aspects. For not only is this capital not "usefully" employed, but its proceeds are spent in large part outside the country. This view rests on a number of assumptions: that these funds would not be used for other "nondevelopmental" purposes; that during the period when savings were being accumulated the funds were not being employed to achieve developmental goals; and that there are no other modernizing ends being achieved through the hadj.

We can first attest that the amounts expended have been high both on a personal and national basis. With the onset of air travel, the costs of the hadj have increased markedly. In Indonesia, where the pilgrimage became a government monopoly in 1970, the cost that year was estimated at Rp 1 million (US $ = about 415 Rp) or approximately $2,400 per person.[16] At 70,000 pilgrims and even maintaining the 1970 cost, that would be almost $17 million annually. In Malaysia at about the same time the individual cost of the pilgrimage, estimated by a Japanese team, was M$1500.[17] Care has to be taken in any estimate of exact costs due to government subsidies, the use of hadj funds for other religious purposes (as they have been employed in Indonesia), overhead, and so forth. As well, regrettably, there have been cases of overcharging pilgrims, particularly in the case of Indonesia. Where profits from the hadj have

TABLE 4.1

Indonesian Pilgrims to Mecca 1892–1940

A.H.	A.D.	Total of pilgrims from Indonesia	Total of pilgrims from overseas	%
1310	1892/1893	8092	90173	9,–
1311	1893/1894	6874	49628	13,9
1312	1894/1895	7128	57503	12,4
1313	1895/1896	11788	62726	18,8
1314	1896/1897	7075	41133	17,2
1315	1897/1898	7895	38247	20,6
1316	1898/1899	7694	36380	21,1
1317	1899/1900	5068		—
1318	1900/1901	7421	unknown	—
1319	1901/1902	6092	id.	—
1320	1902/1903	5679	id.	—
1321	1903/1904	9481	74344	12,8
1322	1904/1905	4964	66451	7,5
1323	1905/1906	6863	68735	10,–
1324	1906/1907	8694	108305	8,–
1325	1907/1908	9319	91142	10,2
1326	1908/1909	10300	69077	14,9
1327	1909/1910	10994	71421	15,4
1328	1910/1911	14234	90051	15,8
1329	1911	24025	83749	28,7
1330	1911/1912	18353	83295	22,–
1331	1912/1913	26321	96924	27,2
1332	1913/1914	28427	56855	50,–
1333	1914/1915	—	—	—
1334	1915/1916	—	—	—
1335	1916/1917	72	8585	0.8
1336	1917/1918	48	7020	0.7
1337	1918/1919	1123	22101	5,1
1338	1919/1920	14805	59370	24,9
1339	1920/1921	28795	60786	47,4
1340	1921/1922	22412	unknown	—
1341	1922/1923	22022	86353	25,5
1342	1923/1924	39800	91786	43,4
1343	1924/1925	74	—	—
1344	1925/1926	3474	57957	6,–
1345	1926/1927	52412	123052	42,6
1346	1927/1928	43082	98635	43,7
1347	1928/1929	31405	86021	36,5
1348	1929/1930	33214	84810	39,2
1349	1930/1931	17052	40105	42,5
1350	1931/1932	4385	29065	15,1
1351	1932/1933	2260	20026	11,3
1352	1933/1934	2854	25252	11,3
1353	1934/1935	3693	33898	10,9
1354	1935/1936	4012	33730	11,9
1355	1936/1937	5403	49864	10,8
1356	1937/1938	10327	67224	15,4
1357	1938/1939	10884	59577	18,3
1358	1939/1940	6586	31610	20,8

Source: *Indisch Verslag,* part 2, as far as regards the figures for the years 1878 to 1938. Figures for the years 1939 and 1940: pilgrimage report of the Netherlands Consul in Jeddah with the appendices. From J. Vredenbregt, "The Haddj," *Bijdragen Tot de Taal, Land-en Volkenkunde* 118 (1962):149.

been used for projects such as the construction of the Istiqlal mosque in Jakarta or for various educational institutions, the modernization benefits may be mixed and considerable further research is necessary. [18]

As to the individual pilgrim, he has used a variety of ways to obtain the necessary funds to make the hadj. In his analysis of prewar financing of the hadj in the Netherlands East Indies, J. Vredenbregt[19] saw five major means of financing: (1) savings, particularly among "small-holders"; (2) liquid resources; (3) borrowing; (4) working for wages abroad, particularly in Malaya; and (5) trade on the hadj. Particularly serious economic repercussions for the pilgrim could arise from the sale of property or loans. In the latter case high interest rates at home or the repayment of IOUs made out in Saudi Arabia often led to the forced sale of property. An unusual system was used in Banten where a water buffalo was slaughtered and the meat sold at high prices to villagers who felt social pressure to purchase the meat to finance the pilgrimage (even to the point of pledging their own property).

Both during the colonial period and after independence, governments attempted to limit the worst aspects of financing the hadj. For example, in Malaysia a religious fund has been established to aid savings and to reduce the sale of agricultural land to finance the pilgrimage. The amount in this fund (*Perbadanan Wang Simpanan, Bakal₂ Haji Tanah Malayu*) rose from M$0.4 million in 1962 to M$5.7 million in 1967. In 1974 the Muslim Pilgrims' Corporation had deposits of M$132,803,000.[20] Still, many villagers do not use formal savings institutions and certainly not banks where the issue of *riba* (usury) would be a factor. For these people the sale of land, savings held outside organized financial institutions, and borrowing from relatives would be the usual way of paying for the pilgrimage.

It has been argued that by following this tenet, the Southeast Asian places certain obstacles in the way of modernization. First, in the case of the rural small-holder who saves his or her money over a life-time to take this journey and does not employ an institutionalized means of saving, there is a real question as to whether these accumulating funds could not be used in a manner more conducive to modernization, such as for the education of their children and modernizing agriculture or trades. This affects societal as well as individual modernization, since before state monopolies on the pilgrimage and the airline industry, much of this money was expended outside the country for transportation and costs in Mecca.

However, a reverse effect of the hadj is seen in the middle- or upper-class landowner or shopkeeper who sees in the accumulation of land and other wealth the necessary means of achieving the goal of the pilgrimage.[21] For this individual, the hadj becomes a force for economic achievement and material betterment and all that that might entail.

If the effect of the hadj on capital accumulation for development may have mixed implications, the same may be said for the second major influence of the pilgrimage: its impact on the formation and maintenance of a religioeconomic elite. On the one hand, it has been argued that the hadj reinforces the conservative religioeconomic establishment by reinforcing the status of the more well-to-do landowners and merchants who have been able to afford the pilgrimage. This elite has been described as economically conservative, more prone to support traditionally oriented political parties and programs, and thus not "progressive." It should be noted that the education which these individuals encourage their children to pursue at the higher levels tends to be in the humanities and particularly Islamic studies; yet no longer is there the aversion to secular schooling that previously existed. An example of this pattern was seen by the author at the first graduation of the Malay language Universiti Kebangsaan in Malaysia. No graduates with "Hadji" in their name (publicly denoting their parents' pilgrimage) graduated in science or engineering in that particular class.

However, there are a number of counterarguments to this model of the hadji, without questioning the proposition that many are and remain conservative, particularly among the older small-holders and women. In the first place, there are not always positive reactions in the village to returning pilgrims, particularly to those overly pretentious regarding their new-found status. Those without other proper religious credentials may not receive respect. Rich pilgrims may be considered to have "bought" the hadj and others come back with little more than tales of the trip and souvenirs consisting of pictures, prayer rugs, and cloth.[22] Second, a newer and younger element has begun to take the pilgrimage. Many of these are educated, urban, political, and religious reformists who do not use the title or dress to publicly declare their status. However, in Mecca and the Middle East they take advantage of their stay to make contacts with the general Islamic community and to widen their intellectual vistas. These are individuals often seeking a means of synthesizing their deeply held religious values with modernizing Western education, occupations, and concepts.

This pattern of the hadj being an awakening experience has been commented upon by a number of authors over the years. For example, J. Peacock's work in Java shows that the hadj strengthened theologically reformist views,[23] while others have noted the number of Islamic reformists who were influenced by their pilgrimage. This is not to state that the hadj naturally contributes to political liberalism. Indeed, Peacock and others note that those who have made the hadj tend to support conservative political causes. And, it is no doubt true that the hadj lent status to a new middle class. As Vredenbregt asserted regarding the prewar pattern:

> Accumulation of wealth by commercial activities together with the corresponding ethos of frugality and thrift were a cultural element that offered no connection with the traditional Javanese culture pattern; in fact it meant the rejection of it. But Islam showed the way out. It became the pre-eminent system of values for the new class, the members of which distinguished themselves from their fellow-villagers by their greater economic abilities. These economic criteria also decided the class-position of this social layer which looked for and found a fitting expression of their social status by undertaking the pilgrimage to Mecca; an accomplishment which offered prestige and usually involved the use of status-symbols such as turban or white head-dress. This enhanced prestige and the according status in their turn had an important function regarding the activities of the hadji in the *desa;* more than before he would apply himself to activities that agreed (or were considered to agree) with his (enhanced) status, such as trade and industry, or money-lending or sometimes religious teaching . . . . At the turn of the century this haddj became more and more the symbol of the self-confident Indonesian middle class for whom Islam acquired a unifying and emancipating function, just as it did for the masses. [24]

It should also be noted that the hadj not only provided and still provides a greater sense of unity within the wider Islamic community, but historically contributed to a sense of national consciousness and pride during the years of colonial rule by Kafir governments. Although the Dutch met arriving pilgrims at the port to check on their health, Mecca was a place beyond the control of the colonial authorities, where it was possible to feel equal among brothers and sisters. Thus, in the prewar era, the hadj helped to form a state of national consciousness necessary for the success of the nation-state, one of our prerequisites for modernization. During the ensuing years of independence it may also be somewhat divisive in pluralist societies such as Malaysia. We can only surmise what the contemporary experience means to Malays returning to a country where non-Muslims play such dominant economic roles, particularly after interacting with some of the more radical elements of the Middle East.

In sum then, the hadj has sustained some negative attacks vis-a-vis its relationship to the accumulation and expenditure of funds for "nonproductive" activities and the increased power it may have given conservative forces. However, it also appears to have strengthened the drive for the accumulation of wealth in order to undertake the hadj, broadened the intellectual horizons of many returning pilgrims, and increased a sense of national consciousness. What may be confusing here is a possible disagreement over what fosters modernization. Certainly more equity minded liberal analysts may perceive that increasing religious awareness, when tied to a reinforcement of the status and wealth of the middle class, strengthens forces opposed to change.

Others might argue that the increase in status and the acceleration of an entrepreneurial drive within a largely traditional society are positive moves in the direction of modernization. As will be detailed in a later chapter, perhaps even of more importance has been the reinforcement of Islamic reformism through the hadj. Reformist attitudes downplaying the role of ritual, emphasizing a more individualistic pattern of thinking, and accepting the need to synthesize Islam with Western technology and education were important in establishing the kind of adaptive mind necessary for modernization to succeed.

BUDDHISM

Buddhism has been described by some as not a religion at all, but a code of life, the teachings of one of the world's greatest spiritual leaders. Certainly as a faith whose basic concepts were devoid of ritual, authority, and a Supreme Being, it differs markedly from the Christian-Islamic religions under discussion here. As well, it is a belief system at once very simple and most sophisticated and can be presented here only in its broad outlines. If we go to Buddha's teachings prior to the overlay of centuries of interpretation and institutionalization, we need to begin with the Four Noble Truths, the Eightfold Path, and the Five Precepts. [25]

The Four Noble Truths, taught by Buddha in his first sermon are:

1. All existence is suffering (*dukkha*) involving birth, sickness, old age, death, separation from loved ones, unfulfilled desire, and bondage to what one abhors.

2. Suffering is caused by desire (*tanha*), more properly the need to preserve the individual ego and refusal to accept the impermanence of life.
3. The end of suffering comes through the extinction of desire.
4. The way to achieve this is through the Eightfold Path.

The Eightfold Path provides the way step by step:

1. right knowledge or views, including the Four Noble Truths;
2. right thought which means freeing thought from lust, desire, and ill-will;
3. right speech, meaning the avoidance of falsehood and control of one's passions;
4. right conduct or behavior, focusing on the Five Precepts listed below;
5. right livelihood, relating to occupations which are positive and don't hurt others (Buddha precluded butchers, tax collectors, armament makers, and producers and sellers of alcohol);
6. right efforts means avoiding and eliminating evil thoughts and cultivating good ones;
7. right mindfulness related to meditation, self-examination, and awareness; and
8. right concentration or absorption that arises out of other efforts and meditation.

Buddha provided a specific code of ethics, fewer in number than in the Judeo-Christian and Islamic faiths, but certainly similar in their thrust. They are:

Do not
Kill—most Theravada Buddhists extend this to most animals
Steal
Lie
Be unchaste or sensual
Use alcohol or drugs

Or, as is repeated in Pali by Thai villagers when they call upon the priests to lead the congregation in the Five Precepts:

1. I reverently promise that I will not kill animals myself, nor will I order others to kill them.
2. I reverently promise that I will not myself steal, nor will I order others to steal.
3. I reverently promise not to follow lustful love.
4. I reverently promise not to speak lies, rude or frivolous language, or words which will cause quarrels.
5. I reverently promise to abstain from drinking, smoking, or eating anything that is intoxicating.

These and other teachings of Buddha were written long after his death and out of them have developed a variety of interpretations and schools. Ultimately we will be concentrating on the character of that faith accepted in Burma and Thailand, but first we will address the question as to how these fundamental concepts have affected the modernization process. As was noted in the second chapter, many prewar observers saw Buddhism as otherworldly, antimaterialist, and generally an obstacle to progress. This view has continued into the postwar era as well. As one Vietnamese observer commented, "So far as it teaches the eradication of all desire, and aspiration for non-being, Buddhism is entirely a–economic or anti–economic, since it discourages consumption and production. Its influence on the people's standard of living is thus, on the whole, negative."[26]

However, if we are to assess the impact of original Buddhist doctrine on modernization we face a formidable task. We must initially recognize that Buddha left no strict rules of conduct outside the Five Precepts, gave little attention to the laity, left no school of law, and established "salvation" as an individualistic process. Thus, there are few of the strictures to be found either in the Old Testament or Islamic doctrine and no direct line of authority.

Second, we face the issue raised by Spiro as to the extent to which Buddhism is internalized by the people of Burma and Thailand. If all Buddhists were to follow with care and precision the doctrine of renunciation and emotional detachment then we might expect that this religion would be an insurmountable obstacle to modernization. This true Buddhist would reject all action, empty himself of all self-hood, and seek to abandon all earthly desire. Spiro is probably correct when he asserts that "the doctrines of normative Buddhism only rarely constitute the Buddhism of the faithful" and as to Theravada Buddhism, "Many of its doctrines are only rarely internalized by the members of these societies, because they are either ignored or rejected by the faithful."[27]

At the same time, too many observers have noted particular characteristics of the Buddhist of Southeast Asia to say that there is no impact. Whether this relates to the basic tenets, a re-interpretation of the religion, or other cultural factors is a difficult question about which there is considerable debate. A good deal of what we shall have to say about the influence of Buddhism will come in other chapters, recognizing the lack of internalization of the original doctrine. Since our real question relates to how religion affects modernization, it is not particularly important at this point to differentiate too precisely between "pure" and "popular" Buddhism. However, we can review one obvious element of Buddhism that parallels our earlier analysis of the more ritualistic aspects of Islam.

One of the Five Precepts forbids the taking of life, interpreted by many Buddhists as the taking of all life. Based upon the concept of loving kindness (*metta*), not to take life is a strong belief practiced with varying degrees of strictures in Southeast Asia. In Burma, butchers, cattle farmers, hunters, and fishermen are looked down upon and viewed as not acceptable occupations in Buddhist eyes, although many Burmese eat fish and chicken. This prohibition on taking life has led to a number of problems in modernizing agriculture and medicine, although they have often ultimately been solved by rhetoric sleight-of-hand. In agriculture there have been difficulties in getting farmers to use efficient means of eliminating rodents and insects. It was also necessary to tell the peasant that by spraying his house with DDT it was not his fault that the mosquito died. The elementary health book used by the author to practice his Burmese and distributed by the government to schools stated that the mosquito landed on the wall and "voluntarily died." It also described the microbes that caused illness as vegetable and not living and thus all right to eliminate. The division of opinion on such issues could be seen in 1960 when, upon his return to office, the devout Prime Minister U Nu forbade cattle slaughter, and the army quietly filled the gap for those desiring beef.

On the other hand, in Thailand there has been considerably less attention paid to this precept. The Buddhist Sino-Thais of Bangkok appear almost unaware of the prohibition. In general, Thais are not vegetarians and the government has only forbidden the slaughter of beef on Precept Day. Most village studies find fishing and poultry raising ubiquitous activities of the people. There are various rationalizations for eating meat—the animal is dead anyway—a local Chinese or Indian is asked to kill it—the fish is not killed, it simply dies when out of the water.[28] In this process, the Buddhist displays the same patterns of rationalization found in the adherents of other religions.

With regard to this particular precept, it is thus difficult to say that it has any major effect on modernization, in large part due to its external legitimacy but lack of internalization in practice. We cannot say the same for other parts of the Theravada belief system, including karma, merit, or the role of the monk. These will be considered in other chapters since they reflect the transformations of Buddhism starting in the third century B.C. under King Asoka, through the twelfth and thirteenth centuries A.D. They then would more properly fit under institutionalized or popular beliefs and practices.

We have generally shied away from giving much credence to the impact of fundamental doctrine on contemporary modernization. Most of the reasons for this caution were presented earlier, including similarities in ethical admonitions among the world religions, difficulties in empirically verifying relationships, and the problem of popular internalization of dogma. These points have been supported in varying ways by postwar anthropologists and sociologists who have stressed not only differences between textual and popular religion, but the important variations that exist between values and overt behavior.[29] In the latter case, it is important to recognize that Southeast Asians, like people elsewhere, may conceptualize, publicly promote, and otherwise verbalize religious values that they may practice only intermittently, if at all.

However, all too often both foreigners and locals have written or spoken as though these differences do not exist at all. Norman Jacobs has castigated the former, asserting that: "Certain outsiders, especially westerners, . . . have played what amounts to a "great game" of matching values expressed in texts with actual behavior, or, more typically, behavior they believe it would be nice for Thais to follow in accordance with a scholarly conception of implications from old texts."[30] Of course, the paramount example of such textual analysts was Max Weber who, like so many who followed him, made assumptions about the relationship of religion to behavior and attitudes without the benefits of field research.

However, it has not only been the "scholastics" noted in the first chapter who have played the "great game" as seen by comments of prewar observers of Southeast Asia. In the postwar era, as well, scholars have argued that Islam, Buddhism, or Christianity have been responsible for the acceptance of what they perceive to be aspects of a modern society.

For example, J. Cady and R. Ray have seen in Buddhism the basis for democracy. Ray wrote that "Whoever has cared to enter into its spirit and understand the meaning [of Buddhism] knows very well that it [democracy] is one of those remarkable gifts Buddhism has given to Burma."[31] Increasingly though, as anthropological and sociological research has enlightened our analysis, Western writers have seen the importance of understanding the impact of religion within its historic and cultural environment and have limited their generalizations.

This type of "objective" assessment of a time- and culture-bound religion is not always found acceptable by Southeast Asian Muslim or Buddhist spokesmen. The observation of Jacobs regarding the Thais holds for other peoples as well: "Thais, as almost all believers, are extremely sensitive about any social-scientific and especially sociological study of their religious system. They tend to view such study as a personal assault on themselves by (or inspired by) outsiders who are not interested in, let alone capable of understanding them."[32] More often the rhetoric of the believer has been to deal with matters of faith as part of eternal religious verities. At a more sophisticated level, activists may present efforts to strengthen the role of religion as a drive to return to immutable truths. Thus, a paper on Islamic banking could argue that there is an Islamic banking system that is derived from a deep belief in Allah, His Apostles, Angels, and the teachings inscribed by Muhammad;[33] or we have the writings of the Malay novelist Ahmad Shahnon, who views the superiority of Islam over other religions and notes Islamic innovations.[34] At another level the believer may assert that there is nothing new, that all was explained in the original texts. Thus, in the pre-independence era Indonesian Muslim nationalists could argue that scientific socialism was originally presented in the Koran and Hadith,[35] or in the postwar period Geertz could find an "advanced" Kiayi who would state "The Declaration of the Rights of Man, the secret of atomic power and the principles of scientific medicine are all to be found in the Koran."[36] These comments reflect the firm belief among adherents of these faiths that there is but one immutable and true faith and that it is now being expressed in Southeast Asia. Even those seeking to reinterpret particular aspects of these religions do not feel that they are straying from the core of these beliefs.[37]

In this volume, we have obviously joined those who see a changing pattern of belief and practice and find it futile to either sift out what are the "pure" elements of these faiths or to assess the relationships between the fundamental spiritual core and behavior and attitudes. It is to be noted that when attempting to assess the applicability of basic dogma to modernization we turned to its more ritualistic elements. This meant comparatively little attention to Christianity and Buddhism and considerably greater concentration on the more ritualistically oriented Islam. It would have been possible to assess other Koranic admonitions regarding marriage, inheritance, and the like, but these have been judged either tangential to our quest or too overlain with contemporary interpretations to be analyzed at this point.

The major influence of religion on modernization in Southeast Asia appears to come primarily from popular beliefs and practices, the institutionalization of the faith, and efforts to manipulate religious symbols. If we were dealing with "pure" and "universal" manifestations of religion without the accretion of historic and cultural factors, we would not see the diversity of behavior and attitude that exists in Southeast Asia. S. Alatas stated regarding Islam and capitalism:

> If the capitalist spirit is so closely tied up with the religious attitude, we can expect a uniform pattern of expression among Muslims of common schools and mystical interest. Apparently what is decisive here is not religious but other factors. The factors which released the capitalist spirit among Arab Muslims, Indian Muslims, Minangkabau, Acheh and Bugis Muslims, and also the Chinese, must clearly be of non-religious origin because (a) either they reacted in a different manner despite the same religious and mystical background, or (b) they developed a common capitalist spirit despite differences in religion like the Indian Muslims and the Chinese in Malay.[38]

While these same types of differences and similarities may be found among Theravada Buddhists, we might ask if we do not need a broader definition of religion. This we will investigate in succeeding chapters.

5

Religious Institutions and Modernization

The impact of contemporary religious institutions upon modernization has probably been less than that of such elements as popular practices and the manipulation of religious symbols. In fact, modernization has probably made a greater impact on religion in this area than vice versa. In Southeast Asia the colonial environment, official policies, the traumas of nationalism, and struggles of the postindependence period each in its own way affected these institutions. As well, technological change created new social issues which religious institutions had to confront if they were to keep pace with the problems challenging their adherents. In this chapter we will concentrate upon three aspects of the contemporary religious institutions: the role and structure of the hierarchy, the activities of ecclesiastical personnel, and the activities and attitudes of lay groups. A number of issues involving these organizations have been covered in other chapters. To give cohesion to the analysis some ground will have to be covered again, with as little duplication as possible.

RELIGIOUS HIERARCHIES

This section will investigate the organization and public statements of the hierarchies of the region. We will not go into detail as to how each is organized, as that has been described fully elsewhere.[1] Instead, after brief descriptions of patterns of organization we will concentrate on how these have related to the process of modernization. It should be stated at the outset that this aspect of religion has not been very significant in its influence on the path of modernization; rather it has been the reverse.

The most obvious trend in the development of religious hierarchies in Muslim and Buddhist states has been the effort of governments to centralize the administration of religious personnel. Sunni Islam, as such, does not have a hierarchical structure, but in Malaysia the individual states have attempted to organize religious activities more closely within their domain. Among other actions, there have been efforts to gain the support of "establishment" *ulama* who become the religious, and in some cases the political, spokesmen of the government. The federal authorities on their part have sought to intrude into formal state powers through influencing *ulama* thinking. UMNO, the major Malay party, has looked to religious teachers for political backing. In Malaysia there is a Grand Mufti, but his powers are severely limited.

In Burma, the *sangha* hierarchy was all but moribund during the colonial era. The British conquest of the Kingdom took place through three separate military campaigns over sixty years. After the first wars, sections of lower Burma came under British rule and the sangha in those territories were no longer under the control of the leadership in Mandalay. With the final destruction of the kingdom in 1885–86 the hierarchy seriously deteriorated. As the authority of the sangha leadership was not recognized by the colonial regime, the role of the monk in education declined and the legal jurisdiction of the ecclesiastical hierarchy was not accepted by the civil administration. In the process elements of the sangha became undisciplined and authority tended to revert to the local level. A reversal of this trend began during the Japanese occupation, but it was for U Nu to attempt a major re-organization of the sangha hierarchy. A Supreme Patriarch, ecclesiastical council, and a structure for developing discipline within the sangha were formulated. The results were less than totally satisfactory, as discipline was never completely restored during the U Nu period, as evidenced by the many unauthorized antigovernment demonstrations involving monks that took place during both U Nu's and Ne Win's regimes.

In Thailand the long rule of a monarchy recognized as the protector of Buddhism, the absence of an unsettling colonial experience, and well-calculated efforts to assure control over the sangha all created an atmosphere in which continuity and the centralization of authority could take place. Under the Sangha Acts of 1902, 1941, and 1963 a generally well-organized and disciplined structure was established under the aegis of the government in Bangkok. The 1963 act in particular centralized the authority of the sangha and placed it well within the control of the secular administration. According to S. Suksamran, "the Sangha is effectively incorporated into the government structure at the higher and lower levels in such a manner that the government can exercise effective control over Sangha policy and procedure at the higher administrative levels."[2] Figure 5.1 shows this structure.

In assessing the impact of these changes in hierarchical patterns it should be underscored that while this centralization was being attempted, the role of organization had varying influences on modernization. Thus, in Burma during the colonial era the lack of organization of the sangha allowed elements of it to partake in a variety of secular activities that would not have been permitted in other circumstances. The encouragement by these monks of the nationalist movement and their role as indigenous anticolonial symbols were significant factors in the development of Burmese independence. As well, many monks and local sangha organizations became involved in efforts to achieve reforms in agriculture, the tax structure, and other needed economic changes. The absence of centralized authority can also have negative effects, allowing divisiveness among religious personnel and their use in domestic local political struggles, as seen in both Burma and Malaysia.

Overall, however, the relationship of the hierarchical structures to modernization in Southeast Asia appears to be limited. The process of centralization has both positive and negative aspects. It has allowed governments to employ these organizations more effectively in attempting to achieve development and national integration goals. Therefore, as related in chapter 8, with limited success it was possible for the Thai administration to work with elements of the sangha to encourage local development and foster national integration through employing monks to assist villagers in development projects, strengthening the faith of believers, and attempting to convert the hill tribes. In Malaysia the government supported religious groups with more limited, but similar, goals. Central authorities have also tried to improve the education, discipline, and understanding of religious personnel, with the aim of making them more effective in both religious and secular matters.

However, these efforts to give greater structure to the hierarchy also have created difficulties for religious personnel. Howard Kaufman, in his study of a village in Thailand, detailed some of the problems as they affected the place where he lived.[4] The increased power of the Ministry of Religion brought a concomitant decrease in the autonomy and prestige of the *wat* (temple and monastery) and a loss of morale and status among the monks. The development of a national and local structure to control the sangha led in this case to a questioning of the authority

FIGURE 5.1[3]

Administrative Structure of the Sangha
and its Relationship to the Government

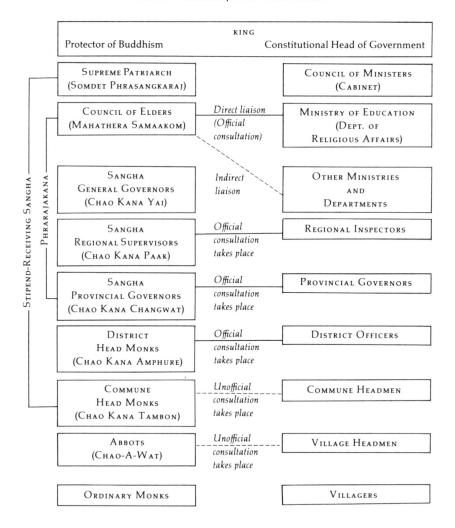

of the abbot and a decline in the role of the monk in the village. In terms of modernization the real issue is whether this substitution of secular power was as useful in providing legitimization for the political structure and desired technological changes. As seen in other studies, success in using the sangha for local development has really been dependent upon the personality of the particular monk or abbot.

In general, though, the religious hierarchies of these countries have tended to concentrate upon nonsecular issues, unless they perceive a major threat to the welfare of their flock or themselves. The pattern has also generally been one of support for the government in power. In Thailand the sangha has not become directly involved with politics and has been under rather tight control with few signs of rebellion. In Burma, where little actual cohesion was achieved, abbots could seemingly always be found to speak for those in power. Thus, after Ne Win took over both the Zawtikaryon and Tipataka Sayadaw made statements supportive of Ne Win and his policies.[5] The Grand Mufti of Malaysia has been a spokesman for the federal government and used in attempts to influence Muslims to support government policy.

Similarly, the Roman Catholic hierarchy in the Philippines has generally been characterized as conservative. Most of its 104 bishops have been criticized by liberal opponents as either politically naive or supporters of the establishment. They are accused of squelching programs and criticism that challenge the government too directly because of innate conservatism, combined with anticommunism and the desire to protect their own positions. Cardinal J. Sin comes in for somewhat less abuse, given his own quarrels with President Marcos, but the left does not think his "critical collaboration" is sufficient and objects to such statements as, "The moment the church advocates a system of government, the church can become a widow in the next generation," and "The church must minister to the left and to the right."[6]

RELIGIOUS PERSONNEL

This section seeks to provide an assessment of the relationship of local religious personnel to modernization. More specifically, it is intended to analyze the role of the Buddhist monk and abbot, Catholic priest, and Muslim ulama and imam at the village level. While changes are taking place in rural areas, aspects of the more volatile urban situation will be viewed in the next chapter. Suffice it to state at this point that while the more traditional patterns of religious leadership remain strong in the villages, what evidence we have shows a decline in their status among the general population of the larger cities.[7]

The Buddhist Monk

While the number of Buddhist monks as a ratio of the populations of Burma and Thailand is apparently declining (see below), it remains quite large when compared to the size of religious personnel in other societies. Most young boys in rural areas are expected to spend at least a short symbolic period as novices and men often will enter the monastery during the Lenten season. In fact, the Thai government gives leave to civil servants for that purpose. At any given time in recent years the number of monks in Burma has run around 100,000, with more than double that number in Thailand (plus another 120,000 novices).

The monk is expected to be at least twenty years old, free of debt and certain illnesses, have the permission of his parents or wife, and agree to follow the vinaya, the disciplinary rules. Accordingly, the monks are not expected to become involved in secular matters, although the actual

TABLE 5.1[8]

Temples, Monks and Novices during the Rainy Season: 1927–1970
in Thailand

Year	Temples	Monks	Novices	Population	Adult Buddhist Males	Monks during Rainy Season		Adult Buddhist Males
1927	16,503	129,698	83,345	11,600,000	2,150,000	1	:	16.5
1937	17,592	149,146	70,800	14,700,000	2,750,000	1	:	18.4
1950	19,704	176,377	75,263	20,000,000	3,740,000	1	:	21.2
1958	21,385	156,111	92,442	24,800,000	4,640,000	1	:	29.7
1961	22,920	152,787	87,335	27,000,000	5,050,000	1	:	33.0
1963	23,184	150,685	83,772	28,500,000	5,330,000	1	:	35.3
1964	23,454	166,975	85,127	29,400,000	5,500,000	1	:	32.9
1966	24,105	175,266	87,661	32,000,000	5,964,000	1	:	34.1
1968	25,116	184,873	108,504	34,000,000	6,358,000	1	:	34.4
1970	25,659	194,561	116,030	36,100,000	6,750,000	1	:	34.7

degree of obedience to the vinaya varies. By far the highest percentage of these monks come from and serve in areas outside Rangoon and Bangkok-Thonburi.[9]

There is consensus among almost all observers that the monk and wat have been central to the Theravada Buddhist community. However, considerable variation can be found in the role and status of monks in different parts of those countries. In most cases the monk has traditionally been viewed with respect and the abbot has been perceived as an individual with stature and spiritual qualities. Nevertheless, there are those who may remain aloof from the village activities or not be held in great esteem. Thus, D. Pfanner noted in his village in Burma that the monks did not participate in or give advice on local matters.[10] In M. Moerman's village in Thailand the monks did not have much personal status, being very young with no monk over thirty and the "abbot" only twenty-two.[11]

In the village the monks may engage in both religious and secular activities. While each man is to seek his own salvation, the monks become intrinsically involved in a wide range of religious ceremonies (marriages, funerals, the opening of new shops or a new house, initiations of boys, etc.), give sermons to the people, and provide religious training to the young. There are also more subtle contributions including providing the laity with role models, giving them a sense of belonging and security, and comforting them in times of stress or misfortune. As well, although properly not within the realm of orthodox Buddhism, the monks participate in animistic practices including blessing charms and amulets to ward off spirits, astrology and fortune telling, folk medicine, and legitimizing some aspects of spirit worship.[12]

Secular functions vary from place to place, depending upon the character and attitudes of the local sangha, the degree of intrusion of modern institutions into traditional roles, and what is expected of the monks locally. In many villages they may give advice on local issues, family or personal problems, provide secular education, and participate in or encourage village development projects. In northeast Thailand, where monks tend to be particularly active, W. Klausner observed them being consulted on community projects, collecting funds for such activities, actually working on the site as "foremen" or contributing manual labor, cooperating with the government in community development and education, arbitrating personal quarrels, providing folk medicine and diagnosing illnesses, giving family and personal advice, acting as a "banker," depositing or loaning funds, giving the village "a symbolic mantle of gentleness" that is "not easily thrown off," acting as astrologer and fortune teller, and functioning as a welfare center, taking care of the poor, problem children and orphans.[13] Again, it should be underscored that these activities can vary markedly from village to village.

The wat or *pongyikyaung* is the center for most of these activities. Suksamran has characterized it as the most important institution in Thai rural life after the family, and "the cardinal and the most integrative institution for the village community."[14] According to H. Kaufman, the wat in his village in Thailand was a counseling agency, primarily for auspicious days for business ventures or social functions, a hospital, a religious school, a community chest from which farmers could rent a variety of goods for special occasions, a free hotel, a news agency with government information posted on a pillar, charity employment, a bank, a clock through the drum and bell, a sports center since the grounds provided the only large area for games, a morgue, a poorhouse, a landlord from whom some villagers rented their home or compound, home for the aged, reservoir for needed water, an asylum for the psychotic, a music school, and, before monks were required to carry identification, a refuge for criminals.[15]

The monks' contribution to modernization needs to be considered in relationship to national integration and community development. Aspects of development programs formulated by the hierarchy with government encouragement and cooperation and the role of the monk in national integration will be assessed in chapter 8. Here emphasis will be placed upon village-level community development activities in which monks act independently from more widely organized operations.

It is not unusual, nor is it universal, to find monks involved in a wide variety of local projects. At one level the monk or abbot may give advice regarding such projects as building roads, digging wells, or improving village structures. This may involve cooperation with government officials who seek the legitimacy of the sangha and hope to encourage the people to perceive these projects as acts of merit. The author has seen this successfully accomplished in Sakol Nakhorn in northeast Thailand where a local military commander obtained the aid of an abbot in a roadbuilding project and in another village a very active abbot was well-known for engaging the populace in such development programs. J. Ingersoll, in a study of a central Thai village, found the local abbot tied into projects ranging from giving advice for a canal to aiding in building a new school. "Practically every official who visited the village wat came to see the head priest to explain his program and hopefully to win the priest's endorsement."[16]

Monks may even engage in manual labor in community development undertakings. Both Klausner and Schecter have provided examples of such activity. According to Klausner, "The northeastern bhikkus are generally very active in aiding the villagers to solve their everyday lay problems. In the northeastern villages, the bhikkus and novices can be seen helping in the construction of a village well, the building of a bridge or small dam, the laying of a new village road, or the erection of a village meeting hall or school."[17]

Schecter gives us the comments of a monk advocate of community development: "We Buddhist monks help the people spiritually but now we are starting to help them physically with community-development projects. Buddhist monks help with wells and dams. I've even told the people not to worry about the police and to cut down logs for a dam. I showed them how to carry on the construction. The people respect the monks. Let them lead the development teams; then they will be successful."[18]

Considerable debate has arisen over the involvement of the sangha in community development programs, particularly when they are fostered by the government. A more detailed review of these objections will be given in chapter 8, and at this time we will concentrate on the relationship of the general role and behavior of the sangha to modernization. Most particularly attention will be focused on criticisms to the very existence of the sangha, coming from Asian Marxists who have often termed clergy in general as parasites and, in some cases, in the same class as prostitutes.[19] These negative assessments have tended to center upon the unproductive nature of sangha activities, the undesirability of the monk as role model, and the traditionalist character of their beliefs.

It is asserted that the monks perform few, if any, useful functions, spending too much of their time in study, meditation, or other religious duties, or are simply lazy. They are materially dependent upon the poor villagers for food, clothing, housing, and other amenities, thus impoverishing those who can ill afford such charity. There is no question that the 300,000 monks, plus novices, in Burma and Thailand do not spend a great deal of their time in pursuits that have a direct bearing on the modernization process; and, as will be analyzed in detail later, it is also true that there is considerable cost to the villager in ceremonies ivolving the sangha and the initiation of boys into the monkhood. Given high underemployment in rural areas, there is at least some question as to the productive alternatives that might be open to these men if they did not continue to lead monastic lives.

Second, it is argued that the monk provides a poor role model for the village youth. Rather than looking to more productive examples, they may choose to follow the path of the monk, selecting an education and career that is not conducive to technological change. It is charged that the poor are particularly vulnerable to being influenced by the monks and abbots who have high status in the village (although some studies show that those at the middle income level are more likely to enter the sangha).[20] The presence of poorly educated monks, activities questionable in terms of the vinaya and the process of secularization have reinforced this negative characterization. This was particularly true in Burma where weak discipline led to sights of monks lined up at the cinema in Rangoon or monks in Mandalay walking about with expensive cameras around their necks.

Even as a role model, the sphere of activity for which he is most respected, the spiritual, may limit the monk's ability to transmit modernity to the people. As well, as J. Mulder has commented, it would be strange if the living habits of the monks' existence were to influence the villagers in sanitation, for example, since they view monastic behavior as peculiar to the monks.[21] To support his position he quotes Klausner's observations that

> The villagers' attitude toward the bhikkhus depends on the situation, and, in certain instances, the villagers view the bhikkhus as a separate group isolated from the ordinary laymen. For example, where an issue involving morality is concerned, the bhikkhus are considered as exemplers of ideal moral conduct and their actions judged against a theoretical ideal that does not apply to laymen. This line of reasoning applies to the bhikkhus' daily living habits in general. In this context, one can understand the seemingly incongruous fact that certain sanitary practices are followed by the bhikkhus but do not reach beyond the wat confines. Despite the bhikkhus' influence, the respect accorded them, and their leadership role in community welfare programs, the villagers do not naturally accept such sanitary reforms merely because the bhikkhus practice them. The villagers feel that such practices as boiling water, using a filter, wearing shoes, and using latrines are reserved for the bhikkhus and identified with their way of life, there is little consideration that such practices might apply to them. The villagers do not see the health factors underlying these practices and associate such acts as part of the Dhamma and rules of discipline of the bhikkhus. The villagers also note with a touch of rural realism that the bhikkhus, by the nature of their life,

can afford to take the pains to carry out such practices as the wearing of shoes and the boiling of water, but the villagers would find it inconvenient to do the same.[22]

Finally, it is argued that the monk is naturally traditional and unsympathetic to modernization. His choice of education and career display his real interests. The dangers to his religion would appear to come from materialism, the increased secularization of society, the loss of age-old functions in education and health to more specialized government personnel, and Marxism and other radical ideologies that are either areligious or antireligious. In these circumstances, it is asserted, the best that can be expected is that the monk will concentrate on his spiritual role since, although there are elements of the sangha that are oriented toward modernity, the sangha as a whole can be expected to inhibit "progress."

A variety of counterarguments can be made underscoring contributions to modernization made by the monks. The most obvious one relates to the increased role of the sangha in community development projects. There is no doubt that these activities have gone much beyond the practices of the prewar years, although they were not absent then. In this role the village monks can provide a respected, legitimizing structure to mobilize the populace toward changes in agriculture, health, education, communications, and the like. An active, modernization-minded abbot in particular can be extremely useful as a promoter, conduit of information, and link with external sources of support. Note that although religious authorities (or personnel; or the clergy) *can* provide these services, in a large proportion of cases this activity is limited. Second, the clergy provide a subtle reinforcement of a sense of unity and security, noted by Klausner, Kaufman, and others. This environment may help to ease the villagers through the traumas of change now being experienced in rural Southeast Asia. Certainly, as will be discussed in the next chapter, there are those who perceive this to be an essential function of the new face of Buddhism.

In sum, the sangha is changing in its involvement in local development and has always given a sense of belonging to the Buddhist villager, but the bulk of the monks remain attached to their more spiritual core. It is that role that the modernizer finds difficult to define in a positive manner.

TABLE 5.2[23]

Ratio of Catholic Priests to Population, Dioceses, and Mission Territory

No. of Catholics per priest (religious & secular)		Mission Territory	Total
Over 10,000 Catholics	3	–	3
From 8,000 to 10,000	5	4	9
From 6,000 to 8,000	11	3	14
From 4,000 to 6,000	6	3	9
Less than 4,000	2	5	7

Roman Catholic Priests

The role of the Roman Catholic priest in Philippine development is significantly different than that of his Buddhist counterpart in terms of closeness to his parishioners, his own and others perception of his role in fostering material change, and the recent extensive nature of his activities in that realm. In the mid 1960s there were less than 4,000 priests in the Philippines, of whom 47 percent were foreigners. This meant an average of 6,000 parishioners per priest, a decrease from 8,300 in 1950. Compare this to one monk to every 34 adult males in Thailand at the same time.

This added up to approximately 15,700 Catholics per parish with a projected increase of 1,000 every five years. In addition there were 5,607 nuns or 4,342 Catholics per nun, about half the ratio of 1950. These figures themselves preclude the more intense relationship between the Buddhist clergy and their laity. This inadequacy has been the focus of much discussion within the hierarchy and populace in the postwar era.

The second significant difference centers upon perceptions of the role of the clergy in social action. There is far less ambivalence in the Philippines among both priests and parishioners, although there can be considerable divergence on aims and methods. Fortunately as well, there are a number of attitude surveys to lend support to any analysis.

It is generally accepted within the Catholic clergy that social action is desirable, although a sizable number do not view it as their primary goal. In a survey of 547 parish priests of the country's 1,868 parishes and representatives of church schools, seminaries, and women's and men's religious communities taken in the early 1970s, 82.81 percent of the parish priests and a majority of the others agreed that, "the priest should initiate social activities in his parish. The priest should not only initiate but also implement the social action program in his parish."[24]

On the other hand, while 320 of the parish priests agreed with the following statement, there was considerable disagreement among the other respondents,

> To parish priests/sisters: Priests or Sisters should primarily concern themselves with moral and spiritual matters rather than with social concern.
> To schools/seminaries: Schools/Seminaries should be primarily concerned with the moral, academic and professional training rather than engaged in social action programs.[25]

The striking aspect of the responses to this question is the rather large numbers that believed social action was more important than traditional spiritual and educational practices.

Other studies in the Philippines reinforce this support for social action. For example, a 1971 survey in one parish found that 95 percent of the priests believed that they should be engaged in development projects in their own parishes.[26] In these and other surveys the clergy suggest a similar set of reasons for involving themselves in social action:

Leadership role
- as a parish, school, seminary or school leader, he should reach out to the people
- people should look up to him
- as a leader he can push the implementation
- he is in the best position and his primary duty
- should be the moving spirit
- he should give support not in words but in works
- a good example as a leader
- a matter of his leadership
- to be more effective among people
- part of his priestly leadership

Part of the church teaching
- comparison with less privileged brethren
- can't preach to empty stomach
- part of the mission of the church
- part of his priestly mission
- part of his training

For credibility
  – to practice what he preaches
  – people's attitudes would be aflamed with priest's involvement
  – people believe more in him
  – for effectivity of the program
To meet the needs of the people
  – show real concern to the people
  – to help people respond to their needs
  – good to look after the needs of the people[27]

These views are reflected in the perceptions of the parishioners who tend to favor an active and development-minded clergy. Various surveys show confidence in clerical involvement in social action and even a belief that the results are better than government projects.[28] Responding to these attitudes and challenges, priests have become increasingly active in social action in the Philippines from giving counsel on development programs to taking to the hills with the insurgents. In the aforementioned survey of 547 priests, 43.1 percent said that social action programs were in existence in their parishes, the most frequently mentioned being:

1. socioeconomic
2. nutrition
3. family life and family planning
4. relief and rehabilitation
5. socioreligious
6. sociopolitical
7. health and sanitation
8. social
9. justice and peace

Different priorities were evident, dependent upon local problems and attitudes.

Some of these social action programs have not found favor with conservative elements of the hierarchy as conflict has arisen between more activist priests and those bishops who wish to control undesirable projects and ideologies. For example, one lay program, the Mindanao-Sulu Pastoral Council (MSPC) was formed in 1971 with the support of southern bishops. Its goal was to emphasize lay leadership and social justice, but the hierarchy perceived the organization as taking an increasingly radical stance vis-à-vis the Filipino establishment. By 1981 the bishops took control of the group. When the staff of the MSPC balked at this the bishops disassociated themselves from the organization.[29] There are those in the clergy and laity that argue that this conservative bent of the hierarchy has aborted the most effective projects aimed at alleviating poverty and the large disparities in income that exist in the islands.

Islamic Religious Personnel

The "clergy" in Islam have distinctly different characteristics than their Buddhist and Christian counterparts. Not only is there no formal hierarchy in Sunni Islam, but there are no official prerequisites to join a priesthood as such. Nor does Islam accept the limitations of the vinaya or the separation of church and state found in the Philippines. We therefore have a less structured pattern with more individual flexibility possible. This does not mean that there are not organizations largely confined to religious personnel or that there are not strong religious and social controls on behavior.

Islamic religious personnel in Southeast Asia fall into three categories, although an individual may be in all three at one time or another. There are religious teachers (ulama or *kiayi*), those in charge of the mosque (*penghulu* or immam), and religious judges (*kathi* or *hakim*). At the village level the ulama and immam or penghulu are the most important in affecting secular matters. Ulama in Indonesia and Malaysia may be men of great knowledge, coming from a long line of scholars and with contacts throughout the Muslim world. At the local level these religious teachers must also lay claim to knowledge of the Koran and Hadith, Islamic history and law, and, of course, Arabic. The ulama's position may also be reinforced by the fact that he is a member of the economic elite and is often related by marriage to elements of the religious and secular powers of the community. In Malaysia the ulama may be supported by state religious councils and immam are now appointed by these councils.

In the rural area the ulama's duties include teaching and directing religious education at various levels, officiating at ceremonies such as funerals, marriages, births, and the opening of new shops or homes, and leading prayer in the mosque. As well, he may be asked for his counsel on personal and village matters and issue informal *fatwa* (rulings) on a variety of subjects. The ulama in both countries have also become deeply involved in local and national political questions. In the Netherlands East Indies they were the core to the foundation of the orthodox political party,

Nahdatul Ulama. In postwar Indonesia reformist ulamas and their more conservative counterparts gravitated to the still active Nahdatul Ulama. With the changes made by the New Order, Muslim political groups were brought together in a new organization, the Partai Persatuan Pembangunan (PPP). Many PPP adherents become members of village boards where they have come into conflict with elements of the government-backed Golkar party. In Malaysia the intensity of the disputes dividing local ulama supporting UMNO from those backing the opposition PMIP-PAS have become legendary. Ulamas have actively entered the political list and condemned their opponents on secular and religious grounds, even terming them infidels and refusing to participate in religious rituals with them.

It is not easy to relate the relationship of the Islamic elite in Southeast Asia to modernization because of these divisions within the ranks. However, many of the same positive and negative points could be made with regard to Muslim religious personnel as were presented earlier with respect to the Buddhist monks. The issue of religious education will be reviewed in another chapter. Suffice it to state here that the bulk of ulama and other Muslim religious personnel at the local level tend to be conservative in their religious and political attitudes and behavior. They have not shown great flexibility in accepting new educational, health, and social changes. Their economic and social ties to the community elite have also tended to make them supporters of the status quo and suspicious of economic or social reforms. Examples of well-known ulama with strong interests in modernization exist, but their ideas are not always reflected at the village level.

LAY RELIGIOUS ORGANIZATIONS

Lay religious organizations have been particularly strong in Muslim Southeast Asia and especially well-organized at an early date in Indonesia. The most well-known of these was the Muhammadiyah, founded in 1912 and continuously active in preaching to Muslims in the Indies through the employment of *muballighs* (missionaries), publications, and education. Islamic reformist in thought, it sought to "make Mulsims better Muslims." The Muhammadiyah was the precursor of similar organizations elsewhere in the region.

While in the prewar era such activities were subsumed under the concept of *tabligh* (preaching), after the war the word *dakwah* or *da'wa* came to be used to denote a wider view of the process of Islamicizing Muslims. In this ideality, lay religious organizations have expanded their conception of what is involved in missionary activities. While there are other types of lay religious groups in the region, this section will concentrate upon the impact of missionary-oriented institutions on modernization. In the process we will not again recount the relationship of such movements to the religious resurgence, but will more narrowly target their specific tasks and aims.

Dakwah in Malaysia and Indonesia have tended to be composed of two broad types, those seeking the conversion of nonbelievers and those attempting to strengthen Islam among Muslims. Other divisions can also be delineated based upon the scope of activities, reformist versus orthodox concepts of Islam, and government versus private. In Malaysia, no major dakwah institution seeks only to convert the "heathen," but PERKIM (The Islamic Welfare and Missionary Association) is best known for its efforts in that field. Based in the Prime Minister's office, PERKIM receives some government funds, but operates primarily from donations, income from its own investments, and foreign aid. With some fifty offices in the nation, it is especially known for its efforts to convert the Chinese and aborigines of East Malaysia. PERKIM has maintained a rather flexible attitude in its proselytizing, accepting the continuance of non-Muslim behavior among converts and not demanding the more intense introspection encouraged by other contemporary dakwah groups. This has led to the charge that it seeks symbolic Muslims, reflecting a government policy of national integration, thus challenging the more "radical" dakwah aims. It should also be noted that PERKIM works among Muslims. Its welfare programs include clinics, kindergartens, and adult education.

Malaysian dakwah targeting the Muslim is best exemplified by three organizations with quite different patterns of behavior: Darul Arqam, Jemaat Tabligh, and ABIM.[30] Darul Arqam is a comparatively small group known for the commune it operates outside Kuala Lumpur. A significant section of its membership comes from the young educated professional class, a group which is also well represented in counterpart organizations throughout the region. In the commune its members wear Arabic clothing, eat in Arabic style, and eschew Western amenities such as television and electric fans.

Darul Arqam has developed a variety of educational, medical, and economic activities that have made it influential beyond its numbers. It maintains a large, highly traditional, religious school where Arabic and fundamental Islamic teaching is emphasized. It operates a clinic that is open to all, using both modern Western and folk medicine. Through these projects it is hoped that adherents will be attracted to the organization. Most apparent beyond the commune are the various economic activities which include small shops and manufacturing concerns, particularly in food processing. Through these it expects to support itself financially, teach Musims to be self-reliant, and provide *(halal)* products.

The Jemaat Tabligh came to Malaya in the 1950s out of India and is part of a worldwide movement. With little organization and no formal leadership, it involves missionary work throughout the country. It is active in both the villages and the universities through discussions, retreats, and other methods that emphasize the more formal and ritualistic aspect of Islam.

By far the best-known dakwah organization in Malaysia is ABIM (Muslim Youth League of Malaysia). Founded in 1971, its membership is estimated to be 35,000, although many more have attended its rallies. Under its former President, Anwar Ibrahim, ABIM was considered politically dangerous to the UMNO establishment, in large part because of its leadership. Structurally, the organization reaches throughout the Peninsula, but is particularly strong in Kuala Lumpur and in the universities. It has established a school system synthesizing both Western and Islamic concepts, not unlike reformist schools in Indonesia. Vocational subjects are also taught and ABIM accepts the social and natural sciences with an Islamic slant. Arabic is compulsory and the curriculum stresses academic subjects. ABIM also made an abortive move into practical economics, developing a cooperative marketing system aimed at the Malay hierarchy, seeking to raise the economic level of the *bumiputera* (sons of the soil, primarily Malays), and advancing Islamic economic concepts.

ABIM has also been active in organizing seminars, lectures, speeches, and demonstrations covering a wide range of subjects. It has attempted to raise the consciousness of Malay Muslims with regard to international Islamic issues and for a time flirted with the Islamic Revolution in Iran. ABIM has had close contact with individuals, organizations, and governments involved in developing a worldwide Islamic network. Anwar Ibrahim, ABIM's former president, was Malaysia's delegate to the World Association of Muslim Youth.

If ABIM's flirtation with international Islam worried the government, the style and views on domestic issues of its leaders, other than Anwar Ibrahim, were even more alarming. ABIM has attracted a young, educated, and committed core that has displayed organizational and media abilities not easily found among more traditional groups. Anwar Ibrahim was recognized as a charismatic leader capable of challenging

UMNO politically and suspected of seeking an alliance with PAS. He has tended to be far more flexible and tolerant in dealing with other communal groups in Malaysia than with other ABIM leaders.[31] In contrast to strong Malay chauvinist comments often heard from the latter, Anwar supported a plural society and emphasized that he only sought to make Muslims better Muslims. While other ABIM officers have been stridently anti-Western in their economic views, he called for a more equitable society with the takeover of some industries, such as palm oil and tin, but not oil. While he denied that he was socialist, his views fit those of Islamic socialists in other countries. His moderate approach and obvious charisma led to his co-optation by the government. He ultimately became Minister of Sports and Culture and later of Agriculture, leaving ABIM to a less moderate leadership.

In Indonesia dakwah is now taking on a new energy as many Muslim leaders see in it a means of countering both government religious-ideological concepts and undesirable aspects of modern ways. The government itself, through the Ministry of Religious Affairs, is also active in the field. Through its offices of Guidance of the Islamic Community and Hadj and care for Islamic institutions, the Ministry carries out Islamic research, publishes the Koran and books on Islam, and works in the prisons and among isolated tribes. These are administered down to the lowest levels of the polity.

There is also a wide variety of private efforts. The Muhammadiyah remains extremely active, operating some 12,400 schools, colleges, and universities throughout the Republic, 9 hospitals, 308 polyclinics, 86 maternity clinics, and 89 orphanages, plus its traditional missionary outreach programs. The Dewan Da'wah Islamiyah Indonesia, under the leadership of former Masjumi leader and Prime Minister, M. Natsir, is reformist in ideology, like the Muhammadiyah. The Dewan publishes considerable literature, operates schools and hopsitals, and sends mis-sionaries throughout the country. Natsir has stated the aims of dakwah as improving the training of "missionaries," intensifying social welfare activities, particularly among the poor, cooperating with other Islamic institutions to improve education, and stimulating cooperation among Muslims.[32]

Also active have been the Nahdatul Ulama and Pendidakan Tinggi Da'wah Islam. Along with its political activities, the more conservative NU has worked through *pesantren* (Islamic boarding school) and its own school system to implement more orthodox religious goals. While there are those within the organization who wish to concentrate on the latter, it remains to be seen if the NU's efforts to challenge more reformist elements will be successful.

The PTDI was established by military officers in 1963 and had as its target ex-military men who might be attracted by communism or militarism. While more modernist then the NU, its anti-communism makes it somewhat more conservative. Both the PTDI and Dewan Da'wah have engaged in efforts to improve village agricultural practices.

A somewhat different organization is the Lembaga Studi Pembangunan or Institute for Development Studies. This private institution is involved in a variety of development programs. As part of their activities its members help to train Muslim teachers in educational and development programs. One of its more interesting projects is the use of the pesantren in cooperative development. As explained in the organization's annual report, its philosophy in this area is,

> To uplift the people from their poverty and backwardness to become complete and respected human beings, there is required a process of humanisation that includes religious education so that they realise their own potential, and how to use God's gifts, together with filling their souls with faith in Islam. There are not yet very many activities with this orientation because the formula and methods are not yet understood. The majority of religious education revolves around faith and worship, while issues such as extending that faith through good actions in the community is barely touched on.
>
> It is quite strategical that Islamic preachers give religious training to the poorer social strata given their respected and influential position in the community.[33]

When assessing the efforts of various lay organizations to seek greater commitment to their particular faith, it is necessary to consider their aims, success in implementation, and the perceptions of other members of the community. The goals of many of these groups would appear conducive to elements of modernization delineated in this volume. The forging of a unity of believers could aid national integration, particularly if accompanied by toleration of other religions. The expansion of dakwah and Buddhist and Christian missionary activities into health, agriculture, manufacturing, and educational fields help to legitimize modernizing behavior through religious support. Most of these organizations have been moderate to reformist in their worldviews and have been sympathetic conduits to change. In the postwar era their leadership has often come from the young and educated elite who are more comfortable in the modern scientific environment and more capable in employing contemporary organizational and media techniques.

However, there are some real questions as to the implementation of often lofty aims and the negative reactions of other elements of the community to their articulated goals. Spokesmen of these organizations often express unrealistically high goals for conversions, thereby raising real fears among nonbelievers. Thus there were the exaggerated predictions of PERKIM that there would be 250,000 converts in Malaysia in the five years after 1976, the glowing accounts of dakwah efforts by the Indonesian Council of Mosques, the floundering of ABIM's attempts at cooperative marketing, and Filipino Christian statements regarding the conversion of Moros.

As well, there has been considerable criticism of the educational quality of the schooling provided by some of these organizations. In Indonesia the reformist leaders themselves have recognized the need to improve the training of teachers and the character of the curriculum. In Malaysia the Darul Arqam school has been charged with being too heavily loaded with traditional Islamic subjects and unlike an urban *pondok*.[34] ABIM schools are said to present the social and physical sciences in a manner that denigrates them as somehow un-Islamic. Still, these educational institutions are often all that is available to poorer students and may be more acceptable to traditional parents who might otherwise be unwilling to send their children to a more secular school.

The most serious negative criticism leveled at the efforts of these lay organizations arises from the alleged divisiveness resulting from the promulgation of religious values by highly committed individuals and groups. This issue will be reviewed in detail in the next chapter, but at this juncture several points need to be noted briefly. Often lay organizations have displayed little tolerance for the rights of other faiths. Some spokesmen for Darul Aqam, ABIM, and even the Muhammadiyah have been critical of Christian missionary activities and called for the conversion of all the people of the nation to Islam.

In Indonesia elements of the Muhammadiyah and Nahdatul Ulama have led challenges to foreign support of Christian efforts while some dakwah leaders in Malaysia have expressed skepticism about the concept of a religiously plural society. This type of comment, when combined with vigorous proselytizing, has worried minority groups within these countries. In Malaysia, in particular, the wedding of Malay and Muslim chauvinism plus the government policy of special economic and educational privileges for the *bumiputera* have made the Chinese and Indian communities uneasy. Against this backdrop, Muslim missionary activities are considered by many of their targets as endangering national unity and their own livelihoods. In polities where religious minorities are smaller and live in more isolated parts of the country, such as Thailand or the Philippines, this is not a central national issue; but missionary activities can increase paranoia and give credence to other complaints.

Of course, if such missionary efforts become successful their ultimate goal will achieve national integration under one faith. Thus, it is argued that PERKIM's labors to convert the Chinese can break down racial tensions and, while Tabligh is often viewed as too Indian or Pakistani, it is attempting to bring to Islam members of every community in Malaysia. The extent to which PERKIM, Tabligh, and their counterparts elsewhere in the region can weaken the perception of the unity of ethnicity and religion, thereby attaining a higher level of national integration, is open to serious question. At this time such a breakthrough is in the distant future and even the converts may be looked upon with suspicion. In Malaysia the Chinese converts are particularly open to question as "rice Muslims." The major impact of these organizations has not been their successful conversions, but the role they have played in the religious resurgence sweeping the region, one of the topics of the next chapter.

The role of the layman in Buddhism traditionally has not been as important as in Christian and Muslim societies. In part this comes from the central role played by the monks and in part from the ease of entering the sangha and participating in that role. Thus, K. Landon could write before the war that the rise of the layman in Thailand was a "new trend"[35] and in 1981 D. Swearer observed that lay associations taking over the responsibilities of the monasteries was a modern development.[36]

This does not mean that lay associations have not played an important role in these countries during the past century. Before the war both Burma and Thailand had their Young Men's Buddhist Associations which emphasized the study and spread of the faith. The YMBA in Burma was patterned directly after the YMCA, but became much more involved in secular nationalist issues than either its Christian or Thai counterparts. Earlier in Burma various lay organizations had been formed to improve Buddhist instruction and to provide an alternative to traditional sangha activities.

The past few decades have seen something of a proliferation of lay associations in both countries as the resurgence of Buddhism has attracted a wider audience. Thus, in Burma the Buddha Sasana Nuggaha Ahpwe (BSNA) was founded in 1947 with the aims of working for the progress, expansion, and stability of Buddhism, helping in the scholarship and practice of Buddhism, and establishing a building to house the Buddhist scriptures.[37] The group not only built a series of structures to act as a clinic, prayer hall, and meditation center that was the precursor of the Kaba Aye Peace Pagoda, but engaged in missionary activity among the hill tribes and promoted meditation centers.

This and other Buddhist lay organizations in Southeast Asia have been predominately involved in interests similar to dakwah. They have sought to reinforce understanding of Buddhism and to proselytize among the nonbelievers. However, these activities have neither been as widespread as in the Muslim societies or become involved in secular activities to the same degree. But they too have attempted to expand religion beyond its traditional boundaries. Swearer sees a danger to the sangha in this, asking rhetorically, "What justification remains for the monastic order if laypersons are becoming meditation teachers and performing social services once rendered by the monastery when it was the most important organization outside the family."[38] The probability is that lay associations in Burma and Thailand are far from being a serious challenge to the sangha today. The greater danger comes from unfriendly state authorities as seen in Burma, Laos, and Cambodia.

Roman Catholic lay organizations have a long history throughout the Catholic world. In the Philippines such associations have been active with and without the sanction of the church. Some have emphasized religious priorities, while others have centered on social action. The best example of the more religious type would be the pastoral and parish councils which were formed to advise on lay religious matters (many lay leaders would say decide as well as advise). Working in conjunction with the church, these councils have displayed comparatively more interest in subjects dealing with the family, religion, and education than in social action. It would appear that the hierarchy would like to see it maintain these interests rather than launch into more sensitive areas.

More directly targeting development objectives have been the church supported Social Action Centers (SACs). The primary motives of these groups have been economic development and social justice. In the former realm they have sought to improve agriculture (from pig-farming to irrigation), health, nutrition, sanitation, and family planning and to establish health centers, cooperatives, and credit unions.[39] In the area of social justice there have been calls for eliminating economic inequities and increasing the ability of the people to affect decisions. Different SACs vary in their priorities with some such as those on Luzon emphasizing economic development and the Mindanao SACs pressing for social action. Thus the former calls for the provision of health and welfare services, relief and rehabilitation, the development of socioeconomic institutions, promotion of self-help projects in education and training, and the development of housing and resettlement. The Mindanao SACs made such statements as,

> to promote movements and organizations for the Little Man respon-
>   sive to their socio-economic needs and to equality;
> education for the development of people's leadership in organizations
>   for social change and progress;
> conscientization and organization of smaller communities;
> conscientization: people are made aware of their capacities for
>   alleviating their plight;
> conscientization, cooperative development, family enrichment,
>   and social justice;
> development, justice and peace;
> total human development and and the promotion of justice;
> to enable the weak and the poor to gain strength and better provide
>   for themselves and thus attain more human dignity;
> to help man in his struggle for equality and participation in
>   decision making and thus attain for himself dignity and freedom
>   and eventually form together with others a Christian Community;
> to concretize and actualize among the masses the Gospel message
>   of Justice and among the rich the awareness and application of
>   the Gospel. [40]

In sum, although it is difficult to generalize about the role of religious institutions in the process of modernization, recent years have seen expanded efforts toward modernization by both lay organizations and clergy. Technological change remains only a marginal interest to the vast majority of the religious in Southeast Asia, but changes are underway.

6

Popular Beliefs

Religion as it is perceived and practiced in Southeast Asia today
is the result of the accretion of new tenets and the interpretation
of old ones. Each major faith displays considerable heterogeneity by way
of sect, the degree of the influence of animism and other religious beliefs,
and levels of secularization, each of which underscores its variance from
the fundamental dogmas discussed in the preceding pages. This chapter
does not seek to address the myriad of belief systems that inhabit the
religion, but to concentrate upon several areas that appear to be related
to the process of modernization. These include Buddhist views of merit
and karma, characterizations of Southeast Asians as "otherworldly" or
fatalist, the religious resurgence, and contemporary intellectual concepts of
the role of religion as it pertains to modernization.

All of these factors have been targets of conflicting interpretations
among both scholars and the general public. Reasons for these differences
involve the limited amount of data available on many of these issues,
a lack of clarity in the meaning of terms such as "otherworldly" or
"fundamentalist," and the nature of many recent changes in the role of
religion in these societies. In the last instance, while the escalation of
the religious resurgence during the past decade has its antecedents in
earlier years, its present impact has markedly changed perceptions and
interpretations of the role of religion in modernization.

POPULAR BUDDHIST BELIEFS

As we saw in the last chapter, a rigid acceptance of the fundamental
dogma of Buddhism would probably straitjacket modernization, leading

the believer to reject the materialism of this life. However, as interpreted by the average Burmese or Thai today, individual expectations are quite different and can bring us to different interpretations of the relationship of Buddhism to modernization. This is particularly true when perceptions of karma and merit are addressed. Central to popular Theravada Buddhism is the belief in a series of births and rebirths and that one's present situation is the result of experience in past lives. Former good or bad behaviour shapes the conditions of life today and good or bad behaviour in this life leads to merit or demerit affecting future rebirth. This is not a totally fatalistic doctrine, for as Bhikku U Thittila commented, "man has a certian amount of free will; he can modify his actions and affect his future."[1]

In orthodox Buddhism the ultimate aim of man was the end of suffering and the attainment of Nirvana. While one element of the Theravada community may center its thoughts on the achievement of this goal, for the average Thai or Burmese, Nirvana is perceived more as a heavenly paradise and the more immediate aim is rebirth to a more pleasurable life and the avoidance of retribution for acts of demerit. The objective is thus more materialistic in form.

Undesirable behavior can lead to rebirth as a lesser being or even the terrors of hell. Such acts of demerit include killing, stealing, lying, drink, envy, and the abuse of others. Merit is accumulated through proper behaviour and more specifically through certain recognized acts. Often quoted is H. Kaufman's list of acts of merit based upon his observations in the central plains of Thailand:

1. becoming a monk;
2. contributing enough money for the construction of a wat;
3. having a son ordained as a monk;
4. making excursions to Buddhist shrines;
5. making contributions toward the repair of a wat;
6. giving food, daily, to the monks and giving food on holy days;
7. becoming a novice;
8. attending the wat on all holy days and obeying the eight laws on those days;
9. obeying the five precepts at all times; and
10. giving money and clothing to the monks at the Kathin festival.[2]

Working in northeast Thailand, S. Tambiah provided a somewhat different list:

1. completing financing of the building of a wat;
2. either becoming a monk or having a son become a monk;

3. contributing money to repair a wat or making Kathin gifts;
4. giving food daily to monks;
5. observing every *wanphra* (holy day); and
6. strictly observing the five precepts. [3]

More recently, efforts have been made by the government and hierarchy to add community development to these lists. However, generally, the emphasis has been on support of the sangha and religious giving.

It is not the intention here to describe in detail the intricacies of popular views on karma and merit. For such analyses the reader is directed to the works of M. Spiro and S. Tambiah. [4] Rather, the subject of this section is the validity of some of the charges made that popular Buddhism inhibits the process of modernization by emphasizing nonmaterialist values, weakening ambition, and fostering a lack of social concience.

Materialism

In theory, the Theravada Buddhist, like his counterparts in most religions, rejects an emphasis upon materialism. The Southeast Asian Buddhist has often been described as "otherworldly" and uninterested in worldly goods. This view is often fostered by those who decry the material baggage brought by the West and warn that it can destroy the value of both the nation and the individual. Upon leaving Burma in 1960, several Burmese friends told the author of their regret that he was returning to the United States where rampant materialism would limit his religious "progress". Yet this disapproval of materialism does not appear to mesh with the reality of popular attitudes. There seems to be strong interest in acquiring radios, televisions, bicycles, automobiles, running water, electricity, and other amenities of modern life. When Spiro asked Burmese villagers "what do you desire for your next existence?", the second choice after Nirvana was to be rich. [5] At the same time, while saving for the acquisition of such goods can be limited by high expenditures for religious giving and ceremonies, in many cases it may simply be a long-term investment in a better life in the future. There have also been more mundane reasons for not purchasing material goods, such as the dangers of thievery, the need to save in case of poor harvests, or fears that ostentation might attract the government tax collector. As well, conspicuous consumption is usually frowned upon in rural areas.

Lack of Ambition

It is argued that since past karma has defined one's place in life, there is little reason for the individual to display much ambition. While the average Thai or Burmese may blame his problems on weather, the government, or the spirits, he is also likely to point to bad karma from misdeeds in the past. However, this does not appear to lead to the heavy collar of fatalism, since it is also important to prepare for the next existence. Thus, as one observer commented:

> The belief in karma may indeed induce an attitude of resignation to the frustrating conditions of one's present existence, even when this view is qualified, as it is in Burma, by the belief in the importance of wisdom and effort as co-determinants of one's life chances. For the Burman, however, the present existence is but a moment in a total "life" of inconceivably long duration. Although his belief in karma might resign him to his present poverty and suffering, the Burman nevertheless aspires to a future of riches and happiness. It is his belief in karma, and the efficacy of merit as a means of improving karma that provides him with the expectation of altering, even dramatically altering, his future life-chances. On the assumption, then, that one's present existence is but a temporary way station in one's total life, it would seem quite obvious that hope, planning, and effort—not resignation, indifference, and quiescence—are the conditions to which the belief in karma are conducive.[6]

It is even possible to argue that there are positive entrepreneurial aspects to merit since on the one hand wealth is perceived as a sign of good karma and on the other it is necessary to have the ability to spend for giving in order to achieve a better next life. Thus, popular Buddhism would appear to encourage saving and investment. The problem is that, unlike Weber's Protestants, the urge to save is not oriented toward investment in "productive" activities, but toward giving for religious purposes. Thus, as will be detailed in chapter 7, heavy expenditures in this area can have negative consequences for modernization. Noting these consequences, Spiro commented, "It takes little imagination to realize that, if even part of the economic surplus that so long has been devoted to (giving) had been available instead for economic investment, Burmese economic history might have been significantly different."[7]

Individualism and Social Conscience

Finally, it is charged that Buddhism encourages selfish individualism and a weak social conscience. Observers have long noted a high level of individualism in Burmese and Thai society and the difficulty of achieving cooperative action.[8] There have been some who have attributed this, at least in part, to Buddhism. It is true that the religion emphasizes salvation through one's own efforts and that acts of merit are made to develop one's own welfare. Buddha said, "Work out your own salvation with diligence," and the scriptures read, "By oneself is evil done; By oneself one suffers; By oneself is evil left undone; By oneself one is purified." As H. Phillips describes this pattern, "it is imperative to point out that the principal tenet of Hinayana Buddhism is the complete psychological freedom, isolation, and responsibility of every person."[9] Still, it is a difficult point to make, given other factors that have made the populace suspicious of cooperative efforts (such as government manipulation).

More potent is the argument that Theravada Buddhism does not encourage giving for secular reasons. Merit is primarily to be gained through the support of the religious, including building or repairing wats and feeding and clothing the monks. Aid to the poor, support of hospitals, and other secular charities have traditionally received comparatively little backing in Burma and Thailand. Projects to achieve such goals must often be given the aura of merit-making to attain success. Government personnel, abbots, and local leaders have at times cast activities in that vein, not always with great success. This continued predeliction toward support for religious giving to the neglect of secular charity can affect modernization to the extent that it inhibits cooperative efforts in the development realm.

"OTHERWORLDLINESS" AND FATALISM

Frequent charges have appeared in both the prewar and postwar literature stating that "progress" in Southeast Asia has been hampered by "otherworldly" and fatalistic tendencies among the people of the region. It is difficult to address the issue of "otherworldliness" since it appears to be a short-hand for a range of attitudes and behaviour from belief in spirits and an overemphasis upon religious dogma to inordinate expenditures of time and money on religious activities. There is no doubt that in theory there is a de-emphasis upon material goods, and that, when compared to their European and American counterparts, the average Buddhist, Muslim, or Christian in the region does appear to have a deeper commitment to matters of faith, and does give more time, energy, and surplus income to religion. However, as to whether this creates a psychological isolation from this universe is another, and far less supportable charge. It is certainly not one founded upon systematic empirical analysis.

More concrete is the description of the Southeast Asian as more dependent upon spiritual forces for defining his present place and future. As discussed elsewhere in this volume, animist spirits are still powerful influences that must be propitiated and in conjunction with interpretations of the dominant world faith can have an effect on medical and agricultural practices. To the extent that the individual or society does not seek to meet problems in a practical manner and looks to external powers, he may not be able to confront "real-world" issues. However, as will be emphasized, this does not appear to be the normal behavior of villagers who usually make decisions on grounds related to highly practical considerations.

More precise have been statements that Christians and Muslims are prone to take fatalistic attitudes towards life and that this has inhibited modernization in the area. Thus, in a controversial article B. Parkinson said of the Malay in Malaysia that,

> The Islamic belief that all things are emanations from God is another important force affecting the Malays' economic behavior, for it tends to make them fatalistic in their approach to life. The Malay is very prone, after receiving a setback, to give up striving, and to say that he has no luck, that it is the will of God. In economic affairs this is most clearly seen in the concept *rezeki*, a person's divinely inspired economic lot. Such an attitude constitutes a significant drag on economic development. For, if the Malays subscribe to this fatalistic view and believe that any individual efforts to improve living

standards are not likely to be successful, then they are not likely
to attempt to master nature, or to strive for their own economic
advancement by initiating changes necessary for it. [10]

Islamic fatalism is allegedly based upon a belief in the powerlessness
of man to define his own destiny, since all that happens is God's will.
Given this determination, the individual is thus not prepared to take risks,
too easily accepts his fate, supports the present social order rather than
seeking to change it, and is generally weakened in his resolve to exert
himself. In the Malay case, it is supposedly reinforced by a messianic
tradition that looks to a "golden age" defined in traditional rather than
modern terms. "In other words, it does not seem to envisage a commercial
or industrial community with all the trappings of material wealth, and
any economic changes that merely promise to lead toward this end are
therefore not accepted with quite the exuberance as they might be in
the West." [11]

Filipino Catholics have been similarly described as fatalistic, seeing
their lives determined by God. According to one Catholic prelate this
belief is founded upon views concerning "the world and man's relation
to it: man is governed by a set of forces beyond his control." [12] This
is perceived by modernists as shirking one's duty and withdrawing from
personal responsibility, which is detrimental to development and makes
it difficult to start and maintain socioeconomic projects.

In the case of the Philippines we actually have some empirical
evidence of fatalistic attitudes. In a survey of the municipality of Vigan
reported in 1975 there was the following question and response:
"Everything going on in this place is God's will, therefore nothing can
be done about our situation here. Do you agree or disagree?"

Agree	36.7%
Disagree	47.9
No Answer	15.4 [13]

Those in the professions and services displayed the greatest
disapproval of the assertion, while people in business and the handicrafts
had the highest percentage of agreement. It could be argued that similar
surveys in more rural areas would elicit even higher levels of fatalistic
belief.

The difficulties in assessing the relationship of popular religion to
modernization are based upon both methodological problems and the

apparent great diversity of attitudes in the region. In the first instance not only is there comparatively little empirical data, but there is the problem noted in previous chapters of having to come to grips with the internalization of beliefs and their impact upon behaviour. In the case of diversity, there are too many examples of adherents to the same religion displaying different perceptions of modernization and its utility. Thus, we have Chinese in Burma and Thailand who have accepted local Buddhist beliefs and are legendary in their entrepreneurial skills and Pakistani and Indian Muslims who display similar attributes in Malaysia and Indonesia.[14] As previously argued by Alatas, the capitalist spirit has differed in Southeast Asia among Muslims in spite of similarity in religious belief.[15]

This is not to state that Muslims, Christians, and Buddhists may not be "otherwordly" or fatalistic and that this might not hamper modernization. Many are, and they do! However, it does mean that it is necessary to analyze the relationship of popular belief to modernization on a more discrete basis. Popular belief becomes important to our task when viewed within the more circumscribed limits of more local belief systems. Within that smaller community, behavior results from an amalgam of religious contexts, some orthodox and others not. One must consider holistically the relationship to the outside world and a host of internal factors, rather than to simply refer to the impact of Christianity, Islam, or Buddhism. As F. Lynch noted regarding the Philippines, "Concrete religious behavior (beliefs, attitudes, practices) of a Catholic is a function not only of official doctrine and practice, universal or particular, but also to the culture in which he is reared, and the community in which he dwells."[16] In these circumstances a much more complex and often inconsistent pattern appears upon the map of Southeast Asia.

THE RELIGIOUS RESURGENCE

Southeast Asia has experienced a marked resurgence in interest in religion in recent years which has further complicated issues of modernization. These developments have their antecedents in prewar and early postwar movements, but the changes that have appeared recently seem to display a different character in terms of intensity, aims, and leadership. This resurgence has been most obvious in Malaysia, but has shown itself in different guises throughout the region. This section will detail the

Malaysian pattern and then briefly review developments in Indonesia and Thailand.

During the 1970s and 1980s the externalities of Islamic influence became increasingly apparent in Malaysia.[17] The media provided more time for religious programs from prayer to Koranic reading contests. The rhetoric of politicians stressed Islamic issues more frequently. The government attempted to make Muslim holidays more national in scope. More women began to dress in what was perceived to be more modest clothing and civil servants were asked to dress conservatively. International Muslim meetings became regular events in Malaysia and the country showed greater consideration for the international Islamic cause. There was a growth in dakwah organizations emphasizing proselytizing among nonbelievers and an increased understanding among the faithful. These developments and others made the political parties even more cognizant of religious issues and Muslim parties fostered policies designed to meet the demands of their constituents.

Observers for more than a century have noted that to be a Malay was to be a Muslim and that the political, social, and economic life of the nation have been based upon this symbiotic relationship. Given this intertwining of religion and ethnicity, it is possible to delineate those factors responsible for the growth in Islamic intensity. The Islamic resurgence in Malaysia can largely be attributed to the changing character of the society, the influence of education, international forces, and government policy. In the first instance, the process of modernization has increasingly brought rural Malays into an urban setting and distributed Western culture and artifacts into the villages. This has led to both an ideological and ethnic confrontation. In the cities the Malay has found it necessary to compete with the more modern Chinese and Indian communities, raising his consciousness of his own identity. It has also shown the Malay the disparities in income and life-styles that persist in the society, thereby increasing their demands for a larger role in the system. On the ideological side, the Muslim has been faced with a culture and values that are often perceived as alien and even antithetical to his own. This too has underscored his sense of separate identity.

Second, young Malays have entered colleges and universities in increasing numbers where they have been confronted by peoples and cultures different from their own—whether at home or abroad. However, rather than becoming assimilated into this new environment, many of these youth have become even more closely attached to their religious foundations. They returned to society more deeply conscious of their

Islamic identities and prepared to become involved in religious organizations committed to increasing the role of Islam in the nation.

The resurgence of Islam elsewhere in the Muslim world has had
an impact upon Malaysia's Muslim population as well. Pride is taken
in the increasing role Muslim nations play on the world stage. Funds
from Middle Eastern countries have aided educational and dakwah
activities. Efforts to develop a greater role for Islam in the political and
economic arena in places such as Iran and Pakistan have not been
overlooked by religious activists in Malaysia. From all of these has come
an enlarged pride in Islam and a reinforcement of a sense of being part
of a wider and increasingly powerful community of the faithful.

Finally, the government itself has given impetus to the resurgence.
As it has symbolically and rhetorically attempted to show itself as the
protector of Islamic interests, it has also further intensified a sense of
Islamic identity. Ironically, the leadership generally does not wish to foster
the religious compartmentalization of the country, but political pressure
has led it to mount policies that may aid in doing just that.

Given these forces providing strength to the resurgence, two
questions arise: what are the perceptions of modernization among the
participants in the movement and what impact have these developments
had on modernization? The characteristic that appears to dominate the
relationship between the resurgents and modernization is ambivalence.
On the one hand, Muslims of all kinds appear willing to accept the
amenities of modernization, and the leadership of the resurgents employs
modern means of communications to develop and distribute its ideas.
Admittedly there are those fringe elements that eschew televisions, radios,
and other modern artifacts, but they remain a small minority. Yet, there
are also more widespread negative reactions to many aspects of modernization. An overemphasis upon materialism, immorality as exhibited on
television, the films, and literature, the great national enemy, drugs, or
the weakening of family life are all castigated by both the general public
and the Muslim leadership and are perceived as being influenced by
non-Muslim sources.

This incongruence has led to intellectual efforts to seek modernization within an Islamic context. Often the rhetoric is vague and imprecise,
attacking the "evil" elements of change and arguing that technological
development can be attained within Islamic values. The government in
particular has sought to emphasize the point that its development
programs can and do take place in a manner that does not sacrifice
spiritual values. Anwar Ibrahim, youth leader and later government
minister, stated that, "The Muslim must be able to live in a manner true

to his faith; in other words, he must be in full control of the entire complex of systems—economic, social, political—that run his life."[18]

This desire to control one's own life and to live within an Islamic context has expanded into areas of anti-imperialism and support for social justice—two areas that are seen as closely interconnected. There are elements of dependency and neocolonialist theory in the rhetoric of many in this group as they see dangers in both the continued dominance of Western capitalism and a conspiracy between foreign capitalism and the domestic establishment. As well, Islamic youth leaders and the Muslim political opposition have sought to speak for the poor peasantry and have accused the government of formulating development plans that have established a Malay capitalist class rather than helping the disadvantaged. Care has been taken not to define these views as socialist or Marxist, but to place them within the context of traditional Islamic values as understood in a modern environment.

Caution also must be taken not to characterize the entire resurgent movement as politically and economically radical. Some groups such as the Darul Arqam and Tabligh (see chapter 5) either remain outside such political and social action or are involved in entrepreneurial activities themselves—within the confines of Islam. Even within the now radical opposition party, PAS, local leaders often have strong economic interests and are allied with regional and village elites.

It may be too early to assess the impact of the Malaysian Islamic resurgence on the process of modernization. To this point the movement appears to be more a reaction to modernization than a crucial influence upon it. Those fringe groups that have been involved in violent attacks on other religions and the government have only given the latter a further rationalization for urging moderation.[19] Other organizations which have chosen to remain outside the mainstream of political and economic life have had a restricted impact. The Islamic political opposition continues to be a small minority in Parliament and controls no state government. This does not mean that PAS or activist resurgent organizations do not influence national policy. The perception that they might weaken its electoral support is a major factor in shaping the government's Islamic policies. The rhetoric, symbolic gestures, and Islamically oriented projects are in part a response to such pressures.

The one serious impact that can be observed has been the fear generated among non-Muslims that they would no longer play a competitive role in the new Malaysia. Less apparent is the basis for charges that the resurgence has led to a brain and financial drain among dissatisfied Chinese and Indians. Other than this, there appear to be few negative factors today, although there is always the possibility that rhetoric and symbolism may be replaced by more strident action if the government feels sufficiently threatened. Meanwhile, efforts to synthesize Islam and modernization may aid the process of easing the Malay Muslim into a new environment.

The situation in Indonesia is quite different from that in Malaysia. While there is increased Islamic activity in the former, the government remains suspicious, if not antagonistic, toward the growth of an Islamic movement that might weaken its control over the economic and political system. On their part, many Muslims perceive the Suharto regime as attempting to diminish their role and that of their religion in Indonesian society and politics.

Like Malaysia, Indonesia has its fringe elements that have sought to employ violence to achieve extreme religious ends. Similar to Malaysia, their only real importance has been to provide the government with another tool to control the Islamic movement. While there have been mass demonstrations by Muslims rarely have more violent efforts by frustrated Islamic groups involved more than a handful of activists. However, the publicity they have received in the establishment-oriented media has been extensive. In Indonesia during the late 1970s there were charges that the so-called Kommando Jihad was conspiring to overthrow the government. In 1978 the Gerakan Pemuda Islam (Islamic Youth Movement) was accused of planning to burn shopping centers and homes in an effort to implement the Koran. During this period Muslims in Acheh were also said to be working to establish an Islamic state and seeking aid from the Libyans. In 1981 the "Indonesian Islamic Revolution Board" was described as plotting the overthrow of President Suharto and attempting to obtain aid from the Ayatollah Khomeini. However, the most dramatic event took place in 1980 when a group of Muslim "fanatics" commandeered a plane and were slain by Indonesian commando forces at the airport in Bangkok, Thailand.[20] Those responsible for the attack were based in Bandung, where they called for an Islamic state. The leader of the organization had voiced opposition to modernization in the form of television, movies, and other aspects of "yellow culture." In 1985 bombings of stores in Jakarta and of the famed Buddhist Borobadur monument were blamed on Muslim extremists.

In the "nonpolitical" arena Muslims have also perceived the government as attempting to weaken their role. Among the various issues causing friction, the two most prominent have related to education and the place of the Panchasila. The role of religion in education has long been a point of contention between religious and secular forces. More recently, Muslims have worried about government regulations that might decrease the importance of Islam and increase that of Javanese mysticism. Thus, then Minister of Education, Daud Yusof, was charged with trying to intimidate the faithful over such issues as compulsory school attendance during Ramadan. For example, when the religiously oriented Muhammadiyah defied him and refused to close their 12,400 schools during the fast, he threatened to take away their subsidy (which was only US $98,000) and later hinted that he would withdraw governmental recognition if compliance was not achieved. Daud was not the villain with regard to expanding the teaching of Javanese mysticism in the schools and, in fact, opposed the efforts of then Information Minister Ali Murtopo to go in that direction.

However, it has been the role of the Panchasila that has been the critical issue of Muslims who see it as not only supporting agnosticism but as a real danger to their faith. As Michael Morfit has noted:

> The first principle (or *sila*) is a belief in one supreme being *(Sila Ketuhanan yang Maha Eas)*. Thus the Indonesian state is not secular in the Western sense. However, the belief in one supreme being is left as a general statement, broad enough to encompass a wide variety of religions including Islam, Christianity, Hinduism and Buddhism— those "great" religions officially recognized by the state and dealt with by the Department of Religion. This Sila is the source of considerable controversy. More orthodox Muslims have frequently favored an explicit commitment to Islam as the state religion and have felt some dissatisfaction at the phrasing of this Sila. They have also resisted what they see as an attempt on the part of the government to equate mere belief or faith *(kepercayaan)* with a true religion *(agama)*. This objection is aimed at many of the traditional and pre-Islamic beliefs of the Javanese, which are seen as corruptions or denials of the true faith of Islam.[21]

Associating the Panchasila with government plans to support *kepercayaan* beliefs and subvert Islam, Muslim politicians and religious leaders have characterized almost any effort to promote mysticism as an attack on the faith. They have been particularly unhappy with what have appeared to be state attempts to use support of the Panchasila as a litmus test of loyalty to the regime. The critical issue has been whether the state ideology is to be viewed as the only basis of belief, thus denying the paramountcy of Islam. The debate over this issue has led to bitter rhetoric and violence in the streets. Government efforts can be viewed as directed against the perceived dangers of increased Islamic revivalism as well as part of a campaign to establish national unity. While the Panchasila law was promulgated in 1985, it appeared to strengthen religious commitment among many in the Muslim community.

While there has been renewed intellectual interest in Buddhism in Thailand during the postwar years, there has not been the degree of agitation nor have questions of modernization been as salient as in Malaysia or Indonesia. As described previously, some elements of the sangha had become involved in development and other outreach programs during the 1960s. In the early 1970s, the ferment surrounding the end of the Thanom-Praphat regime, the student uprisings, and democratic experimentation brought an increasing number of members of the sangha into the political arena. There came to the fore a group of "political Monks" expressing a wide range of views toward contemporary issues from the extreme right to the extreme left.[22]

On the left were organizations such as the Federation of Buddhists in Thailand, The Young Monks' Front, and the Monks and Novices' Center of Thailand. These relatively small groups tended to espouse left-wing solutions to Thailand's problems, the need for a reorganization of the sangha, greater attention to the underprivileged, and an end to foreign economic power. Their members participated in rallies and demonstrations and assisted like-minded politicians during elections. With the return of the military in 1976 these movements became largely dormant.

Opposing these elements were the more conservative members of the sangha, a number of whom were overtly nationalist and anticommunist in their rhetoric. The most well-known religionationalist leader of the time was Bhikkhu Kitthiwuttho (or Kitthivuddho), an active and articulate spokesman for Thai nationalism. At one level Kitthiwuttho encouraged education, community development, and moral discipline. Through his Spiritual Development Program he sought to amalgamate the spread of Buddhism, nationalism, and development, claiming in 1976 that the organization had: " . . . helped people to understand the responsibilities and duties of good citizenship, elevated the morality of government officials. . . . , strengthened people's adherence to Buddhism . . . , restored and promoted national traditions and customs . . . , raised the people's confidence in government. . . . , helped the people in material development. . . . and, led the people to a proper conception of national security, and the need for self-sacrifice to uphold the monarchy and religion.[23]

An even stronger nationalist tone in Kitthiwuttho can be seen in such statements as "The Buddha taught us that whenever we are frightened we should look at the flag and have steadfast hearts." and his sermon "Killing Communists is Not Demeritorious."[24] Terming communism evil he asserted that killing communists did not constitute killing a living being. With government support he espoused his views widely through mass mobilization campaigns.

Not all Buddhist leaders entered this fray, with many continuing to stress primarily spiritual needs. A more sophisticated approach was taken by Bhikku Buddadasa who encouraged political involvement within Buddhist precepts. He projected a more balanced approach than the "political monks," proposing a spiritual socialism which rejected the materialism of both capitalism and modern socialism. He emphasized the principle of nonattachment in which the people were called upon to work for the entire society and attempt to eliminate materialism. In this he followed more orthodox Buddhist concepts.

These conflicts exemplify a rising interest within the sangha in contemporary problems facing the Thai people and a wrestling with how Buddhism can supply solutions. The majority of monks remain outside this arena and today the expectations for change and ferment of the 1970s is certainly diminished. However, as with the other states we have surveyed, this has been an era of reinterpretation of the relation of religion to public policy issues. Significant numbers of people, and most interestingly many educated youth, in all these societies seek to integrate their faith with civic action and are attempting to synthesize religion with technological change. It is still too early to see the impact of these events and attitudes on modernization, but the direction appears generally positive.

This brief review of the relationship of popular beliefs to modernization underscores the care needed in analyses of this nature. It is essential to delineate the reality of contemporary beliefs from the more formal tenets of the religion and the rhetoric of the activists. Thus, we find that while the formal dogma of Buddhism would appear to provide an insurmountable obstacle to modernization, popular beliefs would seem to allow for possibilities of technological change and entrepreneurial activities. In the case of the religious resurgence now spreading through Southeast Asia, we find not a reactionary Luddite movement intent upon destroying all aspects of modernization, but a highly complex pattern which encompasses a wide range of attitudes and demands from the traditional to the radical. What is apparent is an increasing interest among religious elements of the need to incorporate religious values into contemporary issues. Finally, as exemplified in our discussion of otherworldliness, it is often difficult to assess the extent to which behavior and attitudes reflect religious as against other forces within comparatively integrated societies.

7

Religious Practices and Modernization

There exists today in Southeast Asia a wide range of practices that are at least in part derived from religious beliefs. At one level these are animists, who act according to traditions largely outside the influence of world religions, although in reality their practices tend to merge with elements of more universal faiths. Thus, magic, folk medicine, the propitiation of spirits, tokens of protection, and the like interact with Islamic, Christian, and Buddhist behavior. At a second level we find religions no longer formally accepted having a continuing impact on the presently dominant world religions. It is argued by more orthodox Muslims that if one scratches a Javanese you will soon go through his outer covering of Islam through Hinduism, Buddhism, and ultimately to animism. The influences of these earlier beliefs can be seen in agricultural practices, for example, in east Java. Finally, each of these universal faiths has incorporated a variety of practices not originally delineated at the time of their origination. Some of these relate to organizational characteristics as explained in chapter 5. Those we will be reviewing in this chapter describe activities by individuals and groups, largely, but not entirely, outside the formal structure of the institutionalized "church." Particular emphasis will be given to four aspects of this issue: expenditures for religious purposes, agricultural practices, health, and education.

EXPENDITURES

The general consensus of the literature has been that the effect of religious expenditures on modernization has been primarily negative.

Similar to the alleged impact of the hadj reviewed in chapter 4, it is argued that these are largely unproductive outlays, often by persons who cannot afford the expense. Those who consider these expenditures unacceptable in terms of modernization assert that (1) these funds could be used more productively for modernization purposes such as education or agricultural innovation; (2) they deny the poor basic necessities such as food and housing, maintaining a permanent underclass; and/or (3) they involve the unproductive employment of time in ceremonies, feasts, and so forth. The same methodological problems exist in analyzing the validity of these assertions as were present when we assessed the hadj, for example: (1) what would the individual's income be used for if not for these purposes, and (2) how can we characterize these activities in terms of aiding or inhibiting the modernization process? The second question is easier to deal with and we will consider it as we investigate feasts and other ceremonies, religious buildings and artifacts, and merit in Theravada Buddhism. We have already dealt with the mixed effect of the hadj and zakat and will not return to these aspects of Islam.

Feasts and Ceremonies

The religious practices of Southeast Asia, like those in the rest of the world, are replete with a wide variety of feasts and other ceremonies which have accrued to them over the centuries. Some of these are almost purely animist while others have become an integral part of the ritual of the dominant faith. In Indonesia and Malaysia, feasts (*selamatans* or *kenduri*) are held to celebrate auspicious events in the lives of the individual, kinship group, village, nation, or religion.[1] As with other faiths, many of these relate to life-cycle rituals of birth, adolescence, marriage, and death. Others may fall on important dates such as the Prophet's birthday, giving thanks for surviving an illness, reaching some important attainment, the propitiation of spirits, or agricultural rites. Table 7.1 illustrates the feasts that were held in one Malaysian village during a six month period. The most popular celebration in the Southeast Asian Islamic world comes at the end of the fasting of Ramadan. It is a time for religious ritual, visits to families (which clog the roads, trains, and airlines), special foods, gifts, and days of activity.

The nature of these feasts may vary markedly both within the same area and across the region. The local character of these activities reinforces

TABLE 7.1

Feasts in a Malaysian Village over Six Months

Wedding reception	5	Including two held in houses near Bukit Pegoh
Covenant rite	1	
Sending wedding expenses	3	
Receiving wedding expenses	3	
Circumcision	1	Two other circumcision feasts were held with weddings
Commemoration of death	1	
Pilgrimage	1	Two occasions, when a woman departed on the pilgrimage and when she returned home safely
Entering a new house	2	
Erecting house framework	3	
Entering a university and safe travel	1	
Passing the Malaysian Certificate of Education	2	
Homecoming	1	
Seven-month pregnancy	1	
Kenduri arwah	1	

these variations, a particularly important factor among more isolated communities such as the pagans. At some feasts only light refreshments may be provided while others are quite elaborate. They may be brief, such as those normally associated with birth, or last for extensive periods, as is the case for some weddings of wealthier families. Those invited may only be the family or the invitation list may extend to the village and beyond.

There are similar types of activities in Buddhist countries of the region, although, with the exception of the Festival of Lights and New Years, they tend to be more subdued.[3] Life-cycle ceremonies are to be found in Burma and Thailand although by far the most eventful one—the temporary initiation of boys into the monkhood—does not exist in Islam. More complex in Burma than elsewhere, the initiation ceremonies include several days of activities including food provided to the monks and laymen, offerings, special clothes, and entertainment. New Year's is a multiday festival including both religious and secular elements, a major part of which is the throwing of water on seemingly all concerned, supposedly to cleanse the often unsuspecting recipient morally and spiritually.

In the Philippines there are the frequent fiestas to celebrate holy days, national days, harvests, and life-cycle events, but there is also the lengthy Christmas period when urban centers appear largely involved in festivities. For example, Illocano rice farmers have one to two harvest fiestas, the first following the May harvest ostensibly to honor the Virgin Mary. There are games, food, beauty contests, a special mass, refurbishing of the chapel, and other religious and secular activities.[4] Also individual barrios have their own patron saints, and as no two neighboring barrios have the same fiesta day, and people visit more than one fiesta, a good deal of celebrating goes on.

Seemingly, almost every budding young anthropologist's dissertation gives extensive attention to the variety of feasts and ceremonies that take place in their village, often with consideration given to the extent to which these are Christian, Muslim, Buddhist, pagan, or some admixture thereof. The degree of purity of these activities is not the question here except for the level of secularism. Of some importance to our analysis as well is the rejection by many religious reformers, especially Muslims, of these feasts as "un-Islamic." The extent to which they do not participate and urge others to follow their lead can, of course, diminish the impact of these events in terms of community involvement and legitimacy. Thus, Peacock found in his Javanese sample that 60 to 80 percent of his Muslim reformist respondents did not attend life-cycle *selamatans*, less than either the Islamic traditionalists or Javanese syncretists.[5] When considering the influence of such activities on modernization it would probably be correct to postulate that it is greater among those in the rural populace less affected by external religious patterns.

Given the wide variety of religious practices present throughout the region, it is impossible to provide extensive cross-national cost figures for these feasts and ceremonies. A few generalizations can be made and then followed with some specific examples. First, it would appear that expenditures on these activities, as a percentage of income, with some variation in terms of specific occasion, fall most heavily on the poorest elements of the community. There have been numerous reports of virtual bankruptcy or the expenditure of long-term savings for weddings, initiations of boys into the monkhood, and death rituals. Second, the rich tend to give more in dollar terms, but percentages of wealth can vary markedly across communities. In many cases the rural rich may sacrifice heavily, to the point where wealth is pictured as simply adding further burdens on the individual. Finally, care needs to be taken in generalizing too far as to the religious content of expenditures. In many cases a legitimate holy day may be exploited for commercial purposes, as Christmas or Easter in the United States, or a ceremony or feast may have only a thin overlay of religion as in some harvest fiestas in the Philippines. However, what follows are a few examples given in village studies to illustrate the costs of various feasts and ceremonies.

Douglas Miles, in his report on an Indonesian Borneo community as of 1961–63, found that pagans tended to spend more than Muslims, particularly for funeral feasts where they were likely to overextend themselves financially.[6] Wealthier pagans might have celebrations for over a month after a death. Both Muslims and pagans tended to compete among themselves in ceremonial display, although the former were involved in less elaborate functions and gave gifts of more symbolic value.

M. Spiro, in his study of a Burmese village where the average family income was K1,000 (US $200), found that considerable cost went into initiation ceremonies.[7] Expenditures ranged from K200 for the very poor to K5000 for the rich. Other cases in Burma at the high end were from K2200 to K10,000 with an unusually expensive initiation reported to be K100,000. Part of these costs were offset by contributions and sponsorship, but the amount remained high given family income. In addition, there was a collective offering of robes to the monks, in which a family might become involved in five or six times a year for a total of K4,200 to K10,000, expenditures on funerals, daily feeding of the monks, contributions to the repair and construction of pagodas, and other religious events.

In one village, in 1961, the cost to the entire community for eight initiation ceremonies (K24,000), one collective offering of robes (K1,200), and the daily feeding of monks (K4,600) was estimated at K29,600 (not counting K12,000 for a pilgrimage to the Arakan temple in Mandalay. Spiro reports that a typical upper Burma village might spend 30 to 40 percent of its disposable cash for religious purposes and that his village put out 25 percent.[8] Manning Nash, in his study of another upper Burmese village, stated that yearly expenditures for religious purposes were 14 percent of annual outlay for rich families, 4 percent for moderate, and 2 percent for poor families.[9] In Thailand, J. Amyot in a detailed analysis of income and expenditures level found that "charity and ceremonies" was the highest single nonfood item (14.3 percent) for the total village.[10] This percentage was inflated by heavy giving by a few families making the average family contribution, with these larger amounts not counted, B450 (US $22.50) rather than B1400 with average income.

Peter Wilson, in his description of a Malay village in Malaysia, notes the high cost of celebrating Hari Raya Puasa (the end of Ramadan).[11] The cakes made during the last week of fasting have many costly ingredients and efforts are to have something new in the house in expectation of guests. In some cases, he reports, the costs ran to nearly M $500, although this included special home purchases. It is a relatively more expensive activity at that time of the year given the smaller income often available at the end of Ramadan during which the pace of work slackens. Wilson found that families would go into debt for Hari Raya or ritual feasts (Kenduri).

In the Philippines, reported costs for fiestas tend to be lower, in part because sums expended become subsumed under other items. Thus, one finds that economic and social surveys entailing detailed analyses of income and expenditures show very little spent on religious activities. G. Rivera and R. McMillan's study of 749 farm households of central Luzon, with average expenditures of ₱797 listed only ₱6 for miscellaneous, including burials, weddings, taxes, and gifts.[12] A. Pal and R. Polson's survey of the Dumaguete trade area does not mention religious expenditures in their extensive analysis.[13] Yet, we know that fiestas often include food, gambling, religious offerings, and the like. At the same time Philippine Christians do not tend to give as freely for merit gaining activities as do the Theravada Buddhists or have to expend funds for the hadj or zakat as do many Muslims.

Summing up to this point, we find that feasts and other ceremonies in Southeast Asia: (1) are extensively followed in all religious groups, although life-cycle ceremonies are less accepted by urban and reformist elements (except perhaps weddings which have a more secular aspect); (2) expenditures for these activities are a major drain on family incomes; and (3) these costs vary according to income and religious persuasion.

Buildings and Artifacts

In these societies, a considerable amount of money and effort may go into the construction, repair, and maintenance of religious edifices and the purchase of religious artifacts. Some of the costs of the former are subsidized by the governments concerned. In Malaysia both general tax money and state controlled zakat funds have gone into the construction and repair of mosques, religious schools, and ancillary buildings. In Burma and Thailand, government funds have gone for the same purposes, although not in as systematic a manner, providing for special projects rather than the nation-wide program of the Malaysians.[14] Thus, in Burma Former Primer Minister U Nu obtained state support for the building of the Kaba Aye or World Peace Pagoda, and in Thailand royal patronage has been received by the shrines of Phra Patham, Phra That Nakhon Sithammarat, and Phra That Doi Suthep.[15]

However, beyond this official largess, local groups may expend high levels of expendable income on mosques, churches, or shrines in both labor and cash. Spiro notes that during Buddhist lent emmisaries from neighboring towns and villages come to seek contributions for reconstructing various monasteries. Beyond these collective sums, individuals built their own monasteries, pagodas, and other religious buildings. One rich villager spent K10,000 constructing a monastery while another family gave to such efforts as repairing a monastery (K1,600) and rest house (K1,200).[16] On a visit to any major pagoda in Southeast Asia one will usually see a well-filled contribution box. As Manning Nash describes the hierarchy of meritorious acts, three of the first five are related to the pagoda or monastery

1. to build a pagoda
2. to act as sponsor for a novice monk
3. to build a monastery (and donate it to a monk)
4. to donate a well or bell to a monastery
5. to feed a group of monks.[17]

There are also individual donations for the beautification of pagodas and as an example the public will purchase tin foil like squares of gold to put on statues of Buddha, walls, and so forth. Major shrines allegedly have treasures of gold and jewels in ornamentation. In the 1950s the Burmese Communist Party called for the melting of the gold on the country's most famous pagoda, the Shwe Dagon. The government, as part of a well-orchestrated anticommunist campaign, widely publicized this proposal, leading the communists to state that this idea was a hoax to embarrass the party.[18]

Muslim villagers also become heavily involved in constructing and maintaining their religious buildings. Often this is done in the villages through the efforts of cooperative groups consisting of relatives and/or people from the same neighborhood or village who gather together to repair mosques or prayer houses. Funding for construction frequently comes through the efforts of local religious and secular leaders, although in Malaysia this is heavily subsidized. For example, Kuchiba et al. described a village in which M$2,400 (US $800) was raised through the efforts of the headman and immam with the government providing the remaining M$44,600. This support was looked upon with suspicion by villagers who believed that the ruling party was buying votes. [19]

Of less public consequence and of inestimable value is the wearing of amulets or religious jewelry in Buddhist, pagan, and Christian societies to proclaim one's faith, and/or obtain protection. In rural Burma these may be strips of bamboo or pieces of metal over which a Buddhist incantation has been made. While these are of little intrinsic value, the same cannot be said of the less frequently worn silver or gold tokens of invulnerability or the more elaborate Buddha amulets or Christian crosses worn by wealthier individuals in Thailand and the Philippines.

The Impact

In assessing the impact of these expenditures on modernization we cannot adequately answer the first question posed at the beginning of this chapter regarding what these expenditures would be used for if not for the aforementioned religious purposes. There have simply not been the kind of scientific attitudinal surveys necessary to provide evidence on any scale. When asked, the answer from most villagers is usually one of incredulity at the senselessness of the question. Hence, we must look to the second query in an attempt to understand how contemporary practices appear to influence the modernization process.

There are a number of positive factors favorable to the enhancement of modernization that can be posited. First, it can be argued that at least part of these expenditures of money and effort advance community goals useful to modernization. For example Buddhist, Christian, and Muslim societies provide feasts attended by both rich and poor, but sponsored by the former. At the more elaborate of these gatherings a wide variety of food is available. It has been argued that in Indonesia these selamatans often provide the meat necessary for good nutrition to poorer families unable to afford such luxuries. It is charged that efforts by Islamic reformists to do away with these feasts, decrying them as "un-Islamic," are contributing to a decline in a balanced diet among poorer villagers. [20] To the extent that this is true, traditional feasts are a source of better health, an obvious need for an active citizenry.

The maintenance and construction of religious buildings also meet other community needs by supplying a center for religious as well as secular purposes. C. Keyes notes that in north-northeast Thailand these structures and their furniture are used by the community as a whole as well as providing a form of vocational education: "Even the wealth used for the construction of religious edifices or for the purchase of religious goods support some labor and some who have specialized skills. Some wealth thus expended may help provide for communal facilities, whereas other wealth so used actually supports those who are in the process of acquiring modern education."[21] A similar statement could be made for Muslim and Christian centers which are employed in the same way. For example, a visit to Al Azhar mosque in Jakarta will show various classes and seminars, women's and youth group functions, semipolitical discussions, sports activities, and the like. Prayer halls and churches in towns and villages may not be as rich in their offerings, but they do provide an important service.

Corollary to this communal aspect of religious structures is the extent to which they and ritual feasts are a means of strengthening local solidarity and extending the horizons of the villagers. In the former case, cooperative efforts at construction, repair, and maintenance of buildings and preparing and holding ceremonies reinforce group unity. As F. Lynch noted regarding fiestas in the Philippines, "Socially, the fiesta functions to renew community and kinship ties, to reinforce status and prestige, to bolster existing authority, and to express the system of reciprocal obligations."[22] As well, efforts to obtain aid from the outside and presentations by emissaries from beyond the village for aid in their activities open new doors and establish new and wider networks of obligation. As S. Husin Ali comments, regarding activities in Malaysia, "Thus the feasts not only help to strengthen primary group solidarity among the village members, but they also have the potential when they are sufficiently big, to include guests from the adjacent villages, of bringing those from different villages into closer contact."[23] There are also elements of status in these activities. Expenditures can emphasize the importance of material well-being, and, it is argued, accelerate entrepreneurial drives similar to those interpreted to arise from the wish to take the hadj. In a semi-Weberian fashion it is postulated that feasts and contributions for religious purposes show the populace that wealth is necessary to complete one's religious duties and the fact is that the rich give more than the poor. On the one hand, then, in Buddhist societies this example of a wealthy man or woman gaining merit through his or her gifts may be, as Keyes says, "indicative of previous good Karma whose consequences are now being manifest."[24] As well, given the status obtained through contributions and sponsoring feasts and ceremonies, an achievement oriented individual will have further reason to attain wealth in order to increase his prestige. In turn those acts allow him to expand his contacts and network of obligations. Thus, in Indonesia the wealthy will host large selamatans to which important people are invited from within and without the area, thereby establishing relationships that can be important for secular interests.

Others as well may be encouraged to participate more in the modern sector. An intriguing example of such a pattern is described by Miles, who reports that the high cost of ceremonies caused by the need for commercial products (kerosene, cloth, sugar, alcohol, etc.) have brought Borneo pagans out of the hills and into more modern sectors of society.[25] Their reasons relate to better access to markets and an improved ability to increase rice output thereby accumulating more capital to pay for ceremonies. Again, as with the hadj the relationship to such entrepreneurial and materialist-oriented ambitions depends upon the analyst's definition of modernization.

Finally, there is another issue of definition and modernization that could run throughout this volume. As noted in earlier chapters, rationalism has been presented by many social scientists as an element in the process of modernization. We have largely rejected it as a point of analysis due to its imprecision and difficulty in operationalization. However, it is worth noting that there are those who argue that the kind of expenditures of wealth and time discussed here are not signs of irrational or improvident behavior, but well-reasoned investments for the future. As Spiro presented eloquently in an early article on Burmese Buddhism,

> Instead of increasing his capital by saving his earnings, the Burman who wishes to satisfy his desire for material pleasure can choose instead to increase his merit by spending his earnings—on religion. For although capital is increased by savings, merit is increased by religious spending, and surely, from what has already been said, religious spending is the Burman's soundest financial investment. As in the case of secular finance, however, the profitability of the investment is a function not only of the soundness of the investment property (contributions to monks are sounder investments than contributions to laymen) but also of the quantity of the savings invested (a K 2 contribution, all things being equal, yields more merit than a contribution of K 1). It is this that accounts, at least in part, for the inordinately high Burmese investment in religion. From the returns on this investment—in the form of accumulated merit—he

can reasonably expect that his material desires will be wonderfully, even ecstatically, gratified in a future existence, if not as a blissful inhabitant of one of the Buddhist heavens, then as a wealthy man in the human world.[26]

Without the element of karma, similar comments could be made regarding the reasoning of adherents to other religions.

While many of these positive aspects of religious expenditures are persuasive, there remain cogent arguments reinforcing the negative elements noted at the beginning of this chapter. This rebuttal centers on the employment of money and time to achieve goals which will not appreciably enhance modernization as we have defined it.

There is no question that large amounts of money go for religious purposes in Southeast Asia. Whether one reads the data of Harvey, Zimmerman, or Wells on Thailand, Spiro or Nash on Burma, or the extensive village studies on other parts of the region, there can be little doubt that religious expenditures involve a major portion of the expendable income of the people of the area. While these outputs fall more heavily on the rural population, it is important to underscore the extent of government spending in this sector and the fact that often taxation for such purposes comes from the wider community. Thus, we earlier noted that while locals aided in building a religious edifice in Malaysia, some 90 percent of the cost was borne by the government. K. Wells, in his book on Thai rites and practices, found that in 1958 the budget of the Department of Religious Affairs was B13,451,543 (21 baht = US $1), over 95 percent of which went into Buddhist programs.[27]

In addition, historically there has been income derived from the ownership of land by religious orders. The extensive property held by the Spanish friars prior to the American period was notorious and a factor in the development of Filipino nationalism. For example, the first five charges in a fifteen charge indictment of the friars by Isabelo De Los Reyes related to agricultural practices of the orders.[28]

1. The Friars, from year to year, increased the rate of the land rent, despite the serious commercial and agricultural crises through which the country had been passing for a decade, the rice crops having been destroyed by locusts, the coffee plants by an insect much more terrible, and the prices reduced of abaca, sugar, and other products of the Philippines.
2. Besides the land rent, the friars exacted, by what right is not known, a surtax on trees planted by the tenants on the lands they

TABLE 7.2

Budget for Support of Religions
Thailand

	1950	1958
Temple repairs, reconstruction	3,000,000 baht	9,000,000 baht
Pali, Dhamma schools	400,000	500,000
Buddhist associations	25,000	100,000
Buddhist universities, two		400,000
Grant to Muslim organizations	30,000	495,000*
Grant to Christian organizations	10,000	45,000†
Total	3,465,000 baht	10,540,000 baht‡
(21 baht = $1.00)		

Educational Statistics, Academic year 1958, pp. 273, 274. Quoted in Tambiah, *World Congress,* p. 378.

* For repairs, reconstruction, excluding the school for Muslims at Bank Sue which is maintained by the government.
† For repairs, reconstruction, given to Roman Catholic and Protestant denominations.
‡ The total expenditure was 21,630,000 baht in 1957, the Buddhist Jubilee Year 2500. The sum of 4,200,000 baht was allocated to erect a Thai temple at the shrine of Buddhagaya, India.

TABLE 7.3

Budget for Support of Monks and Novices
Thailand

	1950	1958
Salaries	3,522,000 baht	4,422,000 baht*
Administration of sangha	8,323,000	10,988,000
Kathin ceremonies, gifts of robes	50,000	220,000
Fans for monks, to indicate rank	48,000	658,000
Preaching	25,000	40,000
International meetings		35,000
Grants for foreign students		120,000†
Total	11,968,000 baht	16,483,000 baht

* This covers the monthly allowances, *nitayabhatt,* of monks of high rank or monks who have special administrative duties. In 1959 there were 6570 such monks, and their allowances varied from sixty to one thousand baht per month.
† A number of Buddhist monks from Cambodia and Laos were given an opportunity to study at the Buddhist universities in Bangkok.

had leased, instead of being grateful for this favor which constituted improvement of such lands.

3. The friars, instead of using the legal measure when receiving the tax in kind, computed the rice in sacks of 30 to 33 gantas instead of 25, which was the legal content of a cavan, or sack of rice.

4. The friars arbitrarily fixed the prices of products when accepted by them in lieu of specie.

5. In addition to these abuses, the friars not infrequently confiscated the lands which the Filipinos had inherited from their forefathers, and all that was needed to do this was simply to include such lands in the maps of the friars; or else despotically order a tenant to vacate a farm which he had improved for years by hard labor and heavy investment.

Not open to similar criticism in Thailand but still an important source of income have been lands held by monastic orders in the country. In 1958 this amounted to 431,320 rai (1 rai = .4 acre) of which some 80 percent was used for religious and educational purposes.[29] Land held by religious organizations is certainly not unique to the Spanish Philippines or contemporary Thailand and has generally been obtained through gifts from the faithful. However, it is difficult to assess the exact amount of such personal donations.

While some of these funds go into modern education, general communal development, health programs, and other activities that could easily fall under the rubric of modernization, a sizable proportion are expended on less "productive" projects. Expenditures on such things as pagodas, churches and mosques, monks' meals and clothes, ceremonies, and the hadj could be used more effectively if the goal was the attainment of a secular oriented technologically advanced society. Certainly the traditional Thai pattern of building new pagodas rather than repairing the old ones or U Nu's call for the construction of 60,000 sand pagodas in Burma to gain merit are questionable handmaidens to technological change. This has certainly been the view of more secularist socialist governments in Burma and Indochina, even for those who see religions as aiding individual salvation, karma, and contentment.

Similar comments can be made regarding the expenditure of time on religious activities. While the rural population of Southeast Asia tends to be underemployed and has greater flexibility in how it uses its days and hours, there is little question that ceremonies, the building and repair of religious edifices, and other religious-oriented events or projects take a considerable portion of the lives of villagers. For example, a study of ten barrios in a single year (1958) in Negros Oriental in the Philippines found that each household attended a mean of 5.25 fiestas annually.[30] This meant 10.50 days spent in attendance at fiestas in neighboring barrios, plus 4 days preparing for a fiesta in their own barrio for a total of 15.50 days a year. If one adds to this other social activities and Sundays, the author found that 122 days were taken off work, a high percentage of them dealing with religious activities centrally or tangentially.

Any cost-benefit study of religious expenditures related to technological change must address a series of imponderables. What proportion of the income of believers goes into religious expenditures? While we have a good deal of illustrative evidence to show that it is considerable, the very personal and local nature of much of it makes any macro analysis difficult. How do these expenditures enhance or inhibit technological change? In many cases they do appear to have a positive impact such as nutritional aid to the poor during ceremonies, providing community services, and fostering entrepreneurship. On the other hand, a large percentage of such expenditures are for activities that cannot be seen to have any direct positive impact on the process of modernization. Whether they have a negative impact is more difficult to ascertain. We have referred to the central problem of alternate uses of religiously related funds and time. There is the issue commented upon in chapter 6 as to the general *weltanschaung* created by emphases on merit and otherworldly goals. There are questions that simply cannot be answered adequately such as the premise that religious activities of all kinds raise morality thereby weakening the forces of corruption and the misuse of office.[31] In sum, we have a mixed bag in which positive and negative factors are interspersed with questions for which there is insufficient evidence to give unqualified answers.

AGRICULTURE

Academicians, foreign advisors, and capital-based bureaucrats have long accused the Southeast Asian peasant of being burdened by tradition and superstition in his agricultural practices. His reluctance to try new seeds, chemical fertilizers, insecticides, and modern irrigation techniques have all too often been attributed to irrational, status quo oriented value systems. As Geoffrey Hainsworth notes in the introductory chapter to his book on village-level modernization in Southeast Asia, in the traditional dualistic approach to development, "The nation can be described as containing two *types of people:* rural based-urban based, farmers-nonfarmers, Westernized, aboriginal-migrant, need-subordinate-need achievers, risk averse-risk acceptive, nonsavers-savers, workers-capitalists, and so forth. The behavior or propensity of the first type of person is seen as inimical to modernization while the second is adaptive and progressive."[32]

Local religions have taken at least partial blame for unprogressive attitudes and behavior as some agricultural practices have been explained on religious grounds and religious leaders have been perceived as the spokesmen for premodern values. But, perhaps more importantly, the central role played by religion in the traditional village leads the outsider to attribute to it a multitude of actions and attitudes rather than to more diffuse factors. The tendency of the villager to put issues in religious terms can further cloud perceptions. However, the often ill-focused views noted in chapter 2 have been revised under the scrutiny of postwar anthropologists and sociologists. These studies and some of the author's own research have found that the old picture was badly flawed, both in terms of the impact of particular agricultural practices and the influence of "irrational" forces on the villagers' actions.

No doubt there have been and still are numerous specific agricultural practices derived from religious precepts that at best have not been useful in the modernization process. However, as a general rule they have not had a seriously deleterious effect on production. Thus, in some areas of Java, rice was harvested with a small inefficient knife so as not to alert the rice spirits,[33] in Burma there were difficulties in getting the peasant to use pesticides and U Nu's government banned cattle slaughter when such acts would improve herds used for draft animals and provide much needed exports from the hides, and there have been charges that Malay practices with rice seedlings, because of spirit beliefs, can endanger the crop.[34] In the Philippines both positive and negative elements of folk belief have been noted. In the former case, rituals may give a sense of control over nature, and celebrations make the work easier. They can even provide security, such as the corn ritual in Dulag where, as the corn bears fruit, an Awog is placed in the field to keep people from stealing the young crop. However there are also negative aspects, including not assessing the real reasons for problems with crops and blaming local spirits.[35] In each of these cases counterarguments have been made showing that the practice either was not widespread or may not have created the claimed problem in agricultural production.

More important has been the second charge that religiotraditional beliefs have forestalled innovations in agriculture. There can be no doubt that Southeast Asian farmers have shown reluctance in accepting new ideas, as have farmers throughout the world. In this region this has in part been due to different priorities, to a greater emphasis on time given other pursuits, to an aversion to certain types of work, even, in the case of rice, to an aesthetic preference for the long stemmed old varieties over the stubby Green Revolution types. It may even be a matter of taste, such as the northeast Thai villagers liking of brown, less healthy pond water to the clearer groundwater coming from deep wells. At the same time there is no doubt that folk beliefs can inhibit important changes. Thus, a survey by F. Sycip in the Philippines found that innovations in swine culture were limited by the acceptance of hog batteries, castration, artificial insemination, the use of mixed feeds, and using up-graded pork for consumption.[36]

However, even greater emphasis should be given to pragmatic rational choices by the peasant.[37] Having generally lived in relative isolation from markets and government protection, largely dependent upon his own abilities to feed his family and limited in his capital, the peasant has been reluctant to take risks with what little he has. For example, in his own work in northeast Thailand, the author found that an unwillingness to employ modern agricultural innovations was not due to being locked into a belief in a status quo based upon premodern values. Rather it was due to the fact that with a small annual income, the need to feed his family in the absence of other work opportunities, the relatively high cost of new seeds, insecticides, and chemical fertilizers, the dangers of debt and the well-known unpredictability of the rainfall in the region, the peasant simply did not want to take a chance. It was the richer landowners with sufficient capital and government contacts who were the innovators. Given sufficient support for his endeavors in the form of information, subsidies, protected markets, and intelligent government programs, the Southeast Asian peasant has displayed as much willingness to accept change as farmers elsewhere.

HEALTH

We have previously noted the relationship of the prohibition to taking life in Theravada Buddhist countries to health practices. Here we can briefly explore two other issues, folk or traditional medicine and birth control. Assuming that a healthy society is a positive factor for modernization and the increasing spectre of overpopulation in Southeast

Asia has negative connotations, we can address the role played by religion regarding these issues.

It is not our intention to provide an extensive review of the field of folk medicine in Southeast Asia today. The reader is recommended to such literature as M. Jaspan's *Traditional Medical Theory in Southeast Asia*, R. Winzeler's "Malay Religion and Politics in Kelantan", and Phya Anuman Rajadhon's descriptions of birth and child rearing.[38] Briefly stated, while primarily animist in origin and character, folk medicine throughout the region has been inlaid with Buddhist, Islamic, and Christian elements. At times scriptural passages are employed as part of the ritual or Buddhist monks, Catholic priests, or learned and pious Muslims may act as intermediaries to spirits or lead the ceremony.

Differing in specifics throughout the area, much of folk medicine is predicated on a belief in spirits and sorcery, interlaid with astrology and witchcraft. Illness can come from offending a particular spirit or result from the act of a malevolent spirit. In some societies a sorcerer may cast a spell, while in others difficulties can come from being out of harmony with cosmic forces, or the loss of one's "vital essence." A wide variety of methods are used to overcome illness. Herbal medicines, exorcists to eliminate spirits, mediums to contact them, not eating certain foods to realign oneself with the cosmos, bribing or threatening spirits, specialists in sorcery, or the repetition of Koranic passages—each may be used in one place or another.

How effective these methods are in treating illness is certainly a matter of considerable dispute in Southeast Asia. While folk medicine is slowly declining in the region, it remains strong in rural areas, and even sophisticated urban people are likely to employ it in conjunction with more modern methods. To the extent that traditional beliefs may delay or otherwise inhibit more effective modern efforts such as malaria eradication campaigns or prenatal care, they can weaken the nation's health. Certainly with the expansion of health programs (although progress is still less than satisfactory in many rural areas) there has been a dramatic drop in infant mortality and crude death rates. Thus, the infant mortality rates of Burma and Thailand dropped from 139.3 and 44.7 per thousand respectively in 1962 to 62.8 and 25.5 per thousand in 1970.[39] Without rejecting the efficacy of traditional remedies, it would appear that most of this decline came from the more widespread use of modern medical techniques. However, as C. Keyes has quite correctly noted, the resistance of folk medicine to accepting many aspects of modern health care is very minor when compared to difficulties in getting such care into the countryside.[40] As with agriculture, the peasant displays far greater flexibility than he has normally been given credit for.

The issue of family planning as it relates to religion is difficult to assess in much of Southeast Asia due to differences of opinion regarding theological bases for action and insufficient data from the field. While there is no doubt in the Philippines as to the views of the Roman Catholic hierarchy on contraception and abortion, varied interpretations are to be found in Muslim and Buddhist societies. Thus, A. Wichmann has argued that "Buddhist belief and philosophy in Burma constitute a well-nigh insuperable obstacle to even a consideration of population-control measures, to say nothing of implementing population-control measures."[41] On the other hand, in his study of Sri Lanka and Thailand T O. Ling found that while abortion is considered unthinkable in both countries, Sri Lankan opinion was divided on contraception and the Thais saw nothing in Buddhist doctrine against it.[42] Certainly there are religious arguments that can be made on both sides regarding contraception with proponents noting popular belief in some areas that child-bearing is a sign of Buddha's blessings and opponents looking to the prohibition against taking life. Less cogent would appear to be Ling's comments that Buddhism inhibits industrialization and urbanization and leads to social differentiation between the sexes affecting the education of women, all of which have consequences for higher fertility. Some survey evidence is available from Sri Lanka (whose Buddhism is similar to Burma and Thailand). In a study of the attitudes of monks in the early 1950s, B. Ryan found that the great majority of those who were highly educated found no inconsistency between Buddhist concepts and contraception, while those with the least education were opposed. Neither group appeared to consider the issue very important.[43]

While the Koran is the only one of the major sacred scriptures that provides specific advice on birth control, Islamic tenets have generally been pictured as supportive of high fertility. The acceptance of polygamy, the undesirability of celibacy, the drive to expand the faithful, and tendency toward fatalism are all noted. However, there is considerable disagreement among Muslim scholars as to the conditions of contraception, such as when the woman is in danger.[44]

Nevertheless, as powerful a religiously oriented argument against family planning as any has been the perceived danger of low population growth in one's own community in contrast to other competitive groups. Thus in Thailand during the 1960s Minister of Interior Praphat would not support birth control, pointing to the hundreds of millions of Chinese communists to the north. In Malaysia the need to maintain its plurality over the non-Muslim Chinese and Indians has been inserted into family planning discussions by some Malay Muslims.

Certainly whatever the theological or politicoreligious arguments forwarded, the women of these countries have not found "insuperable obstacles" to birth control practices. During Marshal Sarit's days in office, locally advertised birth control clinics opened as pilot projects were extremely successful in attracting women to them as were later U.S. aid sponsored programs in Indonesia. In the former case 150,000 women annually, or 2.5 percent of females between the ages of 15 and 44, were fitted with IUD or oral contraceptives, in spite of a lack of advertising in the public media.[45] In Indonesia the number of family clinics increased from 1,465 in 1970 to 2,719 in 1975 and the number of accepters from 181,059 to 3,486,303. Family planning in the Philippines initially moved slowly. Introduced by Protestant missionaries in the 1920s and quietly begun by the Manila Health Department in the 1960s, it finally took off with government support in the 1970s. By the mid-1970s some 17 percent of married women, ages 15 to 44, were practicing birth control with new acceptances rising from 42,800 annually in 1968 to 733,100 in 1974.[46] These programs have been primarily urban based, but village studies also show an interest in contraception. A survey of village life near Manila found that 64.7 percent of the respondents had heard of family planning, of whom 34 percent wanted to know more and 13.4 percent (13 out of 150 respondents) were practicing it.

We still do not have sufficient evidence to show conclusively the impact of religion on family planning. Other intervening variables such as economic class, rural life-style, and education cloud the picture too much. Certainly there is illustrative evidence of the rejection of birth control measures on the articulated basis of religious belief, but it is also obvious that women who apparently perceive themselves as good Muslims or Buddhists have come to family planning clinics in large numbers. It would generally appear that again, the Southeast Asian tends to be practical in these matters. For example a survey in Indonesia found that while a high percentage of persons equated abortion with murder, most thought birth control acceptable to avoid overcrowding in populous areas. Perhaps most interesting, while 68.2 percent agreed that "birth control practices conflict with the Islamic and Christian religions," 83.5 percent of the respondents felt that it could be practiced by people having too many children. Another recent survey in the Philippines found that religious and moral reasons ranked fourth (2.7 percent of respondents) for not practicing birth control behind wanting more children (24.8 percent), no need for family planning (21.4 percent) and no time/too much trouble (6.3 percent). However, the authors of the study did not deny the importance of religion. While admitting that no proper testing had been done of the religious factor in the Philippines, they considered that it could not be separated from other traditional forces.[47]

EDUCATION

One of the prerequisites for modernization set forth at the beginning of this volume was the availability of an educational system conducive to the achievement of technological change. In this area, as in others, religion in contemporary Southeast Asia presents a far more complicated picture than it once did. The role it has played in the education of the youth of the region has gone through major transitions during the past century. From the paramount place in the learning process, emphasizing primarily traditional religious values and subjects, it was challenged by Western values, methods, and concepts during the colonial period. It is now attempting to synthesize what it considers useful from the new with those values which it is believed must be retained. In this section we will briefly describe traditional Buddhist and Islamic education and its effects on modernization and then turn to the contemporary situation. Finally, the impact of Christian efforts will be reviewed.

Traditional education in Theravada Buddhist and Islamic societies of Southeast Asia was almost entirely in the hands of religious personnel and its content appeared to offer little support for the modernization process. In Burma and Thailand education was the monopoly of the monks and was predicated on preparing boys for the sangha—girls received no formal schooling. At the lower level instruction was in the vernacular language of the country as well as Pali (the scriptural language of Theravada Buddhism) and the curriculum covered the sacred scriptures, some elements of Buddhist cosmology, and, at times, some history, traditional medicine, literature, and so forth. If the boy showed promise, he might go to regional or national religious institutions in order to expand his knowledge of Pali and ability to interpret the scriptures, hopefully ultimately to pass the national examinations in the presence of the king.

In Indonesia and old Malaya education was also primarily for boys and had a largely religious content. While the specifics of primary and secondary schooling varied widely through the Malay world, initial religious education was usually for both sexes in the home, with an emphasis on learning how to recite the Koran. Local primary and even secondary schools were also based upon Islamic learning, reinforcing the ability to read and recite the Koran in proper Arabic and learning one's prayers, with some additional instruction in the vernacular (with Malay taught in Jawi, the Arabic script), history, theology, and basic arithmetic. Again, if the student showed promise and the family had the funds, he might move to a higher level of religious training where he could advance his Arabic and, rather than simply learning the Koran by rote, be able to begin to intepret the sacred scriptures, hoping ultimately to go to the Middle East for further study.

This form of education was usually all that was available for children in the villages and towns of Southeast Asia and it did function to provide some limited literacy and secular material along with its major task of transmitting the fundamentals of Islam and Buddhism. However, as a basis of advancing modernization, it was often deficient. While it can be argued that the mind was disciplined by this manner of teaching, the emphasis on rote learning was not the best means of developing analytic abilities, and Pali and Arabic were not useful tools for dealing with the latest aspects of technological change. The secular subjects were often ill-taught by poorly trained personnel and the normal short period involved for most boys in the educational process meant that functional literacy in any language was difficult to obtain and retain. Of course, by largely ignoring the education of young females, half of the population was left unprepared to effectively enter the modern sector or advance to higher education in any form. Finally, as these institutions began to be challenged by Western ideas and parents sought instruction more attuned to the colonial environment, often taught in Christian missionary schools, local religious teachers tended to see secular education as an evil to be damned in all its aspects. Thus, there was the danger of the local school becoming isolated from the changes that were taking place in the larger society and establishing a mind-set adverse to all things Western.

Under the challenge of colonialism and demands for an education more suitable to upward mobility in the new environment, two changes in religious education took place. First, there has been a decline in the role and status of local religious schools. This is particularly true in urban and commercial centers. In the Muslim countries the village religious schools lost students to secular institutions and were often seen as less salient to the needs of better students. In Burma, prior to the final conquest of the country by the British in 1885, monastery schools reportedly had enrollments of no less than fifty to sixty students each. In the ensuing decades of colonial rule the average number of students dropped to less than ten and the period of schooling became considerably shorter.[48]

In Thailand the monarchy began developing state schools in the late nineteenth century and in the past fifty years this has been accelerated to the point where most education takes place within government schools.

Nevertheless, it would be inaccurate to assert that religion has been eliminated from the educational process—far from it. In both Islamic and Buddhist countries religious schools remain active at all levels. In Indonesia and Malaysia elementary and secondary religious schools, while enjoying less status than previously, still involve large numbers of children. In the early 1970s in Indonesia, the government reported that there were 4,174 *pesantren* (secondary religious), 851 public and 22,886 private *madrasah* (mixed religious–secular), and 274,555 *pengajian* (village religious) schools.[49] A scholarly review gave the following government figures: 25,000 madrasah with 2,980,000 students; 23,000 madrasah dinayah (part-time religious-oriented subjects) with 3,520,000 students; and 11,000 pesantren with 2,240,000 students. Students in these schools composed 17 to 37 percent of the school-going population. The general subjects taught in the madrasah cover local and world geography, health, and Indonesian history and language. However, other languages suffer, given the emphasis on Arabic and that general courses tend to be inferior to state schools.[50] In Thailand at the same time about half of the primary schools in the country were housed in wats where about 20 percent of the primary school population was taught by monks and laymen.[51] As late as 1952, 73 percent of Burmese schools providing education according to government standards were on monastery property, where traditional education had not completely lost its hold. General Ne Win has since nationalized almost all schools and the role of the monks has been downplayed.

As well, religion is today taught in government supported secular schools in most of the countries under discussion. In Burma U Nu helped promulgate a law providing Buddhist education in state schools until he suspended the subject over a controversy as to whether Islam and Christianity could also be taught to their adherents. General Ne Win's government has not reinstated it. In Malaysia, since independence, when there are fifteen or more Muslims in a school an Islamic religious teacher is to be provided, paid for by state and federal funds, and a course in "Islamic Religious Knowledge" is now required in all lower standard grades. In Indonesia the teaching of Islam is compulsory in all government schools from primary grades to the university. In Thailand students are taught that Buddhism, king, and country are closely interrelated. Only in the Philippines today is the separation of church and state long established, but only after three centuries of Spanish colonial–Catholic Church cooperation and the establishment of a strong private Catholic educational system.

However, the second major change that has overtaken the educational system of the region has been the gradual admixture of secular subjects and teacher training into religious schools, at times in cooperation with religious authorities and often against their wishes. In Thailand the government has encouraged monks to obtain teacher training while in Malaysia the state departments of religion have attempted to regulate the type of teachers used in religious schools and the federal government has tentatively tried to upgrade the education of local religious leaders. As well, the curriculum of these schools has seen the addition of more secular subjects. Thus, in Malaysia, while the *Al Madrasah* schools have seen declining support from parents seeking better preparation for the new society in secular institutions, they do provide a combination of Islamic and secular education. Similarly, in Indonesia some 30 to 50 percent of madrasah schooling is in general subject matter and pesantren schools are showing signs of changing.

The impact of these new inputs into the curricula and teacher training have provided mixed results in terms of modernization. In the first place, the process of renovation has been uneven as not all religious schools have accepted such changes gracefully. Even with reforms, the secular modernizer may still question the significant amount of time spent on religious subjects in elementary Islamic and Buddhists schools and even in the madrasahs. Questions could also be asked regarding "lost" time in government sanctioned religious classes in state run schools. At the elementary level, in particular, government efforts to upgrade curricula and teachers have shown only limited success and there is little question that the products of these institutions find it difficult to compete in the better intermediate and tertiary schools. However, this is a legitimate complaint against education in most rural settings, although account must be taken of parental rejection of religious schools on the grounds that they do not prepare their children for today's job market. This decline in the status of religious schools is an observable fact and reinforced by surveys of popular attitudes,[52] and the overly traditional focus of their teaching appears to be the main cause of this weakening.

There are positive elements as well, aside from the increase in "practical" courses. Where state run schools have not been available they can provide the only institutional education for the rural youth. Where parents have been suspicious of the taint of immorality and worldly influences in the secular schools these religious institutions can both give their children a combination of religious and general subjects and form a bridge between the new and the old.[53] Given the dangers of a dual educational system dividing the rural traditional youth from their more secular urban counterparts, this can be important as a matter of national integration. More simply these religious schools may be the only means of getting the child to school and keeping him or her there.

More difficult to assess are the arguments of many religious spokesmen that the education given in these more traditional schools develops discipline, moral character, and commitment, all necessary to achieve in any task in this world. It is asserted that modern secular education has no interest in fundamental moral values, that religious education produces the whole individual, and that without a foundation of values the student is unable to understand his role in the wider community.[54] Some of the advocates of this position see secularization as posing the real danger to both religion and other desirable national goals. To meet this present threat it is essential to control education of the youth. However, religious communities have been divided as to what kind of education, the return to the basic religious principles of the past or some sort of integration of selected elements of Western concepts and methods with fundamental religious values. The manner in which this debate has been played out can be understood in part by examining efforts to "reform" Islamic tertiary education in Malaysia, although illustrations could be drawn from any of the countries under consideration.

In earlier years Muslim students wishing to advance their education in Islam looked to the Middle East. The first Islamic institution of higher learning in the country was established at Klang in 1955. The Muslim College was religious reformist in nature and provided instruction in religion with little attention to secular subjects. Among its aims were,

> (a) the prevention of aspects of Western civilization that bring about a deviation of Muslims from the teachings of the religion, (b) to meet the need for religious teachers well versed in the precepts and tenets of Islam so as to prepare Malay children adequately for the demands of modern life in accordance with the true teachings of the Islamic religion, (c) to lay the foundation for higher learning in Islam that is truly modern, (d) to institute standardization in all religious schools whether Malay or Arabic and also to raise standards, and (e) to spread the tenets and teachings of Islam as well as to correct and reform errors in religious practice and observances found among the Islamic community.[55]

Disagreement surfaced between those who wished to retain the institution as one solely oriented toward religious education as against those who sought to integrate Islamic teachings within the mainstream of secular advances. This was and is an issue within the Islamic community between those who believe that change can come within a purely Muslim context and those who believe that for Islam to survive it must relate to contemporary challenges more directly. In 1966 the Muslim College came under the Ministry of Education and the arts and sciences divisions were added to the curricula. Since that time religious higher education in Malaysia has exhibited two trends. There has been a broadening of Islamic education to include Muslim thinkers of almost all hues. No longer can the Malay Muslim intellectual be accused of being outside the mainstream of modern Islamic thought. Thus, the Islamic Department of the University of Malaya provides a relatively broad curricula in which the students are called upon to read material by Mohammad Qutb, Abu-l-'Ala Mawdudi, M. N. Siddique, Kurshid Ahmad, Afzal-ur-Rahman, Mufti Mohammad Shafi, and a variety of other Muslim and non-Muslim authors.

The second path has been a continuance of efforts to integrate Western science and concepts with Islamic values and aims. Not only does this take place as part of the curricula of the mainstream institutions of higher learning, but Malaysia launched a bold experiment in 1983 with the establishment of the International Islamic University on the outskirts of Kuala Lumpur. With a Malaysian and foreign, Muslim and non-Muslim student body, this institution ultimately seeks to provide a complete university covering law, the arts, and the sciences. Texts by Western specialists are frequently used, but through other readings, lectures, and discussions it is expected that the student will understand the subjects presented within an Islamic framework. Graduates are expected to function in the same job marketplace as their counterparts from the University of Malaya, Sains Malaysia, and Kebangsaan. This is a long way from the original aims of the old Muslim College, and its advocates argue that this must be the future of modernization in Malaysia.

Perhaps the most important handmaiden to modernization in Southeast Asia has been Christian missionary education, its influence ranging across a wide variety of activities. Mission schools brought to the region the first formal training in European languages, arts, and sciences. Thus, the General College at Ayutthaya, Thailand in the seventeenth century was teaching at the standard of a French university with a curriculum including philosophy, theology, history, geography, mathematics, sciences, and classical and modern languages. Later Protestant schools in Thailand offered reading, writing, astronomy, natural sciences, geography, history, moral philosophy, and, of course, a strong dose of religion.[56] Similar courses were being taught throughout the region. Of considerable influence was the contribution of modern medicine and dentistry through hospitals, clinics, and medical schools.

Missionary educational innovations went far beyond the curricula. Missionaries introduced to Southeast Asia innovations such as the printing press, sewing machine, and farm implements. Differing from the traditional Islamic and Buddhist schools they organized the teaching of girls, vocational training, adult education, and the training of lepers, the blind, and disabled. All of this was not lost on community leaders. Members of local elites from Burmese sayadaws, Muslim religious organizations, to Thai kings learned from missionary innovations. Education was more than ever seen as a road to power, and it was noted that it was the more educated European who had conquered.[57] Islamic and Buddhist schools began to borrow the techniques and curricula from the missionaries in order to compete for students. Other institutions and concepts copied were reflected in the Muhammadiyah scouts of Indonesia, the Young Men's Buddhist Association of Burma, orphanages and clinics, methods of conversion, and changes in the educational role of the monks under King Mongkut of Thailand.[58]

It would appear that the overall impact of Christian missionary education in Southeast Asia has had a positive effect on modernization, particularly during the colonial era. While recognizing the mixed nature of their offerings, missionary schools did help to provide the type of education useful to bring their products into the modern sector. Usually the language of instruction was that of the colonial administration and put the student into contact with the mainstream of Western knowledge. While today many of the local vernacular languages, such as Malay-Indonesian, have been modernized and Arabic is the tongue of economic powers in the world, during the colonial years Dutch, French, and English were the languages of modernity. Second, missionary schools tended to present a type of education that was more conducive to modernization than their Buddhist and Muslim counterparts. Certainly we have considerable evidence that parents interested in upward mobility for their children sought to enter them into missionary run institutions, even when they did not accept the religious precepts of these schools.

Another possible positive factor related to this is the very gathering of bright young people in some of the elite Christian-administererd schools of the colonies. Examples of such institutions abound across the region. For example, in Thailand Mater Dei, Saint Joseph Convent, and

Assumption College have long enrolled children from the Thai elite. As one observer remarked, "In a sense Bangkok without Mater Dei girls' school, Assumption College and Saint Joseph Convent, would be like England without Eton and Harrow. Not only the scale but the excellence of Catholic educational activity makes it important to Thailand."[59] Out of this experience was often forged an "old boy" network of individuals who were later to lead the nationalist movements and later independent governments. These linkages were to prove invaluable in gaining the cooperation and trained minds necessary to launch these new ventures.

However, there were negative elements as well. Not all missionary run schools were of high caliber. Some gave extensive religious training and the same criticisms directed against Muslim and Buddhist schools could be made against them including the efficacy of Latin. The most powerful charge that can be made is that these places of learning were part of an institution which was to lead to high levels of divisiveness in these polities. To the extent that Christian missionaries were successful in gaining converts in societies dominated by other religions, they left groups not easily integrated into the new nation-states. The very existence of these "unbelievers" was often untenable to religionationalists and their antagonism was all too often reinforced by the rhetoric and actions of the missionaries and their converts. Frequently missionaries were highly deprecatory toward other faiths. Christian minorities in Burma and the Netherlands East Indies closely identified themselves with the colonial administrations; many Christians fought with the colonial armies against the nationalists and in the postindependence years sought autonomy from the new states. While there were Christians who sided with the nationalist movements, they were in the minority and the activities of Ambonese, Minahassan, and Karen converts were far more dramatic. An unfortunate consequence of this divisiveness was the unwillingness of the independent governments to fully include these often highly trained products of Christian institutions into their administrations. This took place just in those formative years when their contributions could have been most useful.

In recent years missionary education has become both less important in training the youth of the area and less attractive to the upwardly mobile seeking parents and students. In part this has been due to the decline in activity as governments have nationalized private schools and curtailed missionary activities. As well, local state institutions have improved considerably, replete with Western trained faculty at the tertiary level and students seeking an advanced degree can now travel abroad for their education.

This leads to a final aspect of the relationship of religion to education that cannot be ignored—the impact of education overseas. It was earlier feared that the experience abroad would lead students to forget their cultural and national heritage. Pictures from the 1920s of members of the nationalist Perhimpunan Indonesia dressed in morning coats in Holland or dandified Malay and Burmese students in London appeared to lend credence to these views. While the magnet of the Western life-style has always been present, recent reactions of Muslim and Buddhist students have been somewhat different. Rather than being subverted by the "decadence" of the West, quite the opposite has taken place. The Malaysian example may be somewhat aberrant, but it is suggestive of the future.

Over the past decade it has become apparent that Muslim Malay students returning from abroad have articulated a stronger adherence to their faith than when they left, often joining various activist Islamic organizations upon their return. It has been jokingly said that the Muslim centers of today are Birmingham, Canberra, Ohio, London, Indiana, Sydney, and other places where foreign students congregate. Among the reasons for these reactions are probably interaction with representatives of other Muslim countries and disenchantment with what they have seen in the West. The Malaysian authorities have been conscious of these developments and the possible dangers to the country's fragile accommodationist plural society posed by committed religious youth. Warnings have been given against becoming involved in "radical" movements, efforts have been made to limit concentrations of Malaysian students abroad, and Muslim students are provided religious orientation before going overseas. However, at this point these recommitted youth are displaying an understanding of modern political and communications techniques rarely seen among older Muslim leaders. And, as noted in chapter 5, their message is that Western technology is acceptable and even desirable, if it can be placed within an Islamic framework.

The four areas covered in this chapter—expenditures, agriculture, health, and education—have been the targets of considerable disagreement in the debate over the relationship of religion to modernization. In each case a range of arguments have been forwarded to display the negative impact of religious practices on the process of modernization. Expenditures on buildings, ceremonies, and other religious giving have been characterized as draining needed funds from desirable material goals. Agricultural practices tied to religion have been condemned for slowing the development of rural areas. Traditional health activities have been called detrimental to the health and well-being of the people.

Religious education has been termed dysfunctional to those wishing to be competitive in the modern world.

In each case there is conflicting evidence supporting a more complex analysis of what is transpiring in the region. Religious expenditures can also encourage entrepreneurial attitudes and behavior as well as provide services needed by the community. It may be that seemingly religiously oriented agricultural practices are actually the result of decisions based upon local conditions such as climate and capital. The reality of contemporary health practices, such as birth control, may not be as seriously hampered by religious considerations as previously thought. Finally, religious education today has been increasingy infused with modern content; historically Christian missionary activities were important purveyors of modernity and provided models for educators from other religions seeking a competitive edge in the contemporary world. Thus, there appears to be considerable evidence to support both sides of the debate and considerable need to review it on a case by case basis.

8

The Manipulation of Religious Symbols

This chapter seeks to analyze the use of religious symbols to achieve modernization as defined in this volume. Its scope is limited to efforts by elites, whether they be local, regional, or national, and is not intended to review long-standing belief systems that may reinforce modernization. Nor will there be an attempt to test the sincerity of these leaders in their employment of religion to achieve their goals. While there is a good deal of impressionistic evidence that a politician like U Nu was a sincere Buddhist and there are charges that his wartime predecessor, Ba Maw, was more cynical in his manipulation of religious symbols, it is clearly not possible to accurately judge the extent to which individual decisions have been made on the basis of religion, expedience, or both.

This chapter will focus upon two issues that have involved the public use of religion to achieve the legitimization of action. The first relates to the utilization of religion to achieve economic and social development programs. The second area of analysis is the application of religion as an ideological base for prewar nationalism and postindependence national unity.

RELIGION AND DEVELOPMENT PROGRAMS

The most widely publicized efforts to employ religion to legitimize development programs in Southeast Asia have been in Burma, Malaysia, and Thailand. The separation of church and state in the Philippines and lack of consensus as to the proper role of Islam in Indonesia have meant that this pattern has not been of importance in those two states. Even

in the countries under consideration such efforts have not been continuous, attesting to both a lack of agreement as to the use of religion
to reach secular goals and the difficulties in implementing such programs.

Burma

In 1952 Prime Minister U Nu launched an eight year development
project called the Pyidawtha (Happy Land) Plan.[1] Rising out of Nu's
desire to establish a socialist welfare state, he promised all Burmese a
house, automobile, and $175 to $200 dollars a month (at a time when
the annual per capita income was less than $75). This was an ambitious
and complex set of programs that sought to restore the country's
war-ravaged economy to its prewar levels and then to increase the GNP
by another one-third. It called for an investment of $1,575 million over
the eight year period of the plan, much of it to be financed through rice
exports. Included in the overall plan were a major industrialization drive,
a set of agricultural targets, land nationalization, education programs, and
a wide range of other development efforts. Ultimately the Pyidawtha
Plan foundered on its own overly optimistic expectations, a drop in rice
prices after the Korean War, continued civil war, and problems of mis-
management.

While a variety of means were exploited to sell the plan to the public,
the interest here is in the utilization of Buddhism by the government
to gain support. An important element of the Pyidawtha Plan was the
involvement of the populace through a series of self-help projects. As
he had in other campaigns, U Nu used the concept of merit to obtain
public participation. By presenting the idea that merit could be obtained
through support of the projects, the government was able to receive aid
in the form of labor, money, enthusiasm, and other volunteer contributions. On the other side of the coin it was stated that not only would
involvement in the plan lead to personal merit, but that the educational
aspects of the program would reinforce religion by promoting the five
Buddhist strengths (intellectual, physical, moral, economic, and social).
If the Pyidawtha Plan had been successfully implemented, it certainly
would have advanced modernization in Burma. However, it had little
chance and the exploitation of religion to foster what were to be peripheral
aspects of the plan was probably of minor importance in its overall success
or failure.

Malaysia

Malay political leaders have long sought to bring their people into the modern sector of the economy. The evidence is clear that the traditional role of the Malay has been as a rural smallholder with education, incomes, and household amenities below that of other communities in the nation, and particularly the Chinese.[2] To change that pattern both rhetoric and action have been directed toward upgrading the standard of living of the Malay. During the 1960s the Malaysian government supported programs to develop the entire society while emphasizing overall growth. Meanwhile, some Malay politicians were urging their constituents to change their work habits in order to compete more effectively and others were quarreling among themselves as to how to develop their people.[3] Following serious race riots in 1969, the Malay dominated government launched the New Economic Policy, the purpose of which was to eliminate disparities among the ethnic communities of the nation. In order to achieve these goals, a host of programs were introduced in the 1970s and 1980s providing subsidies, training, quotas on jobs, education and contracts, and other "affirmative action" policies intended to increase the role of the Malays in the modern sector and allow them to compete effectively with other communities in the country.

It should be emphasized that at no time during this period did the top leadership of the Malay governing elite place religion as the primary motivating factor for their efforts. Their desire to maintain the nation's delicate communal balance made such statements inopportune politically and their more secular personal outlook made such pronouncements uncharacteristic. However, this does not mean that religion has not become increasingly important, with the national elite encouraging the Malay Muslim to enter the modern sector and less prominent or opposition politicians demanding a place for them.

Three types of religious arguments or actions have been utilized by the national leadership to further the development of the Malays. First, Malay Muslim political and religious spokesmen have long told their people that if their community is to survive it must be able to compete with the more modernized Chinese and Indian populace or else remain a permanent underclass in their own homeland. Given the perception of the interrelationship between religion and ethnicity in Malaysia, a weakened position of one would entail a loss of power for the other. Thus, involvement in the modern sector and successful competition with non-Malays translates into a defense of Islam. While this position has been publicly articulated by successive prime ministers, it has not been absent from speeches by politicians at party gatherings or even statements by cabinet ministers.

A second view encouraged by the current prime minister, Mohammad Mahathir, is that economic development must include a moral commitment and that it is possible and necessary for modernization to take place within an Islamic framework of values. In 1982 he proclaimed a "Look East" policy in which Japan and South Korea were presented as models of how development could be achieved while still retaining traditional values.[4] This position probably reflects an effort to establish a defense against those conservative Muslim political opponents who have accused the government of reaching for Western-oriented modernization at the expense of Islamic values. It also says to the individual Malay that it is possible to enter the modern sector without falling to the decadence of the West. Again, modernization and Islam are seen as reinforcing one another.

Finally, the Malaysian government has formulated a number of programs that at least give the appearance of placing its development plans within an institutional Islamic framework. Until recent years, issues such as insurance, interest, banking, lotteries, and other questionable activities have elicited more rhetoric than actual measures, and even recent programs retain a high level of symbolism. Still, in 1982 an Islamic insurance company and Islamic pawn shops were approved and in 1983 Malaysia's first "no-interest" Islamic bank was opened.[5] Its inauguration was widely publicized with prominent Malay officials pictured making deposits. Initially it appeared that this might be the forerunner of a host of such institutions leading to the Islamization of the country's banking system, but the government turned out to be considerably more cautious. The more symbolic nature of the bank was expressed by both the Finance Minister and the Prime Minister. The former noted that the commercial success of the institution was secondary and Mahathir's comments probably reflect his views of Islamic economics as a whole: "There should not be any fear that suddenly there is the intrusion of a very radical system. It is not going to hurt anybody. But it will certainly satisfy a group of Muslims who feel that it is wrong for them to accept interest."[6]

The various attempts of the Malaysian government to exploit religion as a factor in development have both positive and negative connotations. They have made the process more palatable for Malay Muslims fearing a deterioration of religious values. Also, given fears of Chinese economic dominance, justification in the name of Islam may actually encourage Malay Muslims to compete more fully in the modern sector. However, on the negative side there has been an increase in fears expressed by other communities that they would not be allowed to succeed in the new Malaysia. The tendency of Malay politicians at lower levels to "out-Islam" one another raises spectres of a full-scale movement toward an Islamic economy or the freezing out of nonbelievers from the economic system. Early comments regarding Islamic banking worried many non-Muslims in the financial world and initial developments in the New Economic Policy led to some capital and brain drain.[7] Thus, there has been the danger that while individual Malays may modernize, the state as a whole might be seriously weakened economically. This has necessitated a careful balancing act by the Malay leadership in power as it has attempted to assuage the fears of non-Muslims and at the same time sought to maintain the support of its own ethnic-religious constituency.

Thailand

Thai efforts to employ religion in the development field have both been more subtle and based upon greater private initiative than in the Burmese and Malaysian cases. The Royal Thai government has been cognizant of the inherent dangers of politicizing the religious orders and it was only with an increased consciousness of possible communist subversion that it began to involve the sangha in its programs. The basic thrust of these activities was the employment of religious personnel in programs of community development and national integration. We will review the former at this time and turn to the latter later in this chapter when issues of national unity are considered, recognizing that this division is somewhat arbitrary. These activities have been well described by S. Tambiah, S. Suksamran, and C. Keyes and will only be reviewed briefly here.[8]

To many in government and the central offices of the sangha, the utilization of monks in development must have appeared an obvious solution to legitimizing rural programs. As noted in chapter 5, members of the sangha usually enjoy high status in rural areas and are often called upon to lend their advice on local matters and pass on information from the outside. The wat itself is the center of the community in most Thai villages. As Suksamran notes, there were other reasons the hierarchy thought the monks should become involved in modernization and national integration activities:

> 1. As monks virtually depend upon the community for material support, the monks have a responsibility for its welfare.

2. The king and government give the monks protection and support and in return the monks should render aid and be loyal to the interest of the nation.
3. There are dangers to Buddhism from internal and external enemies and thus the sangha's involvement not only helps the government but also restores Buddhism.
4. The sangha itself must adjust and adapt to meet the forces of modernization facing Thailand or become moribund.
5. Nation-building and modernization are a form of merit-making in themselves and should be encouraged.[9]

A variety of programs were launched in the 1960s that brought the sangha directly into the development field in cooperation with the government. A good example of such an undertaking was the Training Project for Encouraging the Participation of Monks in Community Development, launched with the encouragement of the Department of Religion and the cooperation of the two Buddhist universities, Mahachula and Mahamakut. The reason for its establishment was:

It is apparent that at present national development is a principal policy of the government and it has been actively carried out. In order to fulfil this end the government has to be dependent on, and have the co-operation of, other institutions. The Sangha, which has been in existence as long as the nation itself, is one of those institutions. It has taken part in promoting the progress and prosperity of the nation within the bounds of Dhamma and *Vinaya* ever since. In an age of accelerated development, the Sangha would be an even greater asset to the nation. Only if the monks acquire substantial knowledge, and only if they clearly understand the philosophy, objectives and methods in development laid down by the government, will the Sangha's co-operation be fruitful.[10]

The project's objectives were:

(1) To maintain and promote the monks' status as a refuge of the people by providing them with religious education and general knowledge concerning community development. (2) To encourage monks and novices to participate in community development and thus help existing community development programmes to achieve their aims. (3) To promote unity among the Thai people and thus help to promote national and religious security.[11]

Trainees included 144 monks chosen from the provinces and another 100 volunteer monks graduated from the two Buddhist universities. They received extensive training in religion, history, and courses in development such as sanitation, home economics, public health, vocational promotion, and first aid. Graduates were sent back to their native provinces or, as with those from the universities, to where they were requested. In the villages the monks were advised to:

> —teach villagers to sacrifice their personal interests for communal interests based on the principle of *Dana* (giving)
> —encourage and create the people's feeling of loyalty to the nation, religion and the king;
> —lead the people in such village developments as the construction of bridges, roads, wells, rest houses, schools and other public properties, and in the repairing of the old ones;
> —advise villagers to eat nutritious food; give advice concerning health, sanitation and education. [12]

There were also other development programs in which the sangha was involved. It was encouraged to cooperate with the major anticommunist development undertaking in Thailand, the Accelerated Rural Development program (ARD). Formed in the northeast and north in the mid-1960s, ARD was established around a massive road-building effort through which rural areas were to be opened to commerce and government services such as health, education, and agriculture. Heavily supported by aid from the United States it was meant to fight communism through development. The role of the monk was to provide advice and evaluation and to encourage the people to cooperate with the operation.

Beyond these more institutionalized activities, both civil and military officers have attempted to engage the villager in a variety of development projects by gaining the cooperation of the local abbot or monks. It was hoped that villagers would be more willing to join with the government if the local monks backed the project, particularly if it could be justified in terms of gaining merit. As noted in chapter 5, this was of mixed success. [13]

Still there has been considerable debate as to the effectiveness of the sangha in forwarding development objectives, aside from the question of the political desirability of their involvement in government ordained programs or the propriety of bringing the monks into secular affairs. First, it should be noted that while many village-based monks do participate in local development activities through advice, consultation, and, at times, administration, the number involved in the aforementioned nationally sanctioned community development programs was relatively small. In 1966, at the time of the promulgation of many of these activities, there were 262,923 monks and novices. Tambiah reports that from 1963–66 Mahachula University sent 63 monk-graduates to work in 26 provinces and about 47 to 23 provinces in 1967–68. Mahamakut University in 1969 and 1970 had 29 and 19 graduates respectively and 300 since its founding. Even if we take the Thammthud program, which although primarily established to propagate Buddhism to the border provinces also carried out some development activities, the number of monks swelled by only 1,816 in 1969 and 2,105 in 1971. Add to this the 144 monks in the Training Project for Encouraging the Participation of Monks in Community Development and we still have less than 1 percent of all the nation's monks and novices.

The great opportunity and difficulty in such programs is the very role and legitimacy of the monk in rural Thailand. The core of the sangha's legitimacy has been the purity of its religious actions. Thai monks are expected to lead a life separate from and above the rest of society, and this role is carefully defined. There are thus two dangers to engaging the sangha in secular development schemes. One is failure. Given the religious role of the monk, there is not always support for him in more mundane development activities. As was noted in a previous chapter, there are some parts of Thailand where the monk does not have high status. However, even where he does, problems may arise. M. Moerman recounted one abortive effort to use the sangha to get the people to act in an isolated village in northern Thailand.

> The government attempts to use the ecclesiastical hierarchy to control the villagers. When Ban Ping was unwilling to help construct a new school building the district administrative officer came to the village with the district abbot. The abbot preached a sermon in which he told the congregation that schools and roads make as much merit as temples because they bring about progress and call for cooperation. Just in case the villagers had missed the point, the district administrative officers summarized the appropriate part of the sermon. Afterward, some villagers admitted that a road might make merit but their explanation was that without one people could lose their way or be attacked by thieves. Some admitted that a school might make merit but their explanation was that only after passing the fourth grade can a boy become ordained. All insisted that nothing makes as much merit as a temple and since a new vihara was then

under construction in Ban Ping they could not afford to divert any efforts for the benefit of the school.

The other difficulty arises from the almost ubiquitous suspicion that the Thai peasant has of government authorities. The king may be revered, but local officials have traditionally been viewed as arrogant, greedy, and uncaring. This was particularly true of the more isolated areas of north and northeast Thailand where the major thrust of development projects took place. In fact, it was not until the appearance of these programs in the 1960s that this picture began to change. Thus, by cooperating with the secular authorities, the Buddhist hierarchy itself could become tainted and lose some of its legitimacy. While this might not seriously affect Thailand's overall development efforts, it could jeopardize the campaign to foster national unity in the name of king, country, and Buddhism.

It would appear that at least in the short run, the use of religious symbols to increase support for development programs has generally produced positive results. However, this cannot save undertakings that are badly conceived and implemented, such as the Pyidawtha Plan, or that draw religious personnel too far from accepted spiritual roles. Finally, considerable care must be taken by governments to protect religion where it provides a foundation for legitimacy and stability in the society. Politicization or blatant manipulation may seriously weaken the value of a national asset.

RELIGION AND NATIONAL UNITY

We have proposed that the existence of a modern nation-state is necessary to successfully achieve technological change. This is not to argue that international organizations are not helpful or that in the best of all possible worlds a wider base would not be more effective. However, in the world as it is, the type of administrative system required for technological change seems only possible within the nation-state. It can be argued that the earlier colonial system also provided a foundation for administrative efficiency, but rising nationalism made that alternative out of the question. Given these premises, we can delineate two areas in which religious symbols have been utilized: in the promotion of nationalist movements and in attaining and maintaining national integration after independence.

Religion and Nationalism

In the development of the nationalist movements of three of the four former colonized states under discussion, Burma, Indonesia, and the Philippines, religion played an early and perhaps crucial role, by providing ideological focus and leadership. Having written extensively on religion and nationalism in Southeast Asia, I will merely summarize these findings in the following pages.[15]

Given the heterogeneity of societies in the region, religion was able to be a unifying concept where most of the populace adhered to a single broad faith. In the early years of the nationalist movements differences within these religions tended to be submerged in the desire to rid the polity of the foreign interlopers. Where there was no such umbrella faith, particular groups could unify behind their own religion often leading to divisiveness rather than unity. This was the case of Malaya, with half the population Malay Muslim and the rest primarily Chinese and Indian. As the nationalist movements developed and independence was achieved, religious consensus tended to weaken in the former situation while religious differences intensified in the latter.

In fact, there would appear to have been a number of stages of religionationalism in Southeast Asia. The first reaction to colonial rule tended to be atavistic, as the people sought to return to the old ways. This attitude was often reflected in small-scale uprisings led by local religious leaders. This was followed by elitist religiocultural organizations with nationalist underpinnings which took an opposite position toward Western ways, copying them in many aspects. Examples would be the Young Men's Buddhist Association in Burma and Budi Utomo in the Netherlands East Indies. The next stage was the formation of mass religious and nationalist parties that tried to appeal to the general populace. Such organizations were Sarekat Islam in the Indies and the General Council of Burmese Associations. However, these efforts tended to be short-lived as the nationalist movements fell under more secular leadership that was not averse to using religion to foster political goals. This group dominated the latter years of the nationalist struggles and the formative years of independence. In recent years, we have seen another stage, the reassertion of religious values in reaction to Western-oriented secularism and materialism. Why religion played such an important role in the pre-independence years can be seen by analyzing its attraction as a unifying force in Indonesia, Burma, and the Philippines.

INDONESIA

The colony which the Dutch ruled for some three centuries had never existed as a single political unit prior to its conquest, although the Mataram and Majapahit empires had controlled large sections of what was to become Indonesia. Within its borders lived a multitude of separate and often isolated ethnic groups reflecting a myriad of languages, customs, and loyalties. Lacking any natural unifying factor to lend cohesion to this varied populace, Islam, as the faith of some 90 percent of the archipelago, provided a foundation for unity. To many elements of the society ethnicity and religion were one. Thus, Dutch scholars could point to Islam as a "nationality matter," "the nationality," and "a national symbol"[16] of the Javanese, and H. O. S. Tjokroaminoto, the noted leader of Sarekat Islam could see Islam as a "binding social factor and national symbol."[17] It did not matter at the time that there appeared to be major differences in practice and concept among the colony's Muslims from the orthodox faithful of Acheh to the heavily Hindu influenced Javanese.

The nationalist leaders could play upon the pride and problems, the anger and resentment of the Islamic community. As Tjokroaminoto said at a party meeting in 1914, Islam was being employed by his movement as a "rope, as a binding means" to bring the people together.[18] There was not much need to employ artificial means to generate dissatisfaction in the name of Islam. The average Muslim saw himself ruled by a *kafir* government, his economy dominated by Dutch entrepreneurs and Chinese middlemen, and education coming increasingly under the control of secular and Christian interests. Nationalists could argue that, as a superior religion, it was untenable that Muslims should continue to be treated in such a manner by kafirs. While Marxists could assert that religion did not provide a proper class basis for national liberation, Muslim leaders could rebut that there were only two classes in the Indies, the rich, Christian Dutch and the poor, Muslim Indonesians.[19]

BURMA

Similar comments could be made regarding British controlled Burma although the issue of heterogeneity was less salient. There had been a Burmese kingdom prior to the British conquest. The fact that the final subjugation of Upper Burma took place only in 1885–86 left many

Burmese with recent memories of an independent country with Buddhism supreme and protected. Like the people of the Indies, the Buddhists of Burma experienced a Christian colonial government, a foreign-dominated economy, in this case with Indian moneylenders owning half the agricultural land of lower Burma, and a steady weakening of monastery education under the challenge of Christian and secular schools. To many Buddhists it was a question as to how an individual could effectively improve his karma in such a society. As U Ottuma, the country's foremost monk-politician stated, "At present we want Burma. I think you want it as much as I do. When Lord Buddha was alive, man had a predilection for Nirvana. There is nothing left now. The reason why it is so is because the Government is English."[20] Christian minority leaders and missionaries also made statements that inflamed the situation as when the Karen spokesman, San C. Po, proudly asserted that the Karens affectionately called the missionaries "their 'Mother' under the protection of the British Government whom they rightly call their 'Father'."[21] Or there was the missionary who reportedly wished to convert the hill tribes, "to ring Burma, around, as it were with a Christian Army gathered among the hill peoples, and to compel Burma to surrender to Christ."[22] Little wonder that years later a Burmese writer could declare that Buddhism could act as a new weapon for the nationalists which "served to provide a means towards both national unity and a new form of organized resistance to foreign rule."[23]

THE PHILIPPINES

The Spanish-dominated Philippines offered a distinctly different religious picture than did Burma and the Indies. Through several centuries of conversions, approximately 90 percent of the Filipinos were Roman Catholic by the nineteenth century. Thus, the religion of the ruler and ruled was the same. In spite of this, religion became a critical issue in the nationalist movement in the islands, this time in the guise of anticlericism. The nationalist movement grew up around opposition to the Catholic clergy, not the Church, for as one group of exiled nationalists stated, "We desire that Christianity, basis of present civilization, be the symbol and solid foundation of religious institutions, but without coercion or imposition . . . "[24]

This anticlericism was based upon opposition to the clergy's role in the economic, political, and moral life of the colony. As noted in chapter 5, the clerical orders had acquired major land-holdings and were accused of using their economic power to control and subjugate the Filipinos.

According to the Taft commission, friar agricultural lands, excepting religious buildings, totalled 403,713 acres, accounting for some of the best land and some 48 percent of the total cultivated lands in Tagalog areas.[25] Not only was this accretion of land attacked, but the friars were also charged with the misappropriation of property, unfair labor practices towards tenants, evading taxes, and using their power and contacts with the Spanish administration to gain monopoly advantages.

In the political realm, the Philippine Commission noted that "there is scarcely any branch of the municipal government in which the reverend parochial priest does not play an important part,"[26] and then proceeded to list some fourteen areas of power:

a. assists in choosing the members of the municipal tribunal;
b. revises the act and makes sure that the officials are properly elected;
c. signs the certificate of election;
d. assists and supervises the drawing of lots whenever that is necessary to determine who shall go out of office first;
e. signs a statement certifying to the result of the drawing of lots;
f. assists the municipal tribunal and the twelve delegates in choosing or nominating the cabeza de barangay;
g. becomes a member of the provincial council when there is only one foreign vicar in the province;
h. assists the tribunal in deciding upon the questions relative to taxes and imposts;
i. signs the estimates of permanent receipts and expenditures;
j. assists the tribunal in deciding upon the construction of public works;
k. assists in making any modification in the estimates of permanent receipts or expenditures;
l. assists in deciding upon any extraordinary expenditures of the tribunal;
m. gives his opinion on the accounts presented to him by the tribunal before the same are sent to the provincial council;
n. has the power to decide at what hour the meetings of the tribunal in which he is to take part shall be held."[27]

Aside from these specific duties, which were not always carried out, there were also charges of collusion between the orders and the colonial administration, with both allegedly having the same economic and political interests in dominating the Filipino people.

Finally, there were accusations that local priests used their positions to carry out acts of gross immorality, seducing the women of the village and acquiring wealth for their own self-aggrandizement. The reaction of both sides was often virulent, as exemplified by the following comments of a Spanish Friar in 1897 and the Filipino nationalist Aguinaldo. Writing about the Filipinos, the friar asserted: "They brilliantly set forth the savage instincts and bestial inclinations of those faithful imitators of apes . . . As neither Spain nor the friars can change the ethnological character of the race, so inferior to ours, it will be idle to desire to apply them the same laws as to us . . . The only liberty the Indians want is the liberty of the savages."[28] Aguinaldo in his Manifesto from Biak-Na Bata wrote, "Look at our homes, their landmarks and lands watered with the sweat of our forefathers are taken away by the insatiable friars, despots and plunderers of the fruits of our soil, while they proclaim their poverty and chastity."[29]

Anticlericism thus became the battlecry of the nationalists of the late nineteenth century. Their antagonism was at times brilliantly and other times bluntly put forth in the novels of J. Rizal, such as *Noli Me Tangere* and *El Filibusterismo*, the charges of M. del Pilar's *Monastic Supremacy in the Philippines*, and the fiery manifesto of the Katipunan. To many in the Philippines, the Catholic clergy and Spanish colonial administration were inseparable opponents to their freedom. They would accept the later words of the Philippine Commission that, "The truth is that the whole government of Spain in the islands rested on the friars. To use the expression of the provincial of the Augustinians, the friars were 'the pedestal or foundation of the sovereignty of Spain in the islands' which being removed "the whole structure would topple over.'"[30]

Religion and Nationalist Organization

The religions of Southeast Asia also provided a ready-made group prepared to furnish both leaders and followers. Monks, hadjis and kiayis, and Filipino priests all supplied members to the cause. Without going into the myriad of organizations, manifestoes, and manueverings that characterized this activity, we can outline the who, what, and why.[31] The "who" in Burma were elements of the sangha who either individually or as part of political organizations involved themselves in the movement at all levels. It is difficult to estimate the exact numbers participating as both they and secular nationalist spokesmen tended to exaggerate sangha support. However, they were sizable enough to draw strong reactions from the colonial administration and more conservative clergy, both wishing them to concentrate on traditional religious activities. Since no hiercharchy exists in Sunni Islam, religious leaders involved in the nationalist movement in the Indies included Muslim teachers, ulama, immam and politicized hadjis. Again, there was no unanimity in support of anti-Dutch activities, as Modernists tending to be more nationalist oriented and the orthodox somewhat fearful that the success of the nationalist movement could lead to Modernist domination. As in Burma, other religious leaders remained indifferent to political issues and continued to be principally engaged in teaching and spiritual matters. In the Philippines, the "who" were the Filipino clergy and Masonic orders. Of the 3,044 Catholic clergy in the Philippines in 1896–98, only 675 were natives.[32] Often poorly educated and badly treated by the Spanish clerics, they generally acted as assistants and ministered to considerably fewer people per parish than their Spanish counterparts. The Filipino Masons were active in leading the anticlerical campaign in the islands. Initially established in 1891, the Preamble of the first Filipino lodge read, "In the Philippines where clericism has made the people its victim, brutalizing its inhabitants, we must organize a council of the order which will free them from the yoke and safeguard them towards progress and civilization, defeating those who are only the spectres of the past and who carry with them ignorance, fanaticism and superstition."[33] It is difficult to estimate the numbers and influence of the Masons, and the Spanish were anxious to exaggerate their power for their own purposes (the latter said there were 25,000).

As to the "what," clerical nationalists engaged in a wide range of activities including speaking for the cause, joining, and at times leading, political organizations, participating in demonstrations, some violent, publishing and writing in newspapers and political tracts, and a variety of other generally secular labors. Comparatively, the Burmese tended to be the most politicized, while the Filipino clergy were the least, probably because of their poor educational backgrounds and the authority of the hierarchy. However, in each of these polities religious personnel were used as symbols of opposition to colonial power. At times their participation was conscious and active while at others the clerics were manipulated by secular nationalists.

The "why" must be obvious from previous discussions of the challenge offered by the colonial system. The diminished role of Muslim and Buddhist religious personnel in the traditional education system and the increasing power of secular and Christian schools was matter of considerable chagrin. The seeming growth of secularist and materialist influences was seen to be generated by the sins of the West and was pictured as a danger to the spiritual foundations of the people. The rhetoric of the Christian minorities of Burma and Thailand and the Spanish Catholics of the Philippines further antagonized indigenous religious leadership. Finally, as U Ottuma and his Islamic and Christian counterparts argued, it was not possible to lead a good religious life within the colonial environment.

Religion and National Unity

In the postindependence years, the governing elites of Southeast Asia continued in their attempts to use religion as a symbol to attain or maintain national integration. In nations with variations in language, ethnicity, custom, level of modernization, religion, and the like, the challenge to unify these disparate elements was at the top of the agenda of these new governments. The immediacy of the problem could be seen at its most virulent form in the violent communal and ideological clashes that plagued the region from the first years of independence. Aside from the bloody Indochina wars, which are not in the purview of this study, civil disturbances were experienced throughout the region. Burma saw the initial beginnings of more than thirty-five years of civil war even before independence was achieved in 1948 and since then there have been revolts by a variety of communist groups plus Mons, Arakanese, Karens, Shans, Chins, and Kachins. Thailand has faced insurgency involving Malay Muslims in the south, communist supported groups in the north, south central and northeast parts of the Kingdom, the hill tribes in the north and conflicts related to spillovers from Burmese, Lao, and Cambodian domestic problems. The Malayan government fought a long communist insurgency even prior to independence and since then has continued to clash with communist insurgents on the Peninsula and for awhile in the Borneo states. In 1969 Malaysia experienced serious race riots. Indonesia saw a host of succession movements in the Outer Islands, a violent Muslim insurgency on Java, and probably hundreds of thousands killed during the crackdown on the Communist Party in 1965–66. Finally, the Philippines has faced both communist-led and Muslim separatist insurgency for more than a generation.

In each of these countries religion proved to be a divisive force, leading to violence, major expenditures on the military, and the involvement of the energies of both the authorities and opposition. These conflicts tended to be the most bitter when a fusion of ethnicity and religion provided identity to dissident elements in juxtaposition to dominant forces in the society.[34]

In Burma the Arakanese Muslims and Karen-led Christians came into bloody conflict with the Buddhist-Burmese authorities in the late 1940s. At one time surrounding the capital for weeks, the Karens were pushed back into the hills where elements continue to war against Rangoon. The Arakanese carried out desultory clashes with the Burmese whom they believed were attempting to deny them their rights and at one time thousands fled to neighboring Islamic Bangladesh.

In Thailand the Malay Muslims in the south were long almost totally neglected by the Thai Buddhists in Bangkok, living lives isolated from Thai culture and political power. It was only in the 1960s that a combination of the move of the defeated Malayan Communist Party into southern Thailand and a growing Malay Muslim secessionist movement stirred the Thai authorities. Since that period the Thais have employed both development programs and military force to handle the situation, not always with great success.

In the Philippines the Muslims Moros were never satisfied with their inferior and isolated status under the Spanish, Americans, or independent state. Fearing the encroachment of Christian settlers, demanding the recognition of their Islamic identity, distrustful of the authorities in Manila, and at various times aided by Libyan, Malaysian, and other Muslim states, the Moros are still fighting.

Newly independent Indonesia had as one of its first test rebellions by Christians in Ambon, Sulawesi, and other parts of the Outer Islands against the government in Jakarta. Many of them having fought with the Dutch in opposition to the nationalists, desirous of secession, autonomy, or even being annexed by the former "motherland," and fearful of losing the once favored position they held under the colonial system, Christian insurgents fought a short-lived war. As well, Muslims, dissatisfied with secularist trends after independence and seeking to form a new Muslim state and society, clashed with authorities in the name of Dar-ul Islam. Neither group is now a viable and active movement. Violence in recent years has also involved limited attacks on Christians, often influenced by strong condemnations by Muslim leaders.[35] In Malaysia the only major communal violence with religious overtones was the race riots of 1969. However, as has been noted previously, the fused nature of Islam and Malay ethnicity is such that it is difficult to disaggregate one from the other. In this case Malay rights appear to bave been the paramount factor.

In the long run these religiously oriented domestic conflicts cost many lives and considerable treasure and probably did little to advance national unity and modernize the society. They were used by governing elites to point out the dangers of disunity and may have allowed the military to modernize their forces, but these were questionable pluses. Perhaps the only important positive results came from government responses to dissatisfaction in terms of education and development programs.

Whatever the success of efforts to ameliorate the problems of communal discord, their continued presence led several governments in the region to employ religion as a means of fostering national unity. Two states did not experiment with such policies extensively. The traditional twentieth-century separation of church and state in the Philippines when combined with recent antagonism between the Catholic hierarchy and President F. Marcos have severely curtailed the use of this tactic. In Indonesia, in the postwar years, Muslims attempted, but failed, to establish Islam as the state religion and foundation of the nation's ideology. Instead the Pantja Sila (or Pancha sila) was ordained giving no special place to Islam. As then President Sukarno explained:

> Not only should the people of Indonesia have belief in God, but every Indonesian should believe in his own particular God. The Christian should worship God according to the teachings of Jesus Christ; Moslems According to the teachings of the Prophet Mohhammed; Buddhist should discharge their religious rites according to their own books.
>
> But let us all have belief in God. The Indonesian state shall be a state where every person can worship God in freedom . . . without "religious egoism." And the State of Indonesia should be a State incorporating the belief in God.[36]

Since that time Muslim leaders have continued to work toward the formation of an Islamic state, but have not been able to obtain the political power to be successful. Today President Suharto is following in his predecessors footsteps in attempting to limit the political role of Islam.

President Sukarno did make one major effort to employ religion for national integration. In the early 1960s he formulated the concept of NASAKOM, an abbreviation for *Nasionalisme* (nationalism), *Agama* (Religion), and *Kommunisme* (Communism) in an effort to forge unity out of three not always cooperative elements of Indonesian political life. According to the President: "Thus all three want freedom and socialism. Thus all three contain progressiveness. For that reason, NASAKOM is a progressive necessity of the Indonesian revolution. Whoever is opposed to NASAKOM is not progressive! Whoever is against NASAKOM in reality cripples the revolution, disbalances the revolution. Whoever is anti-NASAKOM is not fully revolutionary, nay, is historically even contra-revolutionary."[37] This symbol manipulation was part of a series of campaigns launched by Sukarno, each usually with its own acronym. In this case the Indonesian Communist Party found it a useful means of attaining legitimacy and strongly backed the concept, but Muslim politicians tended to ignore it to the degree that it was possible. Sukarno attempted to force NASAKOM on the nation's various political organizations, but it ultimately dropped from view, particularly after the abortive communist-supported coup of 1965.

Burma

If the initial postwar nationalist leader of Burma had not been assassinated just prior to independence, religion probably would not have become the focal point of the national ideology that it did. Aung San believed in the separation of church and state and sought to relegate religion to the realm of the personal. As he stated in 1946: "Religion is a matter of individual conscience, while politics is social science. We must see to it that the individual enjoys his rights, including the right to freedom of religious belief and worship. We must draw a clear line between politics and religion, because the two are not one and the same thing. If we mix religion with politics, then we offend the spirit of religion itself. Politics is pure secular science."[38]

This was not the position of Aung San's successor, U Nu. Often called the "monk-politician," and believed by many to be a Buddha in the becoming, Nu made vigorous efforts to promote his faith. He took it upon himself to follow in the path of the Burmese kings, seeing the state as a proper leader in religious matters. He asserted that "in the matter of religion, as in the realm of politics, leadership . . . is necessary to guide the people in order that they may not fall into error."[39] As we have seen in his welfare policies, he was more than willing to employ Buddhism to achieve his goals. When it came to national unity, an essential ingredient for fragmented Burma, he saw no inconsistency in fostering Buddhism in order to integrate the society. More than once he argued that by expanding the people's understanding of their religion, they would be more tolerant of other faiths and better prepared to work with others. Thus, while some might see his efforts to promote Buddhism as narrowly supporting his own faith, to him they were really attempts to aid the people as a whole.

In this process, U Nu helped to promulgate a series of acts, regulations, and projects. Immediately after independence, the authority of the sangha was officially re-established through the Ecclesiastical Courts Act, educational and examination systems were formulated for the sangha and the Pali University Act was passed, a Ministry of Religion was formed, and the government helped to build the World Peace Pagoda, the Kaba Aye. Beyond these parliamentary acts, U Nu encouraged the restoration of pagodas and the veneration of relics, gave government workers time off for meditation, made efforts to convert non-Buddhists (including Indian Prime Minister J. Nehru!), took an active part in publicly propitiating the *nats*, and motivated his ministers to foster Buddhism at every possible opportunity.

As stated, the Prime Minister saw these efforts as reinforcing national unity. Thus, one of his major activities during his first years as premier was preparing for the Sixth World Buddhist Synod which was held in Rangoon during 1954–56. This massive and expensive ($2 million plus) undertaking was completed at the time of the 2,500th anniversary of Buddha's death and attainment of nirvana. Activities included the building of the Great Cave, a replica of the Sattapanni Cave in India, revisions of the sacred texts, special ceremonies, government acts of commemoration such as the remission of prison sentences, and a variety of programs throughout the country fostered to display a renewed religious strength within Burmese society. The importance of the Synod in Nu's efforts at national integration was put forcefully by D. Smith, "The council's greatest significance was symbolic. It dramatized in unforgettable fashion the government's commitment to the promotion of Buddhism, which was regarded as an essential component of the Burmese national identity. The holding of the council was a supreme act of religious merit from which U Nu, members of the government, the Sangha, and ultimately every Burmese Buddhist derived personal *karmic* benefit."[40]

However, not all of U Nu's projects were so successful or seemingly relevant to his people's needs. For example, just prior to the second military coup he called for the building of 60,000 sand pagodas "to avert pending dangers and to achieve complete peace and tranquility in the Union."[41] On December 9, 1961, between 6:00 a.m. and 8:24 a.m. 60,000 pagodas, each nine cubits in height with nine-tiered brass or iron spires, were built throughout Burma. Perhaps these better reflected U Nu's more populist religious beliefs which included astrology (he made a variety of state decisions, including the time for swearing in the first government, on the advice of astrologers) and the propitiation of nats.

The difficulties of attempting to promote Buddhism while at the same time supporting tolerance for all faiths was best seen in Nu's efforts to promulgate Buddhism as a state religion during the interregnum between the first and second military regimes.[42] Again, the Prime Minister emphasized that rather than fragmenting the people, the reinforcement of Buddhist values would lead to national unity. Secular and minority religious interests saw the legislation quite differently, but did not employ violent means of opposition. Less than seven months before the second coup, on August 26, 1961, Burma became a Buddhist state, the Constitution thus reading, "Buddhism being the religion professed by the great Majority of the citizens of the Union shall be the state religion." Along with it the State Religion Promotion bill was pushed which called for Buddhist education for Buddhist students, including those in teacher training colleges, and encouraged other educational efforts to foster the Buddhist religion, including monastery schools.

There was considerable fear that violence would erupt in Rangoon as these bills made their way through Parliament and riot police and tanks were present during the debates. Disruptions did not take place then, but it was a different story when the government later moved to pass another amendment to the Constitution. This act protected all religions from insult and stated that no child would be taught a religion other than his or her own without the consent of the parents. This time members of the sangha disagreed, seeing in the legislation a watering down of the religious state bill, and actively opposed it. Monks passed resolutions, launched poster campaigns against Nu, marched on his home, picketed Parliament in order to prevent MPs from entering to pass on the act, and later took part in violent anti-Muslim demonstrations that led to property damage, death, injury, and the arrest of almost one hundred members of the sangha. Although the amendment was promulgated, the tensions and disruptions caused by the whole religious state issue were given by the military as a partial reason for the coup of 1962. The officers argued that, rather than leading to unity, religion had fostered disunity.

However, the military had not always eschewed the use of religion for purposes of national integration. During its first period of control in 1958–60, faced with a continuing communist challenge, the Department of Psychological Warfare developed a religious campaign against Marxism.[43] In cooperation with private interests, it formulated separate programs based upon perceptions of how individual religious groups would act. Thus, the Muslims were viewed as being more aggressive, and literature targeting the Islamic community implied the use of violence against the Communists. For the Christian and Buddhist population, less inflammatory rhetoric was used. The military also publicized anti-Buddhist propaganda based upon lecture notes given communist cadres by their leaders. These notes damned Buddhism as an opium of the people and included communist calls for stripping the gold and jewels from the Shwe Dagon Pagoda to use for the welfare of the nation.

In private conversations with those responsible for this campaign, the author found considerable frankness as to variations in tactics based upon religion as well as in belief that it was quite proper to use religion as a weapon against the communists. While the military were proud of their success, pointing to the thousands of religious personnel involved in the campaign and the wide distribution of the pamphlet, Dhammanta-raya, it is difficult to assess what was actually achieved in diminishing communist strength. At least some temporary success was probable, given strong communist reactions to aspects of the campaign such as the charges regarding the desecration of the Shwe Dagon.

When Ne Win came into office again in March 1962, his reactions mirrored more Aung San's belief in the separation of the church and state rather than his predecessor's views. In a series of decrees much of what U Nu accomplished was undone. Cow slaughter was reinstituted, the propitiation of nats was castigated as irrational and programs were launched against the practice, the Ecclesiastical Courts and Pali University acts were repealed, and a monetarization policy seriously cut into the funds held by the sangha.

Tensions rose between sections of the sangha and the govenment as the former accused Ne Win of being more interested in socialism than Buddhism and of fostering a campaign to weaken the role of Buddhism in the society. Ne Win and those around him accused some members of the sangha of being "bogus monks' intent on their own self-aggrandizement and the overthrow of the regime.[44] In the early years of military rule there were monks who publicly charged the government with being against Buddhism and in the name of religion demanded its overthrow, resulting in the incarceration of some ninety-two monks in 1965. Since that time there has been a tentative truce, with the government carrying out symbolic acts of suppport for Buddhism such as having the army clean the temples. As Ne Win got older he also tended to become more religious and the amnesty offered former opponents in his latter years in power seemed to reflect a wish to get his spiritual house in order. However, the general tenor of military policy and rhetoric has been to emphasize the nonpolitical aspects of religion and the promotion of

Buddhism to achieve national unity is no longer an essential element of government ideology.

Malaysia

In Malaysia no consensus on religion exists, but this has not stopped the government from working to reinforce unity within the Islamic community. Over the last fifteen years in particular there has been a steady increase in efforts to rally Muslims around their faith. The reasons for this have been presented in chapter 5, but to briefly reiterate, they include Muslim reactions to what they perceive to be objectionable aspects of Western materialism, the influence of the world-wide Islamic resurgence, and pressure from more narrow Malay Islamic political opponents. In large part to meet this popular and potentially politically dangerous popular upsurge, the Muslim-led government has encouraged a variety of activities with the apparent aim of strengthening the Islamic character of the country. Care has had to be taken not to foster fear among nonbelievers that they are the targets of these programs and rhetoric, but there remains the possibility that symbolic acts may develop an environment demanding fundamental changes.

To the regular visitor to Malaysia over the years the country appears to have a distinctly more Muslim character than it did during the first decade after independence. The media, particularly state run television, provides an increasing amount of Islamic programming. The rhetoric of Malay political leaders of all types involves more references to Islamic issues and the political elite is much more likely to be seen fulfilling their religious obligations. As has already been noted, the government has moved, at least symbolically, toward establishing Muslim economic institutions in banking and insurance. Muslim holidays have been given a more national character. The state has aided dakwah organizations intent upon converting nonbelievers to Islam and then publicized their conversion on national television. In education there have been a host of activities developed to inculcate Muslim values and life-style into the youth, from Koranic reading contests to the new International Islamic University. Finally, Malaysia has become deeply involved in International Islamic organizations and issues, hosting innumerable seminars and gathering and sending representatives throughout the Islamic world.[45]

These efforts have normally been directed towards the Islamic community with the view that a strong Muslim populace is the foundation of an indomitable Malaysia. However, efforts at conversion do impinge upon nonbelievers and lead to questions as to their ultimate fate in the new Malaysia, particularly when questions are raised as to the voluntary nature of such acts. For example, the campaign of Tun Mustapha to convert people in his state when he was Chief Minister of Sabah became a matter of some controversy. Opponents charged that he employed improper political and economic pressure to gain converts, including the refusal to re-issue work permits to Catholic priests, and that he exaggerated his successes. Supporters, including former Prime Minister Tunku Abdul Rahman, have argued that Tun Mustapha did more to bring converts to Islam than any other entity in Malaysia, claiming 96,400 new adherents to the faith.

However, perhaps the most interesting aspect of this controversy was the concept of integration posed in support of these conversions. Mustapha had contended that the people of Sabah had been one race, but had been taught to live as tribes. Both Christians and Mustapha had attempted to convert them, but according to the Tunku, "The essential difference in his approach was that he (Mustapha) could create one racial outlook with the religion of Islam as the base. The Christian missions could win converts to Christianity but they were not able to make the people feel themselves as one race. They might still remain divided, but all could be Muslims. Islam breaks through all barriers of race and colour, so they could become Malays."[46]

There is little doubt that a greater conscious sense of Islamic identity exists today, in part due to government efforts. Given the probable correctness of an early statement by Tunku Abdul Rahman that all the Chinese could not be thrown into the sea, it is difficult to see how much further this process can go without even more seriously exacerbating communal tensions. So far the government has been able to lend credence to its claim to support a plural society, but this very intensification of religious identity within the Muslim community can seriously weaken the possibility of maintaining a system based upon the political consensus of all the communities.

Thailand

Traditionally, Thai kings have been perceived as the protectors and promoters of Buddhism, with a mutually supporting symbiotic relationship between the monarchy and sangha. Religion was an essential element in the national identity of most Thais. However, as described so well by W. Vella in his *Chaiyo*, it was Prince and later King Vajiravudh who first systematically articulated Buddhism as the main buttress to nationalism and who forged the ideology of king, Buddhism, and country.

> Previous Kings had supported Buddhism publicly for somewhat different reasons. They had favored Buddhism as a means of increasing royal virtue, as a means of public welfare, and as a means of adding miraculous power to the state. But Vajiravudh identified Buddhism with patriotism; a devoted Buddhist was a devoted citizen.
> The Buddhist messages of the King consisted of four main elements. First, a good Buddhist was a moral citizen and a strength to the state. Second, a moral state would be strong in competition with other states. Third, for the Thai at least, Buddhism was a better route to morality than any other religion. And, fourth, the Thai had a mission to preserve and protect the Buddhist faith. [47]

The King actively promoted the view that Thais should be proud of their religion which, unlike Christianity, was based upon intelligence rather than superstition and fable; that as the citadel of true Buddhism, it was incumbent upon the people to defend their country, with military means if necessary. During the years that followed, and particularly during the period after the fall of the absolute monarchy in 1932, religion and the monarchy played a smaller role in the national ideology.

It was in the postwar years that Buddhism and the monarchy were reinstated as the pillars of Thai nationalism. Modernization was weakening the former bases of legitimacy and social stability. Communism was increasingly perceived by the Thai establishment as both an internal and external threat. Finally, as communications developed and Bangkok came into closer contact with previously isolated sections of the kingdom, it became obvious that the country was faced with dissatisfied ethnic, religious, and regional minorities.

It was Marshal Sarit, strong-man of the 1950s, who in the early 1960s began a renewed effort to forge Thai nationalism to the monarchy and Buddhism as a challenge to the new forces arising in the Kingdom. Sarit promoted the role of the king ceremonially, and through his efforts and the monarch's own abilities, the king's position grew in symbolic and actual importance. Wider publicity was given the king's religious functions and the mass media and educational system were employed to make the national ideology one founded on the tripod of king, Buddhism, and country. [48] This position was clearly articulated by one of his successors, Prime Minister Thanom Kittikichorn,

At present Thai people in some parts of the country are threatened by communist terrorists, and some people are particularly vulnerable to the propaganda of insurgents. The enemy, whether internal or external, aims at destroying the nation, Buddhism the national religion, and the monarchy which is our national morale and unity. It is obvious, then, the enemy wants to enslave us, to destroy our freedom, our religion, and our king. The enemy is advancing its purposes by inciting the people not to pay respect to and not believe in the Sangha and Buddhism. This really jeopardizes our national security and unity.[49]

In line with this concept, the Royal Thai government introduced two programs targeting areas considered threatened, Buddhists in the northeast and south and "heathens" among the hill tribes.[50] Both of these were initiated in the mid-1960s at a time when there was considerable fear in Bangkok of the encroachment of communism into these very areas. It was a period of increasing insurgency and counter efforts by the Thai government to invent programs to meet these challenges. The so-called Phra Dhammatuta or Thammathud program was based upon the premise that Buddhism was the core to Thai identity and if it became weakened, then so would society as a whole. According to the Director-General of the Department of Religious Affairs, its objectives were:

Nowadays people have less perseverance to practise Dhamma; people's faith and trust in monks had declined; and there have been attempts to introduce and propagandize another 'ism', that is, communism, that jeopardizes and undermines national and religious security and public tranquility; and people's happiness. In order to save people from demoralization, the Department of Religious Affairs is to strengthen people's attachment to Dhamma so that they are edified and not misguided in so doing, the development of Buddhist history has shown that whenever Buddhism had remedied it by calling for devout volunteers whose duty was to make people understand Dhamma, these devout volunteers have been known as 'Dhammatuta'; this was said to be ever successful, as exemplified by the deeds of King Ashoka. The Department of Religious Affairs deems it appropriate to revise the Dhammatuta to assume this task.[51]

This was later clarified by the late Supreme Patriarch as follows:

The direct objective of the Phra Dhammatuta Programme is to follow the Buddha's footsteps and to carry on his purpose; through the strengthening of people's attachment to Dhamma, he maintains, the people will be loyal to the nation, the government and the king; the people will better understand each other, thereby promoting national integration; through national integration people will be unified. Moreover, in an age of accelerated development, the Phra Dhammatuta monks will provide the village with morale and help villagers in development.[52]

More specifically, the program sent monks (802 the first year) after initial training to villages where they were to teach the basic tenets of Buddhism. Their training was rather wide-ranging, as discovered by Tambiah. In 1971 he found fifteen subjects covered in lectures,

1. "Public Law" by an official from the Ministry of Justice.
2. "Gems from Buddhist Scriptures" by an official from Rahjaban-dit Thesathaan.
3. "First Aid" by a doctor from Chulalongkom Hospital.
4. "Ecclesiastical Law" by an official from the Department of Religious Affairs.
5. "Rural Development" by the governor of Nan province.
6. "Comparative Religion" by the secretary general of Maha-makut University.
7. "Meditation Practice" by a famous meditation instructor (Phra Thepsiddhiumni) from Wat Mahathad.
8. "Abhidhamma" by the secretary general of Mahachulalong-korn University.
9. "Criminology" by a police lieutenant.
10. "The Administrative Work of the Monastic Secretary" (lekha wat) by the secretary of Wat Anong, Thonburi.
11. "The Buddhist Monk from a Layman's Point of View" by a noted writer and publisher.
12. "Ecology and Environment" by a teacher from Mahidol University.
13. "Credit Societies" by a headmaster of a Catholic school.
14. "Buddhism and the Modern Man" by Phra Wisudhimoli, the deputy secretary general of Mahachulalongkorn University, a gifted scholar-monk.
15. "History of Buddhism" by an ex-monk and an ex-member of the legislative Assembly representing Roied province.[53]

As missionary monks these members of the sangha were sent to both convert nonbelievers and to strengthen the beliefs of the faithful. As well, some elements of community development were to be transmitted, as the monks attempted to relate the Dhamma to modern problems.

The Phra Dhammajarik or Thammacarik project was directed toward nonbelievers at the border and tribal areas who were perceived by Bangkok as endangered by communism. According to one of the initiators of the program: "the propagation of Buddhism among the hill people of different groups would be likely to advance administrative and development purposes among the tribal people because the integration of people into a large community depends upon the ties of custom and religion."[54] Its objectives were:

1. To develop a belief in Buddhism among the hill people in the North, who have not adhered to or understood Buddhism.
2. To strengthen Buddhist belief among those tribesmen who have never actually made a commitment to Buddhism, and encourage them to take vows as Buddhists.
3. To strengthen the sense of Thai nationality among tribal people and to create loyalty among the tribesmen to the nation, the religion and the king.
4. To create a good understanding and friendly relations between the tribesmen and the government and its officials, and towards the nation, so that they have a feeling of being Thai and of practising Buddhism as other Thais, and so that they regard officials as men who carry out their administrative tasks for the benefit of the tribal people as much as for other Thais.[55]

In the end this missionary project floundered, in part due to a lack of language and cultural knowledge by those attempting to transmit their message to a people isolated and somewhat suspicious of government programs. As well, the development aspects of the program may have been of more interest to the recipients, leading to the formation of temporary "rice Buddhists."

The myriad of programs reviewed in this chapter have obviously had mixed success. At times their failures were due to maladministration, poor planning, or a basic misunderstanding of the problems involved. However, some more general patterns were also salient. Much depended upon the degree of consensus on religious belief as well as on the importance of the issue being faced. Thus, in the prewar years the colonial administration was the kind of enemy that could unite a religious community in spite of differences in concept and practice. This consensus only continued after independence when other targets were present, such as the communists in Thailand or Chinese in Malaysia. No such agreed upon enemy appeared in Indonesia, or at least not one perceived to be sufficiently dangerous to lend coherence to the Islamic movement. However, throughout Southeast Asia religion remains a tempting tool to be used to achieve cherished goals and political leaders will continue to employ it for such purposes.

CONCLUSIONS

Historically, Southeast Asian leaders have found religion to be a fertile ground for fostering secular goals. As noted in this chapter, it has been employed to achieve national unity as well as to forward economic and social development programs. While there have been numerous successes using religious symbols for these ends, several possible disadvantages have also become apparent. First, the countries under review display considerable sectarian diversity and efforts to emphasize one faith can weaken the very unity sought by those initiating these efforts. Thus, the tensions arising over U Nu's short-lived Buddhist state, reactions among Muslims to the Panchasila, and fears among non-Muslims in Malaysia regarding the rising tide of Islamic resurgence.

Second, there is the perceived danger that the employment of religious symbols and personnel can weaken the religion itself by politicizing the faith or at the very least debilitating its spiritual nature. This was an oft-mentioned criticism when Buddhist and Muslim religious elements were involved in pre-independence nationalist movements and later development programs; many, both within and without the clergy, have been uneasy about religious personnel leaving what they believe should be their purely spiritual sphere. The degree of involvement of the religious in contemporary social and political issues remains a point of contention throughout Southeast Asia.

Finally, there is the question of efficacy. Considerable disagreement exists among observers as to the effectiveness of religious personnel in fostering development programs, with specific cases supporting varied views. This was apparent in the review of efforts to employ monks in rural Thailand. Questions have also been raised with regard to the relationship of religion to national unity. In the prewar era, when the Christian colonial government provided a common target, Burmese and

Indonesian nationalists saw in Buddhism and Islam a core around which they could unite. However, even then Christian minorities felt isolated from the independence movement and tended to side with fellow Christians in the colonial regimes. In the postindependence era, when there was no longer the easy target of colonialism, the majority religions began to differ among themselves. Variations in religious intensity, debates over interpretations of dogma, and conflicts among sects were all to challenge efforts to maintain unifying religious symbols.

9

The Impact of Modernization
on Religion

To this point we have assessed the manner in which religion may affect the process of modernization. However, as noted in the first chapter, one of the characteristics of the interrelationship between religion and modernization noted by social scientists was that the progress of the latter leads to secularization. To partially test this hypothesis, this chapter will analyze changes in individual and group religiosity and state-oriented behavior as they correlate with modernization. Any testing of causal relationships in this area needs to be approached with great care since data are often not sufficiently available to make meaningful statements. However, prior to assessing what has developed in the religious environment of Southeast Asia, some comments need to be made regarding the extent to which modernization has actually taken place in the region.

Impressionistically, observers of the scene during the past thirty years have acknowledged that major changes have come about in the area. There are places where time seems to have stood still, but these are more and more to be found in isolated villages—although to some all of Burma and Laos falls into this category. Still many rural areas of Burma, Indonesia, Laos, and Cambodia remain outside the primary thrust of modernization. Elsewhere the environment shows significant differences from even the early postwar years. Capital cities such as Bangkok, Singapore, Jakarta, Kuala Lumpur, and Manila display all the best and worst of the modern urban environment, including air conditioned high-rises, pollution, traffic jams of autos, cycles, buses, and trucks, department stores filled with goods from throughout the world, cinemas and theaters, and so forth. The impact of the auto is attested to by growth of motor cars in Thailand from 8,170 (3,976 in Bangkok) in 1928-29 to 600,000 motorcycles and more than 250,000 autos in 1976 or the growth in Malaysia of autos and motorcycles from 91,143 in 1953 to 1,330,950 in 1977. Or one can follow the crowds into the Sirenah Department Store in Jakarta, Ampang Shopping Center in Kuala Lumpur, Daimaru in Bangkok, or the multistory shopping complexes of Singapore. Even the venerable Bogyoke Market in Rangoon displays electronic equipment of dubious origin, along with more traditional stock. Certainly disparities of income mean that many of the amenities of the modern city are not fully available to all, but even the poorer segments of the populace go to the ubiquitous cinema, listen to the radio, and often see programs on television.

Even at the level of the provincial town, modernization has made its mark in terms of amenities such as electricity, running water, stores stocked with a wide range of commercial goods, and media saturation, now often including government controlled television. Again variations exist both in class and geographic region. These changes tend to be less observable in the village, but development has advanced quickly in some areas, particularly in Malaysia and Thailand. Household expenditure surveys and studies of the stocks in local shops show the intrusion of items such as canned and bottled goods, agricultural supplies, patent medicines, and batteries for radios. Communications have also expanded. When working in northeast Thailand in the mid-1960s, the author found that in some provinces the villagers rarely saw government officials and were unable to travel to the district town in the rainy season, even in a four-wheel drive vehicle. As well, governments have attempted to reinforce national integration through the distribution of radio and television programs, perhaps best illustrated by Indonesia's campaign to bring television to outlying areas of the archipelago.

Beyond these impressions there is considerable statistical evidence of modernization.[1] Three data bases illustrate these changes: education, health, and manufacturing. Some of the figures that follow may be open to uncertainty in terms of their reliability, particularly for the early postwar years, but there can be no question as to the significance of changes that have taken place.

Education

During this century, and more narrowly the past forty years, Southeast Asia has experienced major increases in literacy and school attendance. At the end of the prewar colonial era most of the region's peoples were less than 20 percent literate in any language. In the countries under consideration literacy ranged from a low of 6.4 percent for Indonesians in the Netherlands East Indies to 48.7 percent in the Philippines. Even in the first years after the war literacy figures were low—approximately 60 percent in the Philippines, 67 percent in Thailand, and 35 percent in Burma (Sukarno was to declare that all adult Indonesians were literate, but this was dubious at best). However, the new states of the region launched massive education programs and school growth was remarkable. In the colonial Indies there were only about 250,000 Indonesians in elementary education, 27,000 in secondary, and 637 in higher (not including other Asians). By 1977 there were 14,280,157 students in elementary schools, 1,900,000 in junior high, and 800,000 in high schools. Enrollment in primary and secondary schools in Peninsular Malaysia rose from 572,782 in 1949 to 1,385,351 in 1962, and 2,435,733 in 1976. In Thailand in 1908–09 there were but 12,435 boys and 890 girls in state approved primary and secondary institutions. By 1979 the number was 9,558,910, including 190,026 in higher education. In Burma by 1960–61 there were some 1,941,637 students in primary and secondary schools. Finally, in the Philippines, school enrollment of those ages 7 to 17 doubled from 1948-1957 to some six million.

Even with population growth these advances are astounding. It should also be noted that these students were generally receiving a secular education in which they gained at least the fundamentals for competing in the modern sector.

Health

Evidence of the results of improvements such as better medical facilities, purer water, or preventative medicine can be seen, for example, in statistics on life expectancy and infant mortality. Infant mortality has fallen drastically in the postwar era, in many cases by more than two-thirds. As examples of life expectancy increases, it rose in the Philippines from 30.00 years in 1918 to 60.57 years in 1973. In Thailand between 1947–48 and 1964–65 life expectancy increased for males from 48.7 to 55.2 years and for females from 51.9 to 61.8 years. Much of this progress was derived from other aspects of modernization such as better sanitation, agricultural efficiency, housing, and communications.

Manufacturing

Growth in manufacturing is a sign of the development of a modern economy. However, care needs to be taken in comparing cross-nationally or even over time within a single polity, given differences in how categories are defined. At the same time increases have been significant. In the Philippines, manufacturing employed only 205,809 in 1956 but increased to 1,828,315 (categorized somewhat differently) in 1978. In Malaysia the number of employees almost doubled from 128,500 in 1947 to 252,000 in 1970 and then really expanded in the next decade. In Thailand in 1956 there were 463,030 involved in small manufacturing (of whom 203,680 were unpaid family) and 191,621 in large manufacturing concerns. By 1978 the number was 1,700,000. In the Netherlands East Indies there were 154,988 persons employed in registered factories, while in 1978 Indonesia reported 3,855,560 employed in manufacturing.

Modernization has reached Southeast Asia, admittedly in an uneven fashion with considerable variation based upon class, rural–urban, and national variables. However, it is difficult to find places in the region that have not been influenced by the artifacts of modern technology in terms of goods available, communications, and the means of earning one's livelihood. Given these changes, what has happened to religion during this process?

In attempting to assess whether the religious environment of Southeast Asia has been altered during this era of development, it is difficult to employ the tools available to Western social scientists. Data on church attendance, financial support, and organizational activities are not as accessible as they are in the United States. Often governments have been less than accommodating in allowing scientific surveys of attitudes and even when possible social scientists have generally not taken advantage of the opportunities. In sum, our analysis must often be impressionistic, illustrative, or fragmentary. This does not mean that readily observable changes have not taken place.

In an effort to give structure to our analysis, the categories established by Charles Glock will be utilized plus two additional ones. Glock developed his classification scheme in order to assess religiosity in America.[2] His five points include:

1. experiential—the degree of attachment to the supernatural;
2. ritualistic—ritual, meaning formal church activities; and devotional, meaning prayer, reading of the texts, and other private activities;
3. ideological—the degree of commitment to the religious beliefs of the group:

4. consequential—the impact of religious belief on general behavior; and
5. intellectual—the degree to which the individual has knowledge of formal beliefs.

To these two state-oriented categories are added:

6. political—the degree to which religion influences organized political behavior.
7. legal—the degree to which the state is administered according to religious rules

Each aspect will be reviewed in terms of changes which have taken place in recent decades, emphasizing the extent to which these developments have been related to the process of modernization.

Experiential

The general consensus of observers of Southeast Asia is that the supernatural remains extremely important to adherents to Islam, Christianity, and Buddhism. While there is some growth of skepticism among elements in the elite, it tends to be directed more toward the institutions of the faith rather than its theological basis. Impressionistically it would appear that the outright rejection of the supernatural foundation of the dominant religion is to be found more readily among Christian Filipino intellectuals as against their Buddhist and Muslim counterparts.

There has been a great decline in the legitimacy of animist forces in the region and a number of factors appear to be responsible. Modern medicine and agricultural advances have increased doubts as to the efficacy of traditional practices and, as these innovations have permeated rural society, people have tended to mix the old and new rather than to depend upon traditional powers alone. This pattern has been reinforced by professionals in these fields who have strongly attacked animist beliefs and practices as counterproductive to the health and economic well-being of the populace. As one Filipino writer commented. "If we do not overcome this "animistic belief" in our rural population and if we do not educate and channel their attitudes and motivations properly the remaining animistic practices will greatly handicap the economic development of the country-side."[3]

Second, reformist-minded religious spokesmen have condemned animist attitudes and behavior as impure and reflections of ignorance.

They have both declined to participate in ceremonies involving propitiating the spirits and discouraged others from doing so. Examples of such rejection are to be found among Muslim modernists in Indonesia who vigorously condemned such activities as un-Islamic[4] and Ne Win's campaign against nats after his re-entrance into power in 1962.[5]

Finally, many upwardly mobile members of these societies consider it detrimental to their image to appear to publicly retain animist practices and beliefs. These are perceived as reflecting a less sophisticated and "progressive" way of life rather than the model of the modern man. This does not mean that they may not quietly continue to practice folk medicine or take care not to anger the spirits. In sum, there does not appear to be a significant decline in belief in the supernatural among adherents of the world religions, but animism is, at the very least, not publicly supported to the degree that it was in previous years.

Ritual

There is considerable difficulty in Southeast Asia in assessing the observation of ritual as defined in Western terms. Counterparts of church attendance figures are generally not available nor are surveys delineating obedience to devotions. There is some statistical information on the number of clerics and religious edifices over time as well as general observations by scholars and journalists on attendance at religious gatherings and devotional activities. Taken in isolation, such data would be a poor basis for judging religiosity, but viewed in conjunction with the other six variables they do add to our understanding of the religious environment in the area.

A clear picture does not emerge when viewing the data on Buddhist sangha members and edifices in Burma and Thailand. Estimates of the number of Burmese monks in the 1960s ran from 80,000 to 120,000, with 100,000 an often used figure. Given this wide variation, it is difficult to attest to growth or decline, although the military has not encouraged the sangha during past decades. Under U Nu there was a great deal of government supported building and refurbishing of Buddhist pagodas and monasteries, and discounting the 60,000 sand pagodas constructed in 1961, there appears to have been a major growth in religious structures since independence.

Data are far more accurate for Thailand. S. Tambiah and J. Mulder have provided detailed data on numbers of monks and temples and they show growth, but not as fast as population. Tambiah provides the following table:

TABLE 9.1

Number of Temples, Monks, and Novices in Thailand, 1960–69

Year	Estimated total population of Thailand	Number of temples	Number of monks	Number of novices	Total monks and novices
1960	26,499,000	22,639	159,701	95,838	255,539
1961	27,309,000	22,120	152,787	87,335	240,122
1962	28,152,000	23,322	151,560	85,260	236,820
1963	29,027,000	23,184	150,685	83,772	234,407
1964	29,933,000	23,539	166,680	85,873	252,553
1965	30,870,000	23,700	173,126	88,251	261,377
1966	31,847,000	24,105	175,266	87,661	262,927
1967	32,855,000	24,634	185,921	96,569	282,490
1968	33,855,000	25,116	184,873	108,504	293,377
1969	34,947,000	25,292	189,887	114,927	304,814

From Tambiah, *World Conqueror, p. 266.*

Developing his own figures, Mulder found that the ratio of monks to the male population had deteriorated between 1927 and 1966 from 1:16 to 1:34.1.[7] While accepting this analysis, Tambiah does not see this as a loss of faith among young Thais, but the result of changing educational conditions. As secular government schools have become available to the poor, their boys have not continued to turn to Buddhist schools from which they often entered religious life. In spite of this secular education, Tambiah argues that,

> . . . but I for one see "Buddhism" crudely measured in terms of ritual activity, beliefs, ideology, practices, gift giving, material support of monasteries and religious personnel, on the part of both laymen and government as *expanding* and keeping pace with modernization, urbanization, nationalization, and rising expectations. I should like to argue that the practice of and commitment to Buddhism have not diminished in the face of the enlargement of commercial and industrial segments of the population, both bourgeois and proletarian, and the increasing pull of remote villages into the field of influence of urban cultural values and lifestyles.[8]

Islam does not have a priesthood or comparable hierarchy. There are hadjis, religious teachers, ulama, imman, and so forth. Over time it is possible to develop figures on the number of hadjis, many of whom become religious leaders in their communities. The number of individuals making the hadj provides one indicator of religious interest, and there has been a significant increase in recent years. The annual total of hadjis tripled in Malaysia from 1965–80, and major increases were also observed among Muslim minorities from Thailand and the Philippines. In Indonesia considerably more people made the pilgrimage in the 1970s as against the 1960s but as a percentage of the total population the number was considerabley below the high of the 1920s. To reach that level there would have to be a doubling of the high of 73,000 reached in 1978–79.

With regard to religious edifices, there were 93,650 *masjids* (mosques) and 341,177 *mushalla* (prayer halls) in Indonesia in 1971, with a slight decline in the following years.[9] In Malaysia there has been a major religious building program in recent decades as the government has subsidized and systematized the construction of mosques and prayer halls. In sum, while the figures are mixed and their importance open to question, there has been a continued, and in many areas growing involvement in ritual in terms of religious personnel and places of worship in the Islamic world.

Such growth has not been as apparent in the Christian Philippines. At the end of the Spanish colonial era there were 3,044 Spanish and Filipino clerics serving a population estimated at eight million. As of 1960 the population was 27,087,685, but the number of priests had only grown to 3,671 and the ratio was one priest to 6,180 Roman Catholics.[10] This ratio was less than a third of what it had been in 1898. As with other Catholic countries, there have been difficulties in attracting young men into the priesthood.

More impressionistic has been the evidence supporting attendance at religious observances. In Thailand, Malaysia, and Indonesia observers have noted a significant increase in the number of worshipers, with an appreciable augmentation of young people. In part explained by the religious resurgence in these countries, this attraction is also mirrored in the growth of Islamic and Buddhist organizations. There is also illustrative evidence of the continuance, and in many cases the expansion, of the observation of private religious devotions. For example, where there was once considerable comment regarding laxity in following Islamic religious rituals in Malay villages, observers now note relatively high levels of obedience. As well, there has been an increase in publicity given the performance of religious duties by public figures and the author's own experience has found that in at least Malaysia there has been more private observance by many of these individuals.

In sum, tentative evidence backs Tambiah's conclusion that modernization has not led to a decline in the observance of religious rituals and may have even brought about its expansion.

Ideology

Ideology must really be analyzed at two interrelated levels: individual commitment and national articulation. What we will assess here belongs as well under the rubric of "political," as the individual's commitment to an ideological belief system is to a degree dependent upon the vagaries of politics.

Major changes have taken place in the realm of religious ideology in Southeast Asia during the postwar years and popular support for particular concepts has waxed and waned, in part due to who was in power at the time. It is not always clear as to the depth of popular support for religious or secular ideologies throughout the Third World, and Western observers have often overestimated public endorsement. Experience in Southeast Asia also shows that changes in the national ideology are more likely to reflect political and personality factors than a reaction to the process of modernization. Yet, at the same time that these ephemeral ideologies come and go there can be a continuation, or even intensification, of individual support for religion as a force for group identity. The experiences of the five states under consideration illustrate varying patterns of national and individual ideological development.

BURMA

Personality and power have tended to define the characteristicis of the national ideology, while at the same time, support for Buddhism as the focus of national identity for the majority of Burmans has probably not seriously declined. Under Aung San Buddhism was presented as important to the individual's personal values but separation of religion and politics was encouraged. When U Nu came to power he made every effort to foster Buddhism as a central core of the national ideology, along with socialism and democracy. As well he encouraged personal commitment to the faith and expected that through that effort, national integration would grow. Nu himself became the model of a Buddha in the becoming, and in the 1960 elections, his party's ballot boxes (colored the yellow color of Buddhism) had his picture on them (there were reports of people paying obeisance to his portrait in the polling booths).[11] Observers at the time saw him as forging personal and national commitment to an ideology based upon adherence to the Buddhist faith. When Ne Win came into power in 1962 he returned to Aung San's concept of a separation of religion and politics, and Buddhism no longer played a central role in the national ideology. It is difficult to assess popular attitudes at this point. There have been elements of the sangha expressing opposition to what they believe to be concerted government efforts to weaken Buddhism but little public outcry has been apparent. Yet, there is also no evidence that the average Burmese does not consider Buddhism to be a focal characteristic of his national and personal identity.

PHILIPPINES

The anticlericism of the nationalist movement, emphasis on the separation of the church and state under the Americans and postindependence politicians, and the secularist tendencies of pubic school teachers have all probably weakened the degree of commitment to the beliefs of and identity with the Catholic Church. It is difficult to see if the present tension between the Catholic hierarchy and President Marcos is eroding or strengthening support for the church; probably the latter. As well, the Filipino has been bombarded with Western material values, cultures and education, all of which appear to have had a significant impact upon the nation's youth.

THAILAND

The Thais have long viewed Buddhism as the core to their personal and national identity. To the vast majority, to be a Thai is to be a Buddhist. However, it was the recent Thai kings and postwar military-political leaders who were to systematically foster the ideology of king, Buddhism, and country as a means of reinforcing national integration. In the process, missionary efforts have brought formerly isolated peoples in the Kingdom into the fold in a planned effort to make Buddhism a tool of national ideology. However, the apparent growth of a sense of Thai-Buddhist identity in recent years has also been a reflection of negative reactions to what are considered to be undesirable aspects of modernization. The very intrusion of material goods and values has activated a resurgence of interest in traditional religious tenets as a means of retaining national and personal identity.

INDONESIA

Indonesia is a nation of Muslims divided in their understanding of what is entailed in being an adherent to that faith. Officially, the Pantja Sila, as originally articulated by Sukarno and later restructured by the military, has won out as the national ideology over the protests of the practicing Muslims. This defeat reflects both political weakness and religious fragmentation. Very broadly speaking, Indonesia presents two interpretations of Islam, each with its own ideological core and each probably growing in self-consciousness during the past decades. Among practicing Muslims there is an expanding sense of the need to coalesce around Islamic fundamentals as a defense against the challenge of an unfriendly government and the penetration of unwanted Western values. This effort has been led by some elements of the political and religious elite, dakwah organizations, and youth groups. It has displayed only limited success, given problems of internal consensus and external political pressure. At the same time, the government has sought to instill popular loyalty in the Pantja Sila as the only acceptable ideology of the people and *Kepercayaan* beliefs as the religious model. In the process, this rivalry has probably strengthened group identity within both camps.

MALAYSIA

The role of religion in national and personal ideology in Malaysia is at least equally as complex. Individual commitment to group religious belief has a long history among Malay Muslims. it is almost inconceivable to the average Malay to dissassociate himself from his ethnic and religious heritage and this sense of group identity is probably growing rather than receding, primarily due to modernization, but aided by the political manipulation of religious symbols. As modern Malaya developed, the former, overwhelming prominence of the Malay declined as Chinese and Indians entered the colony to work on plantations and mines. By the time Malaysia was formed, the Malays had slightly less than a majority of the population and the immigrants were perceived as dominating the economy. Not only that, these newcomers and the Europeans brought with them foreign values and customs alien to the indigenous population. These economic and social changes were viewed as challenges to both the ethnic and religious position of the Malay Muslim and galvanized them into a stronger sense of communal identity.

The unity was further reinforced by Malay politicians who contested with one another to appear as the real protectors of the Malay Muslim culture and religion. Combating the efforts of opposition Muslims, the government sought to placate their constituency. However, they also had to meet the fears of non-Muslim members of the coalition and a dual policy resulted. To meet Malay Muslim pressures, the various programs delineated in chapter 8 were formulated to show that the government could meet their needs. To foster continued cooperation among all Malaysians, the national ideology, the Rukenegara, was developed. The latter was a restatement of the concept of the plural society and the need for the removal of sensitive issues from national debate. It remains to be seen which of these ideological views become dominant.

Consequential

As has been discussed previously, any analysis of the impact of religious belief on general behavior is fraught with methodological problems. To what extent is faith internalized by the believer resulting in action based upon its tenets? In Southeast Asia, is it possible to disentangle religion from the totality of the traditional environment? Recognizing what must be the tentativeness of any comments on this subject, several points can be made.

Southeast Asia in the past century has experienced a weakening of the influence of religion on general behavior, and modernization has certainly been a major factor. As has been noted, activities based upon animist belief have declined; however, the impact of the world religions has also apparently decreased as a greater number of Southeast Asians move into the cities and elements of modernization penetrate rural areas. In the narrower environment of the traditional sociey, external distractions were few and religion bulked large in the lives of the people. Most important activities were infused with religious beliefs from life-cycle events to house-raising and agriculture. As the individual moved to the urban environment and the secular world intruded into the village, other activities not linked to religion became important. In the cities, in particular, life became compartmentalized as the individual led much of his existence in the secular world while at the same time remaining committed to his faith as crucial in his personal and even the societal realm.

Recognizing these caveats, it is important to underscore the fact that religion still heavily influences general behavior beyond following rituals and supporting domestic and international ideologies. We have already noted the role many observers believe to be played by such factors as merit, fatalism, the belief in spirits, and feasts. To the rural Southeast Asian, especially, essential activities are still predicated upon religious belief. Secularization has assuredly weakened that influence, but religion remains a powerful force.

Knowledge

We have no cross-national or national surveys that provide us with data on changed knowledge of formal beliefs over time. It is thus not possible to present detailed accountings of how modernization may have affected comprehension. It is possible to make some suppositions based upon changes in religious education. On the one hand, we have observed the general weakening of traditional religious education throughout the region. Primary schools, whether they be taught by Buddhist monks, muslim *guru-ngaji,* or Catholic priests, no longer play the role they once did, as secular education has become dominant throughout Southeast Asia.

Yet, religious education has not died out in these countries and, in fact, in most of them has become more systematically presented, "purer," and more widely distributed. Religion is taught in the public schools of Malaysia, Thailand, and Indonesia, and was in Burma under U Nu, and public schools now reach the vast majority of children in these countries. Buddhist missionaries in Burma and Thailand and dakwah organizations in Malaysia and Indonesia have attempted to both spread their faith to unbelievers and strengthen the understanding of the faithful. The efforts of these groups, as well as the more universal religion taught in the state schools, have probably weakened less orthodox or animist aspects of folk religion. In the process, the recipients of this education are probably learning a "purer" form of their faith than they might have under traditional methods. It may very well be that with the expansion of modern education, the young in Southeast Asia today have a better knowledge of the formal beliefs of their respective religions than at any time previously.

Political

Religion has played varying roles in the political life of Southeast Asia in the postwar years from being center stage to being almost unseen. However, it has rarely been absent and continues to be tempting to aspiring politicians and those seeking group or national identification.

THAILAND

At the national level, religion has not penetrated deeply into the politics of the nation, at least in a conflictual manner. Given the absence of colonial rule that activated religious nationalism elsewhere, a general consensus on the place of Buddhism in the society, and government encouragement of Buddhism as a foundation for national integration, it is not surprising that religious issues have not generated much political controversy. It was only in the far south that elements of the long neglected Malay Muslim population have sought reforms and even separation based upon their ethnic and religious identity. While this issue has led to demands for change and even rebellion in the south and government efforts to meet the situation, it has not dominated politics in Bangkok.

PHILIPPINES

Religion has played a somewhat different role in the Philippines. There has been general agreement on the separation of church and state, but this has not totally inhibited religious bodies from attempting to influence local and national politics. Both local priests and bishops of the Roman Catholic Church have been known to become involved in issues of interest to the Church or to support particular candidates. The hierarchy has called upon the faithful to vote for candidates with high moral character, as it did in 1953, and only recently Cardinal Sin has criticized President Marcos with regard to marshal law and human rights. There have even been cases of priests aiding left-wing insurgents. However, there is no religious party as such, although the Iglesa ni Kristo has tended to vote as a bloc.

In addition, there is the "Moro problem," the demands of the Muslims in the south for a recognition of their rights and identity. However, the Muslim issue has had a greater impact on the Philippines than in Thailand. National politicians in the former have focused more attention on the issue than their Bangkok counterparts due to the levels of violence, external aid to the Muslims, and some cooperation between Moro and Marxist insurgents.

BURMA

The colonial era found religion deeply involved in the nationalist movement and after independence it became a central issue in the politics of the new nation. Even during the war, the Japanese and Burmese administrations used Buddhism to both integrate the country and oppose the enemy. U Nu's years were ones of political-religious disputes centering on the Prime Minister's efforts to expand the role of Buddhism.

Conflicts arose over such questions as the demands of Christian and Muslim minorities for autonomy, the religious state amendments, and religious expenditures. Under Ne Win, civil strife between the minorities and Rangoon continued and sections of the sangha objected to both religious and secular aspects of the new regime, but the government allowed little free expression.

INDONESIA

Indonesia also experienced a strong religionationalist movement and the Japanese attempted to inspire Muslims against the Dutch. In the postwar years, both Muslim and Christian parties developed out of pre-independence organizations and actively participated in the political life of the country. The largest, the Muslim Masjumi, was ultimately banned by President Sukarno for allegedly aiding rebellion against Jakarta, but the other parties continued to be active into the Suharto years. During the past decade, there have been generally successful government efforts to limit the power of opposition parties, but the Muslims remain the Suharto regime's most potent political opponent.

Religion has always generated a variety of political issues involving such questions as the Pantja Sila, minority rights, and education. Muslim politicians have long been at odds with the government over the role the Pantja Sila should play in national life with the former agreeing that it can be one basis for action and the latter wishing to give it monopoly status. In the first years of independence, Christian minority groups sought autonomy or separation from the new republic and political controversy ultimately ended in violence. Finally, Islamic leaders have criticized secular government programs such as Suharto's development efforts, in this case arguing that they do not distribute the nation's wealth fairly throughout the archipelago.

MALAYSIA

Observers have continually asserted that Malaysia's politics cannot be understood outside of the ethnic-religious environment. This is not a question of serious Muslim worries over the influence of the religions of their Chinese and Indian fellow citizens. The core question has been what role Islam is to play in the political, economic, and social life of the nation. Non-Muslim organizations, and particularly those in political opposition, see a danger to Malaysia's plural society in the growing power of Islam. Opposition Muslim politicians in PMIP-PAS argue that the government does not go far enough in protecting the interests of the faithful and demand an expansion in the role of Islam. Within UMNO itself, similar debates rage over the proper function of Islam, with parliamentary backbenchers traditionally seeking to increase the government's involvement in protecting Islamic interests and the leadership attempting to maintain a more limited role for the religion.

Islam, combined with Malay ethnicity, enters the political ring over such issues as education, national economic planning, the role of Muslim personal law, legislation to control immoral practices, and a myriad of other questions. Over the years, the intensity of these debates has not decreased in spite of constitutional limits on public discussion of many aspects of these subjects.

Legal

Here the question is to what extent there are laws and regulations consciously based upon religious tenets. Within this category will be considered efforts to establish a "religious state," ascription in the choice of administrative and political leadership, and religious influence on personal law.

THE RELIGIOUS STATE

The meaning of the concept, religious state, has been a matter of political and theological debate in many polities. However, here we are only so defining countries which have specifically described themselves as a religious state. It should be noted that, similar to the previously analyzed category of political religiosity, the primary factor in delineating the sectarian characteristics of the state has been political power rather than the process of modernization. Three of the countries under review clearly do not describe themselves as religious states. Even going back to the Malolos Republic at the time of the Philippine independence movement, there has been the acceptance of the separation of church and state in the islands. The postwar constitution specifically prohibited the establishment of a state religion.

In spite of Muslim efforts to the contrary, Indonesia has never been an Islamic state by law or political structure. As we have previously noted, Burma was briefly a Buddhist state under U Nu's leadership, but the military dropped it. Even after the new amendment was promulgated to make the country officially a religious state, opponents charged that the new system was really only different in name.

In Thailand, the King, as protector of the Buddhist faith, appoints the Supreme Patriarch, while the Council of Elders is under the Department of Religious Affairs and its Director General is the Secretary General of the Council.[12] Officially, there is no separation of church and state and Buddhism is the official state religion of the Kingdom. However, all other religions have the freedom to practice their faiths in law and reality.

Malaysia is somewhat more complicated.[13] According to the Constitution, "Islam is the religion of the Federation" and the Sultans are the Head of religion in their respective states. While every other religion has the right to manage and practice its religious affairs, Muslims are constitutionally protected from external proseltyzing. At the same time, independent Malaysia has always been faced with debates over the religious state issue. Opposition spokesmen and some UMNO politicians have called for an Islamic state and there have been demands for a constitutional amendment requiring the government to follow the precepts of the Koran and Sharia. More recently both the Prime Minister and Deputy Prime Minister have claimed that they are not opposed to elements of an Islamic state, but both sides have been rather vague in their definitions.[14] The issue remains current and politically sensitive, given the plural nature of the society, the multi-ethnic character of the ruling coalition, and the political power of the Malays.

While modernization played little or no role in the religious state question in the other polities, it has been a factor in Malaysia. There proponents of the concept have argued that the negative effects of Western-style modernization necessitate adherence to an Islamic state in order to protect the Muslim community. Prior to the Islamic resurgence, government opponents charged that following Islamic precepts would weaken Malaysia's efforts to compete in the international marketplace. Specific prohibitions related to Friday closing and *riba* were not supported by government ministers. It is more difficult politically to frontally attack such concepts today.

ASCRIPTIVE CONDITIONS

It has been argued by some social scientists that one of the results of modernization is that government offices are no longer based upon ascriptive definitions. Any analysis of this hypothesis in Southeast Asia immediately presents two problems. First, by ascriptive conditions do we mean legal, as defined by law, or political, as delineated by the power structure? This dichotomy is important, considering the other difficulty. If we are to assess changes over time, then the nature of the colonial administration needs to be considered. While legal ascription was generally not important at the time (except for the highest symbolic office in Great Britain and Spain), political ascription was. Leaving aside Catholic-Protestant divisions in the metropolitan powers, the political reality in the colonies was that the most crucial posts were to be held by European Christians until toward the very end of the colonial era. As a matter of politics, not a modernizing environment, contemporary Southeast Asia also displays ascription based upon power relationships. Malaysian and Indonesian Prime Ministers have been Muslim, Burmese and Thai Buddhist, and Philippine Roman Catholic. Nor has this type of ascription been absent from the choice of military officer corps in the area.

The legal-constitutional limits have been far less restrictive. There has never been a religious requirement for office in the Philippines or Burma, and in the latter prior to 1962 the presidency passed among communal groups. Nor does Indonesia have such a regulation, although all Indonesians must be Muslim, Catholic, Protestant, Hindu, Buddhist, Confucian, or mystical (golongan kepercayaan). In Thailand the king is protector of the faith, but except for sangha offices, there are no restrictions on the religious affiliation of officials or politicians. Malaysia is somewhat more complicated. No administrative or political office as such has legal ascriptive limits, but the Sultans are the protectors of Islam and a quota of certain civil service positions is provided to Malays (read Muslims).

Generally then, in Southeast Asia legal ascriptive requirements are of comparatively little importance while political pressures remain crucial. It is difficult to argue that modernization plays much of a role in this process except that opponents of ascription argue in Weberian terms about the advantages of merit.

PERSONAL LAW

In many states of the world, one of the last areas religious institutions are prepared to relinquish is their influence over personal law, particularly regarding morality and the family. Therefore, in every state in Southeast Asia under discussion religious elements have pressured their governments to pass or prevent legislation in this area. Specific areas such as marriage, divorce, and inheritance have not been as important in Buddhist societies where religious tenets have not been as concrete in these matters. In primarily Catholic Philippines, the hierarchy has been active and generally successful in making its position felt in family law questions.

However, it has been in the Islamic societies of Southeast Asia that religious law has played an important legal role. Islam is comparatively precise in what is expected of the believer, and over the years a religiously oriented judicial system has evolved. Sharia courts have been established to hear cases dealing with immorality and the neglect of ritualistic duties. This has been more sophisticated in contemporary Malaysia where one observer has noted the following areas covered by state law:

> Muslim Law and personal and family law of persons professing the Muslim religion, including the Muslim law relating to succession, testate and intestate, betrothal, marriage, divorce, dower, maintenance, legitimacy, guardianship, gifts, partitions and non–charitable trusts; Muslim Wakfs and the definition and regulation of charitable and religious trusts, the appointment of trustees and the incorporation of persons in respect of Muslim religious and charitable institutions operating wholly within the state; Malay custom; Zakat, Fitrah and Bait-ul-Mal or similar Muslim revenue; mosques or any Muslim public place of worship, creation and punishment of offenses by persons professing the Muslim religion against precepts of that religion, except in regard to matters included in the Federal List; the constitution, organization and procedure of Muslim courts, which shall have jurisdiction only over persons professing the Muslim religion and in respect only of any of the matters included in this paragraph, but shall not have jurisdiction in respect of offences except in so far as conferred by federal law: the control of propagating doctrines and beliefs among persons professing the Muslim religion; the determination of matters of Muslim Law and doctrine and Malay customs. [15]

Another author collected the following state statutes, with attendant fines, not all of which are employed:

> failure to attend Friday prayers at the mosque (M$25);
> consumption of intoxicating liquor (M$50);
> sale to a Muslim or consumption by a Muslim of any food or drink
>   during daylight during the month of Ramadan (M$50);

any Muslim male found in suspicious proximity with any woman who is not his close relative (three months and M $300) (this the khalwat law that, if strictly enforced, outlaws unchaperoned dating practices);

any female Muslim abetting the offense of khalwat (three months and M $300);

sexual intercourse between husband and wife in a manner forbidden by Islam (M $25 for each party);

wilful disobedience by a woman of an order lawfully given by her husband (M $50);

teaching any doctrine of the Muslim religion without written permission of the Malay ruler (one month and M $100);

propagating religious doctrines other than Islam among persons professing the Muslim religion (one year and M $3,000);

teaching false doctrine (three months and M $250);

printing or distributing books or documents repugnant to any lawful Fatwa (official interpretation of doctrine) or contrary to orthodox belief (six months and M $500);

contempt of religious authorities or officials (one month and M $100);

contempt of the law of Islam or its tenets (six months and M $500). [16]

There have also been warnings against Muslims working in the gambling places of Genting Highlands, "deviant" religious behavior that could lose civil servants their jobs, and Muslims calling one another "infidels" in the heat of political battle.

During the constitutional discussions in Indonesia at the end of the war, it looked as though that country might go in the same direction. A compromise was worked out between the secularists and Muslim nationalists called the Jakarta Charter. [17] It stated that while the Pantja Sila was accepted so also was the principle that all Muslims were obliged to follow the Sharia and the president of the new state was to be a Muslim. The Islamic part was not accepted by the nation's leaders, but Muslims have continued to assert that the original charter is a legal document. Although later the Ministry of Religious Affairs was a Muslim base of power, under Suharto the Muslims even lost this, and the Ministry became neutral.

CONCLUSIONS

Over recent decades, no consistent pattern has emerged pertaining to the impact of modernization on religion in Southeast Asia. Some facets of religion have declined in importance during the process of modernization. Animist beliefs appear to be less salient than in earlier years, in part due to the intrusion of modern technology. That same penetration has expanded the horizons of the individual and with it has come some decline in the degree to which religion has had an impact on general behavior. In the process, the adherent has tended to compartmentalize his religious beliefs.

There are other aspects of religion where the impact seems to have been mixed or is not readily observable. It is difficult to ascertain the extent of spiritual belief among the followers of the major religions. The role religion plays in defining the law in Southeast Asia is less than in precolonial days, but the relationship of this slippage to modernization is hard to assess. The establishment of a religious state in Burma, Indonesia, or the Philippines appears improbable in the near future, but Thailand continues to be legally founded upon Buddhism and mixed signals are coming out of Malaysia. In the case of Malaysia, reactions to the penetration of alien values related to modernization have been a factor in intensified efforts to expand Islamic law, but this has not been salient in the other states.

At the other end of the spectrum there may very well be an increase in knowledge of formal beliefs as religion has become part of the curriculum of state schools in many countries. Politically, religion continues to be important throughout the region and debates on such issues as religious education, Islamic economics, and communal rights can still create high tension. However, the area where modernization has probably strengthened religious commitment the most is in the realm of ideology. Under the challenge of Western values, demands for modern goods, and other elements associated with a foreign culture, religious groups have closed ranks in order to protect traditional values and exorcise undesirable imports from the West. As importantly, not only have Buddhist and Islamic organizations sought to convert the "heathen," but they have worked to intensify the understanding of the faithful as to the fundamentals of their religions. The result is a growing number of individuals more conscious of their faiths, more clearly identified in an ideological sense with the cause, and seeking ways to define the role that faith can play in contemporary Southeast Asia.

10

Concluding Reflections

For a variety of reasons the role of religion in Third World societies has all too often been characterized in overly simplistic terms. In part these representations have resulted from historic religious and racial attitudes in the West which frequently displayed little sympathy or empathy regarding Afro-Asian cultures. Some explanation can be found in the values and approaches of academic observers, particularly among secularly oriented social scientists, who tended to see religion as an obstacle to the process of desired change, albeit a temporary one that would decline in the face of modernization. Our ability to properly assess religion in these societies was made difficult as well by poor data and the rapidity of change which challenged earlier analyses. The problem did not arise only from the clouded lens of Western observers. The rhetoric of religious leaders in the region often reinforced the traditionalist or even reactionary picture of these faiths and their adherents and there have been obvious sectarian forces working against modernization.

Certainly recent events have challenged the view that modernization has weakened the force of religion, at least in the short run. Violence in the Arab world and Iran, strife in Northern Ireland, the strength of Christian fundamentalism in the United States, and Sikh demands in India are obvious examples of the continued vitality of sectarian loyalties. In the region under investigation in this volume, Southeast Asia, the postwar years have seen religious violence involving Muslim minorities in Thailand, Burma, and the Philippines, Christian minorities in Burma and Indonesia, Buddhists and Christians in Vietnam, radical Muslim groups in Malaysia and Indonesia, and Muslim–Communist struggles in Indonesia. However, while these conflicts have brought into question previous projections as to the power of religious loyalties, they have also tended to lend credence to those who see religion in simplistic antimodern terms. Contemporary references to Islamic resurgence as a "return to the twelfth century" and "reactionary fanaticism" reinforce these simplistic perceptions.

This study has been an effort to describe a more complex set of phenomena as they pertain to selected states in Southeast Asia. The analysis has centered upon two assumptions prevalent among postwar social scientists regarding the relationship of religion to modernization. The dominant paradigm of these early postwar academics characterized religion as an obstacle to modernization, a process which in its turn would inevitably lead to a decline in the role of religion in society. The results of the analysis in earlier chapters, while not substantiating any consistent patterns defining the role of religion in modernization, do underscore the complexity of the relationship and seriously challenge the received and often accepted wisdom of earlier observers.

The task undertaken in this volume was complicated by a number of often intriguing methodological questions, many of which will continue to be the object of research and speculation. The initial problem was one of definition. The 1950s and 1960s saw a flowering of literature on development and with it a plethora of attempts to define the meaning of modernization. Not only was there no consensus regarding terms, but we also observed the frequent formulation of definitions of modernization that were difficult or impossible to test empirically. At times this problem related to the employment of propositions which were hard to test, such as rational behavior, or to tenets such as "democracy" and "secular" which were included with no clarification as to how the term was to be used. This latter difficulty was often apparent in discussions of the relation of modernization to religion, when authors failed to clarify what aspects of religion were being described. Thus, the initial effort in this study was to delineate modernization in terms of technological development and the maintenance of a modern nation-state and to break down religion into basic tenets, religious institutions, popular beliefs, popular practices, and the manipulation of religious symbols. Later secularization was also systematically defined so as to allow for the analysis of the impact of modernization on religion.

A second set of problems centered upon differences in interpretations of behavior and attitudes. Observers of the roles of religion and modernization in Southeast Asia have reflected a wide and often disparate variety of intellectual approaches from the general colonial view that perceived progress as inevitable, but hindered by the lazy "backward native" and his religion, to the missionary who saw salvation only through his faith, to those contemporary Asian writers who deny that the local population had any debilitating habits and blame colonialism for almost all present and past ills of their societies. These views of the region not only tinted their interpretations, but brought into question their descriptions of reality.

Finally, there are a series of intellectual challenges brought by such questions as to how the analyst can assess the degree to which religious tenets have been internalized, the extent to which religion can be differentiated from the cultural milieu within which it operates, or the sincerity of political actors who employ religious symbols to attain secular goals. Issues of this nature cannot be answered with certainty and must be reviewed on a case by case basis within the constraints of the available data.

Recognizing the validity of these problems, this volume has attempted to array the pros and cons in the debate over the impact of religion on the process of modernization. From the analyses of issues such as religious expenditures, institutions, beliefs, and the manipulation of symbols, it is apparent that cogent arguments can be presented to characterize religion as both a positive and negative force in the modernization process. The following brief review of the results of our investigation in Southeast Asia shows the complex and many faceted nature of these findings.

EXPENDITURES

Buddhists, Muslims, and Christians have long expended significant amounts of time and money on religious activities, including feasts and other celebrations, religious tithes and charity, pilgrimages to Mecca and other holy places, merit making among Buddhists, and the building and maintenance of religious edifices. In each of these cases it can be argued that, if modernization is the sought after goal, these expenditures could be better used to achieve material goals such as education, the modernization of agriculture, better communications, health facilities, and capital investments. As well, time spent by both the clergy and laity could be more usefully employed than in prayer, meditation, religious observances, and other "unproductive" activities if modernization is to be achieved. Of course, what has not been adequately assessed is what the alternate use of time and money would be if not for religious purposes.

It is also possible to forward aspects of religious expenditures that would appear to have positive implications for modernization. The repair and building of religious edifices do provide opportunities for skilled labor. In both Indonesia and Malaysia tithes have been used for development programs. It has been argued that religious feasts fill nutritional needs of the poor which would not be supplied through other means. However, the more intriguing question centers upon whether demands to meet religious obligations foster an entrepreneurial spirit among individuals. There is evidence that some elements of the population are encouraged to increase their income in order to be able to expand their religious giving and that the high costs of some religious observances lead to pressure to produce new income. Beyond this, the ability to support religious institutions, give feasts, and make the hadj can reinforce the status of those who have already attained a certain level of affluence. Prominent members of the local society can use feasts and other religious activities to widen their contacts beyond their village or town and thus strengthen their economic and social positions. The result of all of this can mean changes in traditional means of accruing income and a reinforcement of the status of the entrepreneurial elite. Although these patterns have not been pervasive in the region, they do complicate any clear-cut assessment of the relationship of religious expenditures to modernization.

LEADERSHIP AND INSTITUTIONS

It is charged that religious personnel have been obstacles in themselves to the process of modernization. Left-wing critics and secular planners in particular have termed them parasites, described their activities as unproductive, and characterized them as poor models for the rest of society. On their part, monks, priests, and other religious leaders often see themselves as the torch-bearers of tradition, defending old values and ways from the inroads of the evils of modernization. Perceiving their traditional roles in education eroded, their local leadership challenged, and spiritual values undermined, they have often reacted by rejecting the new ways in a wholesale manner. It is not difficult to find examples of reactionary religious leadership in all five states surveyed, reinforcing the antimodern picture of religious institutions.

However, other data contradict this negative characterization. Traditionally, religious personnel have been engaged in a variety of community activities and the mosque, wat, and church have been the centers of numerous pursuits other than the spiritual. Many of these functions have positive developmental aspects. Today a small but increasing number of religious leaders have become involved in community development projects, particularly in the Philippines and Thailand. In the former, such activities are seen as fundamental by a significant portion of the Roman Catholic clergy. There have also appeared politicized elements within Islam, Christianity, and Buddhism who have encouraged a wide range of solutions to their nation's problems reflecting views across the political spectrum. While the majority of Buddhist and Muslim religious personnel and the Roman Catholic hierarchy in the Philippines remain innately conservative, change is apparent. Religious institutions and personnel can no longer be simply categorized as the torch-bearers of tradition.

POPULAR BELIEFS

Historically, Southeast Asians have been characterized as having belief systems antithetical to modernization. As noted in the second chapter, descriptions of these people as otherworldly, stultified by religion and supersition, and spiritually rather than materialistically oriented were frequent in the prewar years. This view is not dead, as exemplified by more recent charges that religious beliefs have caused the peasant to forego needed agricultural innovations. No doubt the rural Southeast Asian has not accepted change easily, but serious questions can be raised as to the reasons for this pattern. (Factors other than religion, such as those based upon the character of rural life in general or pragmatic considerations inhibiting the adoption of new innovations, have too often been translated into critiques of religion alone as the chief obstacle to change.) The intimate relationship of religion to social structure and action in the region makes quite difficult any effort to disentangle the one from the other. At many levels religious belief has been a force in delaying change, but very often as an indistinguishable part of a more complicated process.

This tendency to see religion as somehow anti-modern has been particularly misleading with regard to anti-Western or anti-imperialist positions posited by sectarian spokesmen in the prewar and postwar eras. In the colonial period religious nationalism was frequently characterized as reactionary and atavistic. Words such as "fanaticism" and "medieval" were and are used to describe these movements and their adherents.

While there were and are individuals and organizations that fit these descriptions, often religious nationalists compartmentalized their reactions to colonialism. While rejecting political, economic, and cultural domination, they also sought to harness technological change to the religious needs and values of their societies. Leaders of the YMBA, GCBA, and Sarekat Islam were not Luddites intent upon destroying Western technology. More recently this same thinking by foreign observers has led to interpretations of the Islamic resurgence in the region as being thoroughly reactionary. Certainly there are fringe elements who want to return to the times of the Prophet, but one important core to the leadership of the resurgence has come from well-educated youth, often trained overseas, who want technological change within an Islamic context. What they desire, similar to their prewar counterparts, is the elimination of Western economic, political, and cultural control and the establishment of a society based upon their own religious values.

POLITICAL MANIPULATION

The manipulation of religious symbols to achieve political goals has tended to foster modernization, although not without some serious reversals. Religious nationalism at one time provided a forceful and emotional tool to unify often disparate people within heterogeneous societies. In the prewar years it was effectively used by nationalists such as H. O. S. Tjokroaminoto and U Ottuma to rally their people against the colonial governments, while more recently conservative Thai monks have called for the elimination of the enemies of Buddhism, king, and country, all in the name of religion. However, in the postwar era religion has generally proved to be a less powerful unifying tool and, in fact, has often ultimately been a divisive factor. Not only did the independence years display sharp differences among co-religionists that had been previously hidden by unity against the common target of colonialism, but efforts to give official sanction to the faith of the dominant group have tended to lead to internal conflicts. Thus, U Nu's promulgation of Buddhism as the state religion of Burma brought about dissension and was a factor in the military coup that followed, while the attempt to emphasize Islam in Malaysia has increased fears among non-Muslims that their political and economic roles in the society were being threatened.

Southeast Asia has also experienced state-generated efforts to employ religion as a means of encouraging development, both at the local and national levels. We have previously described Thai government programs to use members of the sangha to promote community development in the villages, U Nu's attempts to sell the Pyidawtha Plan through the manipulation of the concept of merit, and the Malaysian emphasis on the modernization of the Malay as a means of protecting Islam. While often achieving some success, these programs have frequently been hampered by misunderstandings among planners and politicians as to the environment which they were supposedly changing. Like many foreign observers, those in the capital city have often displayed overly simplistic knowledge of critical factors such as the role of religious personnel, reasons for peasant action, and the degree of internalization of religious values.

It has also been apparent that religion need not seriously decline in the face of technological change. Its continued strength has at least in part been due to forces not properly recognized by earlier social scientists. Developments insufficiently foreseen included such factors as religious reactions to modernization, the employment of religious symbols, and the interaction of ethnicity and religion. Modernization was supposed to weaken religion. It has lessened the influence of religion in many cases, or has at least led to its being more compartmentalized by individuals rather than dominating their whole life experience. But for a significant portion of the population of the region it has also intensified their faith. Reacting to what are perceived to be dangers to strongly held values and traditional life-styles, people have coalesced around their faiths. As we have seen, the religious resurgence in Malaysia, Indonesia, and Thailand has selectively attacked the materialism of both capitalism and Marxism as well as the alleged immorality associated with each. This growth of religious fervor has not only been apparent among the less advantaged elements, but has also found particular favor among the educated youth. Thus, young physicists, mathematicians, and social scientists see nothing abnormal with combining undisguised support of their religions with the pursuit of their professions.

The ability of political and religious leaders to employ religious symbols was also underestimated by early observers. Neither the attractiveness of their platforms nor the apparent sincerity of their beliefs were recognized by these critics who tended to look more favorably upon secularist politicians expressing positions more closely identified with their own more Western views. To the populace, the seemingly insecure, unfamiliar, and fast-changing environment of the postwar years made them hungry for recognizable values and increasingly their leaders were prepared to play to those desires. Thus, the modernizing establishment as well as its traditionalist opposition perceived the utility of emphasizing and institutionalizing religious symbols.

Finally, the identification of particular ethnic groups with their religion has reinforced both ethnicity and faith, especially when they have perceived themselves as dominated by other religioethnic forces. Thus, this century has experienced religioethnic movements such as the Moros of the Philippines, Malay Muslims of southern Thailand, the Muslim Arakanese and Christian-led Karens of Burma, and the Ambonese of east Indonesia. Even a majority group, the Malays in Malaysia, see themselves as economically exploited by the indigenous Chinese, and have developed a Malay Muslim chauvinism which is frequently reinforced by their political leaders. This combination of sectariansim and ethnicity can be a powerful tool, easily exploited by religious and political leadership.

We cannot expect a significant diminishing of religious fervor in the immediate future in the countries we have been considering, for some of these very forces continue to remain vital and reify one another. Modernization will still confront traditional rural peoples entering the cities or experiencing the intrusion of the outside world into their villages. Much of Southeast Asia is being transformed by the expansion of more efficient means of transportation and communications, bringing rural and urban peoples closer, by the growth of modern cities with their amenities and problems and by increased industrialization and commercialization. Given past reactions of traditional societies to these challenges, we can expect the peoples of Southeast Asia to look to religion for security and identity. We can also expect governments, wishing to achieve modernization, while at the same time appeasing the demands of their constituents, to attempt to make modernization palatable to them by synthesizing it with traditional values. This was exemplified by the Malaysian "Look East" campaign which sought to pattern the country's development after Japan and Korea where it was perceived that traditional values and technological change were compatible.

Second, the youth of Southeast Asia have entered tertiary education at home and abroad at an increasing rate. As we have seen, along with gaining knowledge of Western concepts and technology, many have reaffirmed their religious commitments. The result of this may be the modernization of religious leadership in countries such as Indonesia and Malaysia as these more educated and politically aware elements become involved in religiopolitical organizations. It is also possible that this new elite may be able to bridge the gap between material modernization and spiritual values—at least some are making the effort.

Finally, communal loyalties remain strong within the region with few signs that the relationship between religion and ethnicity is weakening—even in Europe and North America expectations of the demise of communal loyalties have not come to fruition. In these circumstances we will probably see such groups in Southeast Asia continue to look to religion as a means of protecting themselves against encroaching challengers. In these communal conflicts many leaders perceive that not to modernize is to be exploited by the religions of others.

Thus, as we project into the future, religion will remain a powerful force in much of Southeast Asia, at times weakened by the process of modernization at other times strengthened. There are many circumstances in which religion will play its stereotyped role of delaying modernization, but it can also function as handmaiden to this process. However, this possibility of religion acting as a positive force for modernization needs to be viewed with caution by those hoping to manipulate it for the sake of secular goals. Without entering the debate over the desirability of modernization, it would appear useful to conclude this analysis with a review of some of the dangers attendant to employing this seemingly attractive tool.

Considerable evidence is available to discredit the characterization of religion as simply antimodern and observers should take care not to be misled by such external attributes as clothing and style. Yet, there is also the danger of not recognizing that these people have their own agendas and the politicians or planners seeking to manipulate or cooperate with them need to understand those differences. Thus, the secular modernizer must recognize that his religious counterpart may see development as a tool for sectarian ends or may want to restrict some aspects of change when they conflict with deeply held values. Modernization may not be depicted as the seemingly unmitigated good often portrayed by some of its proponents.

Second, there are important political ramifications to using religion and the religious. As the Thai secular authorities queried in the 1960s, is it desirable to politicize the clergy for the sake of development? What of the Burmese, Vietnamese, and Philippine examples of monks and priests involved in antigovernment activities? To the extent that the religious provide legitimacy to the social structure, is it desirable to give them roles different from their traditional ones? Also in the political sphere, is there a danger that by emphasizing religious symbols the government may further strengthen more radical sectarian interests? This has been a practical issue in Malaysia where federal attempts to maintain the government at the forefront of the Islamic cause through the exploitation of religious themes may also be giving credence to more fundamentalist Muslim groups considered dangerous to the state.

Finally, there is the spectre of sectarian conflict unwittingly nourished by those emphasizing religious involvement. This volume has underscored the heterogeneity of belief systems in Southeast Asia and reviewed a number of cases where the raising of religious consciousness has been a factor in sectional strife. Examples include tensions resulting from U Nu's promulgation of the Buddhist state, reactions to political support of the Islamic cause in Malaysia, and recent violence following efforts to press the Panchasila on Indonesian Muslims. Religion can play a vital role in the process of modernization, but those who seek to channel it to their particular ends must recognize the possible consequences.

Glossary

AGAMA: Religion in Indonesian-Malay

BUMIPUTERA: "Son of the Soil"—Malays and other indigenous people in Malaysia

DAKWAH (DA'WAH): Islamic missionary activity. In Malaysia primarily urban

DANA: Concept of giving in Buddhism

DUKKHA: Concept of suffering in Buddhism

FATWA: Official doctrinal ruling by an Islamic religious council which is considered binding

FITRAH: Islamic personal religious tax levied at the end of Ramedan

GOLONGAN KEPERCAYAAAN: Javanese mysticism, one of the recognized beliefs in Indonesia

GURU-NGAJI: Religious teacher

HADJ (HAJJ): Pilgrimage to Mecca—one of Five Pillars of Islam

HADJI (HAJJI): Pilgrim to Mecca

HAKIM: Islamic religious judge

HALAL: Permissible activity, particularly related to types of food

IMMAM (IMAM): Official and leader in mosque

JAWI: Modified Arabic script for Malay

KAFIR: Nonbeliever or infidel (non-Muslim)

KARMA: The law of cause and effect in Buddhism

KATHI (QADI): Islamic magistrate—in Malaysia usually deals with registration of births, deaths, etc.

KENDURI: Ritualistic religious feasts

KEPERCAYAAN: Javanese mystical beliefs

KIAYI: Islamic religious teacher

MADRASAH: Islamic religious school

MASJID: Mosque

METTA: Buddhist concept of loving kindness—the basis for not taking life

MUBALLIGHS: Islamic missionaries (Indonesia)

NATS: Animistic spirits in Burma

MUSHALLA: Islamic prayer hall

PANTJA SILA (PANCHASILA OR PANCASILA): Five principles which have been the basis of the Indonesian ideology under Sukarno and Suharto

PENGAJIAN: Village Islamic schools (Indonesia)

PENGHULU: Name given by the Dutch to the highest ranking mosque official

PESANTREN: Communal Islamic religious educational center

PONDOK: Literally hut—primary Islamic school in rural areas

PONGYIKYAUNG: Buddhist monastery (Burma)

RIBA: Interest (on money)—prohibited in Islamic doctrine

SANGHA: Buddhist monkhood

SAYADAW: Sangha leader or abbot

SELAMATAN: Rituals involving food and prayer associated with religious and life-cycle events

SURAS (SURAHS): Chapters in Koran, of which there are 114

TABLIGH: Islamic religious teaching

TANHA: Concept of desire in Buddhism

ULAMA: Learned Islamic religious leader

VINAYA: Buddhist monastic discipline

WAKAF: Islamic donations for religious purposes

WAPHRA: Buddhist holy day (Thailand)

WAT: Buddhist temple and community center

ZAKAT: Islamic religious tax—in Malaysia only enforced on padi farmers

Notes

1—Religion and Modernization

1. See, for example, Z. Kampf, *On Modernism: The Prospects for Literature and Freedom* (Cambridge: MIT Press, 1967).

2. For what has become a classic in the area, see J. Bury, *The Idea of Progress* (New York: Dover, 1932). Also see R. Nisbet, *Social Change and History* (New York: Oxford University Press, 1969).

3. For reviews of this literature, see S. Huntington, "The Change to Change: Modernization, Development and Politics," *Comparative Politics* 3 (1971): 283–322; J. Bill and R. Hardgrave, *Comparative Politics* (Columbus, Ohio: Merrill, 1973), pp. 43–83; T. Higgott, *Political Development Theory* (London: Croom Helm, 1983); R. Packenham, *Liberal America and the Third World* (Princeton: Princeton University Press, 1973); and M. Bernstein, "Modernization Theory and the Sociological Study of Development," *Journal of Development Studies* 7 (1971): 141–60.

4. D. Lerner, *The Passing of Traditional Society* (New York: Free Press, 1958).

5. D. Lerner, "Modernization: Social Aspects," in *International Encyclopedia of the Social Sciences*, ed. D. Sills (New York: Macmillan and Free Press, 1968) 10: 386–95.

6. M. Levy, *Modernization and the Structures of Society* (Princeton: Princeton University Press, 1966), pp. 35–36.

7. D. Rustow, *A World of Nations: Problems of Political Modernization* (Washington: Brookings, 1967) and C. Black, *The Dynamics of Modernization* (New York: Harper and Row, 1966).

8. J. Scarritt, *Political Development and Cultural Change Theory* (Beverly Hills: Sage, 1972), p. 11.

9. Z. Suda, "The Rate of Social Change and Modernization," in *Directions of Change*, eds. M. Attir, B. Holzner and Z. Suda (Boulder: Westview, 1981), p. 180.

10. D. McClelland, *The Achieving Society* (Princeton: Van Nostrand, 1961) and A. Inkeles and D. Smith, *Becoming Modern: Individual Change in Six Developing Countries* (Cambridge: Cambridge University Press, 1974).

11. J. Vincent, "Anthropology and Political Development," in *Politics and Change in Developing Countries*, ed. C. Leys (Cambridge: Cambridge University Press, 1969), pp.35–63.

12. L. Pye, *Aspects of Political Development* (Boston: Little Brown, 1966), pp. 30–45. He noted (1) political prerequisites of political development, (2) politics typical of an

industrial society, (3) political modernization, (4) operation of a nation-state, (5) administrative and legal development, (6) mass mobilization and participation, (7) building democracy, (8) stability and orderly change, (9) mobilization and power, and (10) part of the process of social change.

13. Quoted in Huntington, "The Change to Change," p. 303.

14. Ibid.

15. J. Coleman. "The Development Syndrome: Differentiation-Equality = Capacity," in *Crises and Sequences in Political Development,* SSRC (Princeton: Princeton University Press, 1971), pp. 73–74.

16. G. Almond and G. Powell, *Comparative Politics: A Developmental Approach* (Boston: Little Brown, 1966), p. 105.

17. A. Daimant, "The Nature of Political Development," in *Political Development and Social Change,* eds. J. Finkle and R. Gable (New York: Wiley, 1966), pp. 92–93.

18. S. Huntington, *Political Order in Changing Societies* (New Haven: Yale University Press, 1968), p. 266.

19. D. Rustow and R. Ward, eds., *Political Modernization in Japan and Turkey* (Princeton: Princeton University Press, 1964), pp. 6–7.

20. See Huntington, "The Change to Change"; Bill and Hardgrave, *Comparative Politics;* Higgott, *Political Development Theory;* Packenham, *Liberal America;* and Bernstein, "Modernizing Theory."

21. Lerner, "Modernization."

22. Bill and Hardgrave, *Comparative Politics,* p. 63.

23. See M. Weber, *The Protestant Ethic and the Spirit of Capitalism* (London: Unwin, 1930); R. Bellah, "Reflections on the Protestant Ethic Analogy in Asia," *The Journal of Social Issues* 19 (1963): 52–60; R. Bellah, ed. *Religion and Progress in Modern Asia* (New York: Free Press, 1965).

24. E. Said, *Orientalism* (New York: Pantheon, 1978).

25. Examples of such dichotomizing are presented in M. Palmer, *Dilemmas in Political Development* (Itasca, Ill: Peacock, 1973), pp. 15–26; Bill and Hardgrave, *Comparative Politics,* pp. 52–57; and J. Gusfield, "Tradition and Modernity: Misplaced Polarities in the Study of Social Change," *American Journal of Sociology* 72 (1967): 351–62.

26. P. Hauser, "Some Cultural and Personal Characteristics of the Less Developed Areas," *Human Organization* 18 (Summer 1959): 78–84.

27. F. Story, *Buddhism Answers the Marxist Challenge* (Rangoon: Burma Buddhist World Mission, n.d.), pp. 6–7.

28. Bury, *The Idea,* pp. 348–49.

29. D. Apter, *The Politics of Modernization* (Chicago: University of Chicago Press, 1966), p. 68.

30. L. Shiner, "The Concept of Secularization in Empirical Research," *Scientific Study of Religion* 6 (1967): 207–20.

31. Rustow and Ward, *Political Modernization.*

32. Lerner, "Modernization."

33. G. Almond and J. Coleman, eds., *Politics of the Developing Areas* (Princeton: Princeton University Press, 1960), p. 537.

34. R. Macridis and B. Brown, eds. *Comparative Politics: Notes and Readings,* 4th ed. (Homewood, Ill: Dorsey, 1972), pp. 387–88.

35. For example, W. W. Rostow noted that in the transitional stage of development modernization means the reduction in the role of religion. W. W. Rostow, *Politics and the Stages of Growth* (Cambridge: Cambridge University Press, 1971).

36. Black, *Dynamics, pp. 26–34.* This section is called "The Agony of Modernization."

37. Hurgronje quoted in H. Bouman, *Enige Beschowing Over de Ontwikkeling van Het Indonesiah Nationalisme op Sumatras Westkust* (Groningen: Wolters, 1949), p. 55.

38. R. Bellah, "Religious Aspects of Modernization in Turkey and Japan," *American Journal of Sociology* 64 (1958): 1–5.

39. J. G. Hardee, "Rationality and Advancing Standards and Levels of Living—A Theoretical Model of Socio-cultural Change," *Philosophical Society Review* 5 (1964): 67.

40. Lerner, *Passing of Traditional Society,* p. 45. Lerner argues that Islam simply cannot contend with the forces of modernization, but that the intellectuals may temporarily sell out to traditional forces.

41. A. Desai, "Need for Revolution of the Concept," in *Essays on Modernization of Underdeveloped Countries,* ed. A. Desai (New York: Humanities Press, 1972), pp. 458–74.

42. Quoted in M. Singer, "The Modernization of Religious Beliefs," in *Modernization: The Dynamics of Growth,* ed. W. Wiener (New York: Basic Books, 1966), pp. 55–67.

43. Nisbet, *Social Change.*

44. Almond and Coleman, *Politics of the Developing Areas.*

45. K. Deutsch, "Social Mobilization and Political Development," *American Political Science Review* 55 (1961): 493–514.

46. Huntington, *Political Order.*

47. J. LaPalombara, ed., *Bureaucracy and Political Development* (Princeton: Princeton University Press, 1963) and LaPalombara and M. Weiner, eds., *Political Parties and Political Development* (Princeton: Princeton University Press, 1966).

48. Lerner, *The Passing of Traditional Society;* Lerner, "Modernization."

49. A. Organski, *Stages of Political Development* (New York: Knopf, 1965).

50. L. Pye and S. Verba, eds., *Political Culture and Political Development* (Princeton: Princeton University Press, 1965).

51. S. Eisenstadt, *From Generation to Generation* (London: Routledge and Kegan Paul, 1956); *Modernization: Protest and Change* (Englewood Cliffs: Prentice-Hall, 1966); and *Tradition, Change and Modernity* (New York: Wiley, 1973).

52. As Huntington noted in his "The Change to Change" that there was consensus that modernization was (1) revolutionary, (2) complex, (3) systematic, (4) global, (5) lengthy, (6) phased, (7) homogenizing, (8) irreversible, and (9) progressive. There was little a Marxist could disagree with in these elements, at least in general terms.

53. E. Durkheim, *The Elementary Forms of Religious Life* (London: Allen and Unwin, 1915).

54. M. Weber, *The Protestant Ethic.*

55. Quoted in J. E. Goldthorpe, *The Sociology of the Third World* (Cambridge: Cambridge University Press, 1975), pp. 231–32.

56. B. Loomer, "Religion and the Mind of the University," in *Liberal Learning and Religion* (New York: Harpers, 1951), p. 149.

57. K. Boulding, *The Impact of the Social Sciences* (New Brunswick: Rutgers University Press, (1966), p. 87.

58. R. Bellah, "Between Religion and the Social Sciences." in *The Culture of Unbelief,* eds. R. Caporale and A. Grumelli (Berkeley: University of California Press, 1971), p. 285.

59. These data are from E. Ladd and S. Lipset, *The Divided Academy* (New York: McGraw-Hill, 1978).

60. K. Underwood, *The Church, The University and Social Policy* (Middletown, Ct.: Wesleyan University Press, 1969), p. 378.

61. Ladd and Lipset, *The Divided Academy,* pp. 112–13.

2—The Inheritance

1. E. Said, *Orientalism* (New York: Pantheon, 1978).

2. H. Isaacs, *Scratches on Our Minds* (New York: John Day, 1958), p. 37.

3. Ibid. p. 12

4. D. and B. Sardesai, *Theses and Dissertations on Southeast Asia* (Ag Zug, Switzerland: Interim Documentation Company, 1970).

5. S. Neuman and S. Singman, "The Southeast Asian Specialist: A Preliminary Report," *The American Behavioral Scientist* 5 (1962): 9–14. This report also showed that 56 of the 90 had done field research and only 16.5 percent had Ph.D.s in political science.

6. See, for example, A. Johns, "The Novel as a Guide to Indonesian Social History," *Bijdragen Tot de Taal-, Land- en Volkenkunde* 115 (1959): 232–48.

7. R. Butwell, *U Nu of Burma* (Stanford: Stanford University Press. 1963), p. 81.

8. J. Van der Kroef, "The Colonial Novel in Indonesia," *Comparative Literature* 10 (1958): 215–31.

9. See, for example, John Crawfurd, *Journal of an Embassy from the Governor General of India to the Courts of Siam and Cochin China Exhibiting a View of the Actual State of Those Kingdoms* (London: Henry Golburn. 1828).

10. J. G. D. Campbell, *Siam in the Twentieth Century* (London: Edward Arnold, 1902).

11. H. W. Smyth, *Five Years in Siam* (London: John Murray, 1898).

12. J. Bowring, *A Visit to the Philippine Islands* (London: Smith, Elder, 1859).

13. Noted in S. Alatas, *The Myth of the Lazy Native* (London: Frank Cass, 1977), pp. 25–29.

14. S. Raffles, *Memoir of the Life and Service of Sir Stamford Raffles*, 2 vols. (London: John Duncan, 1835) and T. Raffles, *The History of Java*, 2 vols. (London: Oxford Unversity Press, 1965) (originally 1817).

15. F. Swettenham, *British Malaya* (London: Allen & Unwin, 1908); *Malay Sketches* (London: Oxford University Press, 1913); and his *The Real Malay* (London: John Lane, 1907).

16. Discussed in Alatas, *Lazy Native*.

17. G. A. Malcolm, *The Government of the Philippines* (Rochester, N.Y.:Lawyers Cooperative Publishing Co., 1916) and his *Commonwealth of the Philippines* (New Century Crofts, 1936).

18. Dean C. Worcester, *The Philippines: Past and Present* (New York: Macmillan, 1914).

19. J. S. Furnivall, *Colonial Policy and Practice* (London: Cambridge University Press, 1948) and his *Netherlands India* (London: Cambridge University Press, 1941).

20. G. Orwell, *Burmese Days* (London: Gollancz, 1935).

21. H. Van Mook, *The Stakes of Democracy in Southeast Asia* (New York: Norton, 1950).

22. J. Brown, *The Dutch East* (London: Kegan, Paul, Trench, Trüber, 1914).

23. Isaacs, *Scratches on Our Minds*, p. 128.

24. Alatas, *Lazy Native*.

25. J. Dautremer, *Burma Under British Rule* (London: Fisher Unwin, 1916), p. 78.

26. J. Nisbet, *Burma Under British Rule—And Before* (London: Archibald Constable, 1901), p. 224.

27. H. Fielding Hall, *A People at School* (London: Macmillan, 1913), pp. 26–27.

28. H. Fielding Hall, *Soul of a People* (London: Macmillan, 1932), p.115.

29. Brown, *The Dutch East*, p. 10.

30. A. Walcott, *Java and Her Neighbors* (London: Putnam's Sons, 1914), p. 327.

31. C. Day, *The Dutch in Java* (London: Oxford University Press, 1966), pp. 355–56.

32. Swettenham, *British Malaya*, p. 136.

33. H. Clifford, *In Court and Kampong* (London: Richards Press, 1897), p. 19.

34. C. H. Seybold, "Nature's Gentlemen," *Asia* 37 (1937):449–51. Also see his "Malay People are Different," *Asia* 37 (1937): 514–16.

35. A. Wright and T. Reid, *The Malay Peninsula* (London: Fisher Unwin, 1912), p. 315.

36. G. J. Younghusband, *The Philippines* (London: Macmillan, 1899), pp.160–61.

37. J. Foreman, *The Philippine Islands* (London: Sampson Low, Marston & Company, 1892), p. 185.

38. A. D. Hall, *The Philippines* (New York: Street & Smith, 1898), p. 105.

39. Ibid. p. 142.

40. J. Campbell, *Siam*, pp. 227–28.

41. Quoted in H. Smith, *Five Years in Siam, pp. 23–24*.

42. E. Young, *The Kingdom of the Yellow Robe* (London: Archibald Constable, 1907), p. 138.

43. For example Justice Malcolm wrote that the Filipino was easy going and prone to imitation. "But in reality the Filipino is industrious—by that I mean industrious under the conditions in which he must live in the tropics," Malcolm, *Commonwealth*, p. 30.

44. Quoted in C. Russell and E. Rodriguez, *The Hero of the Philippines* (New York: Century, 1923), p. 187.

45. Quoted in Alatas, *Lazy Native*, p. 98.

46. Smyth, *Five Years in Siam*, pp. 23–24.

47. Brown, *The Dutch East*, p. 142.

48. A. Ireland, *The Far Eastern Tropics* (London: Archibald Constable, 1915), pp. 115–16.

49. Quoted in Alatas, *Lazy Native*, p. 55.

50. Brown, *The Dutch East*, p.10.

51. See Russell and Rodriguez, *The Hero*.

52. Brown, *The Dutch East*, pp. 156–57.

53. Campbell, *Siam*, p. 235.

54. Ibid. pp. 227–28.

55. F. Hall, *A People at School*, pp. 224–25.

56. W. Harris, *East for Pleasure* (London: Edward Arnold, 1929), pp. 31–32.

57. L. R. Wheeler, *The Modern Malay* (London: Allen and Unwin, 1928), pp. 98–99.

58. G. Gorer, *Bali and Angkor* (London: Michael Joseph, 1936), p. 40.

59. P. Coote, "Malay Psychology," *Asiatic Review* 19 (1923): 285–88.

60. J. R. Crandall, "Social Customs of Malays." *Sociology and Social Research* 12 (1928): 567–72.

61. I. Bird Bishop, *The Golden Cheronese (New York: Putnam, 1883), p. 460*.

62. H. Weinberg, *Manifest Destiny* (Baltimore: Johns Hopkins Press, 1935), pp. 289–96.

63. J. Gunther, *Inside Asia* (New York: Harpers, 1939), pp. 321 and 402.

64. Sir J. G. Scott (Shway Yoe), *The Burman* (London: Macmillan, 1896), p. 553.

65. Ibid. p. 554.

66. W. C. Purser, "Burma in Transition," *International Review of Missions* 17 (1928): 655–62.

67. Nisbet, *Burma*, pp. 153–54.

68. Campbell, *Siam*, p. 250.

69. Wheeler, *The Modern Malay* pp. 98–99.

70. Bishop, *The Golden Cheronese*, p. 461.

71. Campbell, *Siam*, p. 251.

72. In particular see the works of J. Rizal. See Russell and Rodriguez, *The Hero*.

73. F. von der Mehden, *Religion and Nationalism in Southeast Asia* (Madison: University of Wisconsin Press, 1963).

74. Wheeler, *The Modern Malay*, 99ff.

3—Patterns of Analysis

1. *Asia Yearbook 1963* (Hong Kong: Far Eastern Economic Review).

2. L. Pye, *Aspects of Political Development* (Boston: Little Brown, 1966), 33–45.

3. L. Shiner, "The Concept of Secularization in Empirical Research," *Scientific Study of Religion* 6(1967): 207–20.

4. See, for example, Pye, *Aspects of Political Development*; R. Higgott, *Political Development Theory* (London: Croom Helm, 1983); and O. C. O'Brien, "Modernization, Order and the Erosion of a Democratic Ideal: American Political Science 1960–1970," *Journal of Development Studies* 8(1972):351–78.

5. See, for example, D. Rustow and R. Ward, eds., *Political Modernization in Japan and Turkey* (Princeton: Princeton University Press), 1964.

6. For a review of the capacity variable in modernization, as well as their own support of one aspect of capacity as necessary for modernization, see J. Bill and R. Hardgrave, *Comparative Politics* (Columbus, Ohio: C. Merrill, 1973), pp.69–80.

7. J. Gusfield, "Tradition and Modernity: Misplaced Polarities in the Study of Social Change," *American Journal of Sociology* 72(1967): 351–62; R. Bendix "Tradition and Modernity Reconsidered," Comparative Studies in History and Society 9(1967): 292–346; and L. and S. Rudolph, *The Modernity of Tradition: Political Development in India* (Chicago: University of Chicago Press, 1967).

8. For example, see the careful assessment of issues involved in religion and political development in D. Smith, *Religion and Development* (Boston: Little Brown, 1970).

9. C. Glock, "The Religious Revival in America," in *Religion and the Face of America,* ed. J. Zahn (Berkeley: University of California, 1959), pp. 25–42, and R. Stark and C. Glock, *American Piety: The Nature of Religious Commitment* (Berkeley: University of California Press, 1968).

4—Basic Tenets and Modernization

1. D. Smith, *Religion and Political Development* (Boston: Little Brown, 1970).

2. Thray Sithu U Ba Khin, *What Buddhism Is* (Rangoon: Department of Religious Affairs, 1977).

3. H. Smith, *The Religions of Man* (New York: Harper and Brothers, 1958), p. 222.

4. M. Spiro, *Buddhism and Society: A Great Tradition and Its Burmese Vicissitudes* (New York: Harper and Row, 1970), pp. 425–26.

5. H. Smith, *The Religions of Man*, p. 208.

6. H. A. R. Gibb, "Islam" in *The Concise Encyclopedia of Living Faiths*, ed. R. Zaehner (New York: Hawthorne, 1959), p. 189.

7. For a discussion of zakat at the village level see R. Winzeler, "Malay Religious Society and Politics in Kelantan" (Ph.D. diss., Chicago: University of Chicago, 1970), pp. 160–63.

8. T. S. Chee, *Malays and Modernization* (Singapore: University of Singapore Press, 1977), p. 228.

9. G. Kahin, *Nationalism and Revolution in Indonesia* (Ithaca: Cornell University Press, 1952), pp. 307–309.

10. Chee, *Malays*, p. 228.

11. Kahin, *Nationalism*.

12. Malaysia, *Official Yearbook* (Kuala Lumpur: Government Printing Office, 1977), pp. 394–96.

13. Chee, *Malays*, p. 231.

14. J. Vredenbregt, "The Haddj," *Bijdragen Tot de Taal; Land-en Volkenkunde* 118 (1962):149.

15. These statistics taken from Kingdom of Saudi Arabia, *Statistical Yearbook, 1965, 1980, 1981*, and *Statistik Indonesia, 1980, 1981* (Jakarta: Biro Pusat Statistik).

16. D. Noer, *Administration of Islam in Indonesia*, Monograph Series no. 58 (Ithaca: Cornell Modern Indonesia Project, 1978) pp. 59–60.

17. M. Kuchiba, Y. Tsubouchi, and N. Maeda, eds. *Three Malay Villages: A Sociology of Paddy Growers in West Malaysia* (Honolulu: University of Hawaii Press, 1979), p. 100.

18. Noer, *Administration of Islam*, pp. 53–64.

19. Vredenbregt, "The Haddj," pp. 135–38.

20. Chee, *Malays*, p. 250 and Malaysia, Treasury, *The Expenditure Budget, 1975* (Kuala Lumpur, 1975), p. 77.

21. Vredenbregt, "The Haddj," p. 115.

22. See P. Wilson, *A Malay Village and Malaysia* (New Haven: HRAF, 1967), pp. 64–65 and 136.

23. J. Peacock, *Muslim Puritans: Reformist Psychology in Southeast Asian Islam* (Berkeley: University of California Press, 1978), pp. 104–105.

24. Vredenbregt, "The Haddj," pp. 115–17. This point later reinforced by C. Geertz in his writings, as in his *Islam Observed* (New Haven: Yale University Press, 1968).

25. For various analyses and descriptions of Buddhism, see E. Conze, *Buddhism: Its Essence and Development* (New York: Philosophical Library, 1951); P. Carus, *The Gospel of the Buddha* (Chicago: Open Court, 1909); and J. B. Pratt, *The Pilgrimage of Buddhism* (New York: Macmillan, 1928).

26. Nguyen Huy Bao, "The Impact of Religious Ideology," in *Social Research and Problems of Rural Development*, ed. Vu Quoc Thuc (Brussels: UNESCO, 1963), p. 232.

27. Spiro, *Buddhism and Society*, pp. 10–11.

28. For example, see K. Kingshill, *Ku Daeng—The Red Tomb* (Bangkok: Suriyaban, 1976), p. 186 and L. Sharp et al., eds., *Siamese Rice Village* (Bangkok: Cornell Research Center, 1953).

29. For example, Spiro, *Buddhism and Society*; C. Keyes, *The Golden Peninsula* (New York: Macmillan, 1977); and N. Jacobs, *Modernization Without Development* (New York: Praeger, 1971).

30. Jacobs, *Modernization*, pp. 241–42.

31. Quoted in Spiro, *Buddhism and Society*, p. 431.

32. Jacobs, *Modernization*, p. 240.

33. "Banking in Modern Islamic Economic Order," mimeo, n.d., n.a.

34. Chee, *Malays*. See his chapter on "Challenge and Response—The Impact of Literary Elites," pp. 184–215.

35. F. von der Mehden, *Religion and Nationalism in Southeast Asia* (Madison: University of Wisconsin Press, 1963).

36. Geertz, *Islam Observed*, p. 69.

37. There are those who would reject all interpretation, but the present intellectual consensus would not support the kind of conservative views, say, of Maryam Jameelah, an American convert living in Pakistan, who argues that "We Muslims shall grow in strength and vigor not by 'moving with the trend of time' but only by fighting against it." M. Jameelah, *Islam and Modernism* (Lahore: M. Yusuf Khan, 1966), p. 24.

38. S. Alatas, *Modernization and Social Change* (Sydney: Angus and Robertson, 1972), pp. 19–20.

5—Religious Institutions and Modernization

1. For Thailand see Somboom Suksamran, *Political Buddhism in Southeast Asia* (London: Hurst, 1977) and S. Tambiah, *World Conqueror and World Renouncer* (Cambridge University Press, 1976); for Burma see D. Smith, *Religion and Politics in Burma* (Princeton: Princeton University Press, 1965); E. Mendelson, "Religion and Authority in Modern Burma," *The World Today* (March 1960), and his *Sangha and State in Burma*, ed. J. Ferguson (Ithaca: Cornell University Press, 1975). For the Philippines see I. Alonso et al., *The Catholic Church in the Philippines Today* (Manila: Historical Conservation Society, 1968).

2. Suksamran, *Political Buddhism* pp. 42–43.

3. Ibid., p. 44.

4. H. Kaufman, *Bangkhaud: A Community Study in Thailand* (Rutland: C. Tuttle, 1977), pp. 212–13.

5. Maung Maung, *Burma and General Ne Win,* (New York: Asia, 1969), pp. 308–309.

6. *National Catholic Reporter,* September 16, 1983. To contrast this liberal criticism of Cardinal Sin see S. Del Rosario, *A Monograph on Cardinal Sin* (Quezon City: Manlapaz Publishing Company, 1980).

7. B. J. Terwiel, *Monks and Magic,* Scandinavian Institute of Asian Studies Monograph Series, no. 24, 1975 (Copenhagen, 1975).

8. C. Keyes, *The Golden Peninsula* (New York: Macmillan, 1977), pp. 317–18.

9. Tambiah, *World Conqueror,* pp. 270ff.

10. D. Pfanner, "The Buddhist Monk in Rural Burmese Society," in *Anthropological Studies in Theravada Buddhism,* Cultural Report Series no. 13, Southeast Asian Studies (New Haven: Yale University, 1966).

11. M. Moerman, "Ban Ping's Temple: The Center of a 'Loosely Structured' Society," in *Anthropological Studies.*

12. For an extensive analysis of these activities see Terwiel, *Monks and Magic.*

13. W. Klausner, "Popular Buddhism in Northeast Thailand," in *Cross-Cultural Understanding: Epistemology in Anthropology,* ed. F. Northrop and H. Livingston (New York: Harper & Row, 1964), pp. 76–92.

14. Suksamran, *Political Buddhism,* pp. 19–20.

15. H. Kaufman, *Bangkhuad,* pp. 113–15.

16. J. Ingersoll, "The Priest Role in Central Village Thailand," in *Anthropological Studies,* pp. 62–63.

17. Klausner, "Popular Buddhism," p. 75.

18. J. Schecter, *The New Face of Buddha* (New York: Coward McCann, 1967), p. 89.

19. The communists have not been consistent in their attacks on religious leadership, at times apparently considering such criticisms impolitic. Thus, care was taken in both Burma and South Vietnam in the 1960s to be moderate.

20. For varying views of sangha mobility in Thailand, see Tambiah, *World Conqueror*, pp. 288–360.

21. J. Mulder, *Monks, Merit and Motivation*, Center for Southeast Asian Studies (DeKalb: Northern Illinois University, 1969).

22. Klausner, "Popular Buddhism," pp. 82–83. This is a more extensive quote than given in Mulder.

23. Alonso, et al., *The Catholic Church*, pp. 21–25.

24. Asian Social Institute Research Department, *The Church and Development in the Philippines* (Manila: mimeo, 1975), p. 54.

25. Ibid., p. 53.

26. Ibid., p. 47.

27. Ibid., p. 56.

28. Ibid., p. 158.

29. *National Catholic Reporter*, 16 September 1983.

30. For an excellent analysis of dakwah movements in Malaysia, see J. Nagata, *The Reflowering of Malaysian Islam* (Vancouver: University of British Columbia Press, 1984).

31. Interviews with Anwar Ibrahim and ABIM Officers, 1980, 1981 and 1983.

32. See B. Boland, *The Struggle of Islam in Modern Indonesia* (The Hague: Nijhoff, 1971), pp. 191ff and Alfian, "Islamic Modernism in Indonesian Politics: The Muhammadijah during the Dutch Colonial Period (1912–1942)." Ph.D. dissertation (Madison: University of Wisconsin, 1969).

33. Lembaga Studi Pembangunan, *Laporan 1981–1982*, pp. 44–45.

34. Nagata, *The Reflowering*, p. 106.

35. K. Landon, *Siam in Transition* (Chicago: University of Chicago Press, 1939), p. 217.

36. D. Swearer, *Buddhism and Society in Southeast Asia* (Chambersburg, Penn.: Anima Books, 1981), pp. 62–65.

37. Mendelson, *Sangha and State*, pp. 265–68.

38. Swearer, *Buddhism and Society*, p. 64.

39. Asian Social Institute, *The Church and Development*, p. 119.

40. Ibid., p. 118.

6—Popular Beliefs

1. U Thittila, "The Meaning of Buddhism," *Atlantic* 201 (1958):144.

2. H. Kaufman, *Bangkhaud: A Community Study in Thailand* (Rutland: Tuttle, 1977) 183–184.

3. S. Tambiah, "The Ideology of Merit," in *Dialectics in Practical Religion*, ed. E. Leach (Cambridge Papers in Social Anthropology, London: Cambridge University Press, 1968), p. 69.

4. Tambiah, "Ideology of Merit"; and M. Spiro, *Buddhism and Society: A Great Tradition and Its Burmese Vicissitudes* (Berkeley: University of California Press, 1982).

5. Spiro, *Buddhism and Society*, p. 81.

6. M. Spiro, "Buddhism and Economic Action in Burma," *American Anthropologist* 68 (1966):1172.

7. Spiro, *Buddhism and Society*, p. 460.

8. See, for example, M. Nash, *The Golden Road to Modernity* (New York: Wiley, 1965).

9. H. Phillips, *Thai Peasant Personality* (Berkeley: University of California Press, 1965), p. 88.

10. H. Parkinson, "Non-Economic Factors in the Retardation of the Rural Malays," *Modern Asian Studies* 1 (1967):40.

11. Ibid., p. 41.

12. "Attitudes of Vigan Residents Related to Self-reliance and Fatalism," in *The Church and Development in the Philippines* (Manila: Asian Research Institute, 1975), p. 40.

13. Ibid.

14. See J. Nagata, "Muslim Entrepreneurs and the Second Malaysia Plan: Some Socio-economic Considerations," *Asia Research Bulletin* (August 1972): 1139–42.

15. S. Alatas, *Modernization and Social Change in Southeast Asia* (Sydney: Angus and Robertson, 1972), pp. 19–20.

16. F. Lynch, "Organized Religion," in HRAF, *Area Handbook on the Philippines* II (New Haven: HRAF, 1956), p. 666.

17. For a review of these developments see J. Nagata, *The Reflowering of Malaysian Islam* (Vancouver: University of British Columbia Press), 1984.

18. Anwar Ibrahim, "Islamisation—The Malaysian Experience," typed ms., December, 1982.

19. Here reference is to attacks on Hindu temples and the assault on a police station by fanatical fringe groups that sought to form an Islamic state.

20. See the *Far Eastern Economic Review* (28 November 1980).

21. M. Morfit, "Panchasila: The Indonesian State Ideology According to the New Order Government," *Asian Survey* 21 (August 1981):840.

22. Information for this section has been drawn from Soomboon Suksamran, *Buddhism and Politics in Thailand: A Study of Socio-Political Change and Political Activism of the Thai Sangha* (Singapore: Institute of Southeast Asian Studies, 1982) and D. Swearer, *Buddhism and Society in Southeast Asia* (Chambersburg, Pa.: Anima Books, 1981).

23. Suksamran, *Buddhism and Politics*, p. 96.

24. Swearer, *Buddhism and Society*, p. 57.

7—Religious Practices

1. For Malaysia see R. Winzeler, "Malay Religious Society and Politics in Kelantan," Ph.D. diss., University of Chicago, 1970. For Indonesia see R. Jay, *Javanese Villages* (Cambridge: MIT Press, 1969).

2. M. Kuchiba, Y. Tsubouchi, and N. Maeda, eds., *Three Malay Villages: A Sociology of Paddy Growers in West Malaysia* (Honolulu; University of Hawaii Press, 1979), p. 282.

3. See M. Spiro, *Buddhism and Society: A Great Tradition and Its Burmese Vicissitudes* (New York: Harpers, 1970).

4 H. Lewis, *Illocano Rice Farmers* (Honolulu: University of Hawaii Press, 1971), pp. 164ff.

5. J. Peacock, *Muslim Puritans: Reformist Psychology in Southeast Asian Islam* (Berkeley: University of California Press, 1978), p. 44.

6. D. Miles, *Cutlass and Crescent Moon* (Sydney: Center for Asian Studies, University of Sydney, 1976).

7. Spiro, *Buddhism and Society*, pp. 456ff.

8. Ibid., p. 459.

9. M. Nash, *The Golden Road to Modernity* (New York: Wiley & Sons, 1965).

10. J. Amyot, *Village Ayutthaya* (Bangkok: Chulalongkorn University, 1976), pp. 215–16.

11. P. Wilson, *A Malay Village in Malaysia* (New Haven: HRAF, 1967).

12. R. Rivera and R. McMillan, *An Economic and Social Survey of Rural Households of Central Luzon* (Manila: USOM, 1954).

13. A. Pal and R. Polson, *Rural People's Response to Change: Dumaquete Trade Area, Philippines* (Quezon City: New Day, 1973).

14. In the mid-1960s the author followed a government development officer on the east coast of Malaysia and noted that there were specific plans and price ranges depending upon the size of the mosque being built.

15. C. Keyes, *The Golden Peninsula* (New York: Macmillan, 1977).

16. Spiro, *Buddhism and Society*.

17. Nash, *The Golden Road*, p.116.

18. F. von der Mehden, "Burma's Religious Campaign Against Communism," *Pacific Affairs* 33 (1960): 290–99.

19. Kuchiba et al., *Three Malay Villages*, pp. 120–21. It was also charged that the PMIP party in Malaysia used zakat for political purposes.

20. These feasts often provided food to the poor of the village. See C. Geertz, *The Religion of Java* (Glencoe, Illinois: Free Press, 1960), pp. 81–83.

21. Keyes, *The Golden Peninsula*, p. 150.

22. Quoted in Lewis, *Illocano Rice Farmers*.

23. S. Husin Ali, *Malay Peasant Society and Leadership* (Kuala Lumpur: Oxford University Press, 1975), p. 53.

24. Keyes. *The Golden Peninsula*.

25. Miles, *Cutlass*.

26. M. Spiro, "Buddhism and Economic Action in Burma," *American Anthropologist* 68 (1966): 1167–68.

27. K. Wells, *Thai Buddhism: Its Rites and Practices* (Bangkok: The Christian Bookstore, 1960), pp. 26ff. (originally published by Bangkok Times Press, 1939).

28. Quoted in T. Agoncillo, *Revolt of the Masses* (Quezon City: University of the Philippines, 1956), pp. 152–54.

29. Wells, *Thai Buddhism*.

30. A. Pal, "The Resources, Levels of Living and Aspirations of Rural Households in Negros Oriental" (Quezon City: Community Development Research Council, University of the Philippines, 1963), pp. 197–98.

31. See, for example, A. Zarga. "Islamic Economics: An Approach to Human Welfare," in *Studies in Islamic Economics* by K. Ahmad, ed. (Jeddah: International Centre for Research in Islamic Economics, King Abdul Aziz University, 1980), pp. 3–18. He argues that fasting promotes godfearing which in turn improves moral standards, reduces corruption, and thus increases production in time.

32. G. Hainsworth, *Village-Level Modernization in Southeast Asia* (Vancouver: University of British Columbia Press, 1982), p. 22.

33. See Tibor Mende, *South-East Asia Between Two Worlds* (London: Turnstile Press, 1955), p. 12.

34. S. Espiritu and C. Hunt, eds., *Social Foundations of Community Development* (Manila: Garcia, 1964), pp. 386–89.

35. For differing views on this see B. Parkinson, "Non-Economic Factors in the Retardation of the Rural Malays," *Modern Asian Studies* 1 (1967): 31–46 and W. Wilder,

"Islam, Other Factors and Malay Backwardness: Comments on an Argument," *Modern Asian Studies* 2 (1968): 155–64.

36. F. Sycip, "Factors Related to Acceptance or Rejection of Innovations," in *Social Foundations*, by Espiritu and Hunt, pp. 399–403.

37. For analyses and descriptions of the choices facing the peasant see M. Moerman, *Agricultural Change and Peasant Choice in a Thai Village* (Berkeley: University of California Press, 1968) and B. Mabry, "Peasant Economic Behavior in Thailand," *Journal of Southeast Asian Studies* 10 (September 1979): 400–19. In the author's own experience the Thai villager is likely to be more pragmatic in his choices than his Burmese and Javanese counterparts, but only in degree.

38. M. A. Jaspen, *Traditional Medical Theory in Southeast Asia* (Hull: University of Hull, 1969); R. Winzeler, "Malay Religious"; and Phya Anuman Rajadhon, *Life and Ritual in Old Siam*, ed. and trans. by W. Gedney (New Haven: HRAF, 1961).

39. United Nations, *Statistical Yearbook for Asia and Pacific* (Bangkok: ECAFE, 1973).

40 Keyes, *The Golden Peninsula*, p. 130.

41 A. Wichmann, "Burma: Agriculture, Population and Buddhism," *American Journal of Economics and Sociology* 24 (January 1965): 76.

42 T. O. Ling, "Buddhist Factors in Population Growth and Control," *Population Studies* 33 (1969): 53–60.

43. B. Ryan, "Institutional Factors in Sinhalese Fertility," *Milbank Memorial Fund Quarterly* 30 (1952): 359–81.

44. See, for example, F. Lorimer, *Culture and Human Fertility* (Paris: UNESCO, 1954), pp. 186–87.

45. Ling, "Buddhist Factors," p. 57 quotes A. Satterthwaite, "Family Research in Thailand: A Report to the Ministry of Public Health." M. Potts and P. Selman, *Society and Fertility* (Estover, Plymouth: MacDonald and Evans, 1979), pp. 312–13.

46. M. Concepcion and P. Smith, "The Demographic Situation in the Philippines: An Assessment in 1977," East-West Population Institute, no 44, 1977, pp. 32–40 and R. Cuyugan and M. Bonifacio, "Rural Philippine Communities: A Case Study of the Impact of Industrialization," Discussion Paper 69 (Kyoto: Center for Southeast Asian Studies, Kyoto University, 1973), pp. 64–65. A similar type of study in Malaysia showed that 85 percent of the respondents had heard of family planning, 45.2 percent were interested in further information and 12.5 percent of the total (21 out of 168) practiced it. B. Makhzani, "Gombak: A Malay Village East of Kuala Lumpur," CSEAS Discussion Paper 77, 1974, p. 22.

47. R. M. Thomas, "Attitudes Toward Birth Control for Bandung," *Indonesia* 4 (1967): 74–87 and W. Flieger and I. Pagtolun-an, "An Assessment of Fertility and Contraception in Seven Philippine Provinces, "East-West Population Institute, no. 77, 1981, pp. 80–81.

48. Burma, *Report of the Committee to Consider and Report upon Buddhist Pupils in Vernacular Lay Schools under Buddhist Management* (Rangoon: Government Printing office, 1931), pp. 2–3.

49. "Statistics on the Development of Islam in Indonesia," *Islam in Indonesia Today* (Jakarta: Dewan Kemamuran Masjid Indonesia, n. d.), p. 63.

50. K. Orr, M. Billah, and B. Lazarusli, "Education for this Life or for the Life to Come," *Indonesia* 23 (1977): 129. For the considerable variety of Islamic schools in Indonesia see B. Boland, *The Struggle of Islam in Modern Indonesia* (Hague: Nijhoff, 1971), pp. 112–23.

51. R. Lester, *Theravada Buddhism in Southeast Asia* (Ann Arbor: University of Michigan Press, 1973), p. 115.

52. For example, a survey of ranking school systems in three villages in Indonesia found pesantren and madrasah at the bottom of the prestige list of nine. M. Thomas, *Social Strata in Indonesia: A Study of West Java Villages* (Jakarta: V. Antarkarya, 1975), pp. 106–107.

53. Thomas also found in his survey that this is not a general view and that only 23 percent disagreed with the proposition that too high a level of schooling caused a person to be less obedient in the area of religion. Ibid., p. 119. Orr, et al., "Education for this Life," p. 153, found religious parents stating, "The sekolah desar [state school] prepares children for life here and now, the madrasah prepares them for the life hereafter."

54. S. Siddique, "Moulding the Muslim Mind," *Asiaweek, 20 March 1981.*

55. T. S. Chee, "Sociological Aspects of Religious Reform in Malaya," *Review of Southeast Asian Studies* 1 (1971): 31.

56. J. Nguyen Van Khoi, "A Study of the Impact of Christian Missionaries on Education in Thailand, 1662–1910," Ph.D. diss., St. Louis University, 1972. While very favorable to the missionary cause, this is a very useful work.

57. See, for example, P. Pedersen, *Batak Blood and Protestant Soul* (Grand Rapids: Eerdmans, 1970), p. 88.

58. Ibid., pp. 292–93 and D. Noer, *The Modernist Muslim Movement in Indonesia 1900–1942* (Singapore: Oxford University Press, 1973), pp. 44, 78–80, 93, 127, 306, and 314.

59. Quoted in J. Nguyen Van Khoi, "Christian Missionaries," pp. 297–98.

8—Religious Symbols

1. For background on the Pyidawtha Plan see Burma, *Pyidawtha Conference* (Rangoon: Ministry of Information, 1952); Burma, *Pyidawtha* (Rangoon: Economic and Social Board of New Burma, 1954); F. Trager, *Building a Welfare State In Burma, 1948–1956* (New York: Institute of Pacific Relations, 1958); L. Walinsky, *Economic Development in Burma 1951–1960* (New York: Twentieth Century Fund, 1962); and H. Tinker, *The Union of Burma,* 4th ed. (London: Oxford University Press, 1967).

2. There was extensive research on this as part of the development of the NEP. See the regular reviews of the NEP and particularly the Mid-term Review of the Second Malaysia Plan in 1973. Also D. Snodgrass, *Inequality and Economic Development in Malaysia* (Kuala Lumpur: Oxford University Press, 1980).

3. During the 1960s then Deputy Prime Minister Tun Razak called for Malays to follow the "Protestant work ethic" and the UMNO-dominated Alliance was competing with PMIP-controlled state governments in terms of how much they could offer the Malays. See F. R. von der Mehden, "Religion and Politics in Malaya," *Asian Survey* 3(December 1963): 609–15.

4. For aspects of the "Look East" policy, see the *New Straits Times, March 31, April 6, June 14, July 15 and 16, August 29, October 14, November 8, 10, 24.*

5. For information on Islamic banking in Malaysia see the *Far Eastern Economic Review,* 17(December 1982) and *Asiaweek, 30 July 1982.* Later information from interviews with Anwar Ibrahim, June 1983.

6. Quoted in *Asia Record, 1982.*

7. Non-Malay business people were worried regarding a host of incidents in which overly zealous civil servants made business operations more difficult, or a lack of communications made the situation appear far worse than it was.

8. S. Tambiah, *World Conqueror and World Renouncer* (London: Cambridge University Press, 1976); S. Suksamran, *Political Buddhism in Southeast Asia* (London: Hurst, 1977); and C. Keyes, "Buddhism and National Integration in Thailand," *Journal of Asian Studies,* XXX (1971): 551–68.

9. Suksamran, *Political Buddhism,* pp. 65–67. For other information on this program see Tambiah, *World Conqueror.*

10. Suksamran, *Political Buddhism,* pp. 80–81.

11. Ibid., p. 81.

12. Ibid., p. 87.

13. J. Ingersol, "The Priest Role in Central Village Thailand," in *Anthropological Studies of Theravada Buddhism,* ed. M. Nash et al., Cultural Report Series no. 13, Southeast Asian Studies (New Haven: Yale University, 1966), pp. 62–63.

14. M. Moerman, "Ban Ping's Temple: The Center of Loosely Structured Society," in *Anthropological Studies.* It should be recognized that Moerman found the monks in the village very young and the "abbot" was only twenty-two.

15. F. R. von der Mehden, *Religion and Nationalism in Southeast Asia* (Madison: University of Wisconsin Press, 1963).

16. Quoted in ibid., p. 12.

17. Ibid.

18. Ibid.

19. Ibid., pp. 54–71.

20. *New Burma,* 16 September 1921.

21. San C. Po, *Burma and the Karens* (London: Elliot Stock, 1928), p. 58.

22. U Tun Pe, "Christian Missions in Burma," *Burma Speaks* (Rangoon: Government Printing Office, 1950), pp. 85–86.

23. Tin Aung, "The Burmese Struggle for Independence," *New Burma Weekly,* 3 January 1959.

24. T. Kalaw, "State Paper No. 12." *Philippine Social Sciences Review* 3(1930): 208.

25. Figures provided in J. Carroll, *Changing patterns of Social Structure in the Philippines 1896–1963* (Quezon City: Ateneo de Manila University Press, 1968), p. 39.

26. United States, *Reports of the Philippines Commission* (Washington: Government Printing Office, 1900) I, p. 57.

27. Ibid., pp. 57–58.

28. Quoted in J. LeRoy, *The Americans in the Philippines* (Boston: Houghton Mifflin, 1914), I, p. 62.

29. T. Kalaw, "State Paper No 6." *Philippine Social Science Review* 3(1930): 75–77.

30. United States, *Philippine Commission,*p. 43.

31. See F. von der Mehden, *Religion and Nationalism.* pp. 115–46.

32. Carroll. *Changing Patterns.* p. 37.

33. D. Liang, *The Development of Philippine Political Parties* (Hong Kong: South China Morning Post, 1939), p. 28n.

34. See F. R. von der Mehden, *Comparative Political Violence* (Englewood Cliffs: Prentice-Hall, 1973).

35. Anti-Christian attacks took place in the 1960s in Sulawesi, Java, and Sumatra. See H. L. Oey, *Indonesia Facing the 1980s* (Hull: Europress, 1979), pp. 192–213. Muslim political leaders of the time were also actively questioning foreign assistance to missionaries. See ibid., and Lukman Harun's comments to Parliament, July 10, 1967, mimeo, RIMA 4(January, June 1970), p. 42, and L. Harun, "Christians in the Eyes of Muslims," presented at 1983 Theological Consultation of Indonesia, February 14, 1983, mimeo.

36. G. G. Kahin, *Nationalism and Revolution in Indonesia* (Ithaca: Cornell University Press, 1952), p. 125.

37. Quoted in C. Penders, *The Life and Times of Sukarno* (London: Sidgwick and Jackson, 1974), p. 169.

38. Maung Maung, *Aung San of Burma* (Hague: Nijhoff, 1962), p. 127.

39. Quoted in R. Butwell, *U Nu of Burma* (Stanford: Stanford University Press, 1963), p. 65.

40. D. Smith, *Religion and Politics in Burma* (Princeton: Princeton University Press, 1965), p. 165.

41. Ibid., p. 171.

42. Ibid., pp. 230–80 and F. R. von der Mehden, "The Rise and Fall of the Buddhist State in Burma," Mid-West Conference on Asian Affairs, 1964. According to Ba Maw, "U Nu tried to replace political with religious faith and all sorts of superstitions" and this led to his downfall. S. Banerji, "Burma: Coup and Aftermath," *Far Eastern Economic Review* 12 April 1962, pp. 97–101.

43. F. R. von der Mehden, "Burma's Religious Campaign against Communism," *Pacific Affairs*, 33(1960): 290–99.

44. See J. Schecter, *The New Face of Buddha* (New York: Coward-McCann, 1967), pp. 124–29; Maung Maung, *Burma and General Ne Win* (New York: Asia, 1969), pp. 306–09.

45. F. R. von der Mehden, "Islam in Public Life in Malaysia," Asia Society (in press).

46. Tunku Abdul Rahman, *Looking Back* (Kuala Lumpur: Pustaka Antara, 1977), p. 265.

47. W. Vella, *Chaiyo!* (Honolulu: University of Hawaii Press, 1978), p. 216.

48. Sarit also sought to control the sangha in the name of unity; if a deterioration of Buddhism endangered law and order and particularly threatened national stability, his government would have to intervene in sangha affairs "to the utmost degree." S. Suksamran "Political Patronage and Control over the Sangha," Discussion Paper 28 (Singapore: Institute of Southeast Asian Studies, 1981), p. 40.

49. Suksamran, *Political Buddhism*, p. 93.

50. See Tambiah, *World Conqueror;* Keyes, "Buddhism and National Integration"; and Suksamran, *Political Buddhism*.

51. Suksamran, *Political Buddhism*, p. 94.

52. Ibid., p. 52.

53. Tambiah, *World conqueror*, p. 443.

54. Suksamran, *Political Buddhism, p. 104.*

55. Ibid.

9—Impact of Modernization

1. Data for the following were taken from: Burma: *Allegemeine Statistik Des Auslandes, Burma* (Stuttgart: Kohlhammer, 1972) and *Statistical Yearbook of Burma, 1961* (Rangoon: Central Statistics and Economics Department, 1963); Indonesia: *Statistik Indonesia* (Jakarta: Biro Pusat Statistik, various years) and *Statistical Pocketbook of Indonesia, 1941* (Batavia: Central Bureau of Statistics, 1947); Malaysia: *Malaysia Yearbook* (various years) and *Monthly Statistical Bulletin* (Kuala Lumpur: Department of Statistics, various years); Philippines: *Philippine Yearbook* (Manila: National Census and Statistics Office, various years) and M. Mangahas, *Measuring Philippine Development* (Development Academy of the Philippines, 1976); Thailand: *Statistical yearbook, Kingdom of Thailand* (Bangkok: Department of Government Statistics, various years) and *Statistical Handbook of Thailand, 1979* (Bangkok: National Statistical Office, 1979).

2. C. Glock, "The Religious Revival in America," in *Religion and the Face of America,* ed. by J. Zahn (Berkeley: University of California Extension, 1959), pp. 25–42, and R. Stark

and C. Glock, *American Piety: The Nature of Religious Commitment* (Berkeley: University of California Press, 1968).

3. S. Espiritu and C. Hunt, *Social Foundations of Community Development* (Manila: Garcia, 1964), p. 389.

4. J. Peacock, *Muslim Puritans: Reformist Psychology in Southeast Asian Islam* (Berkeley: University of California Press, 1978), p. 44.

5. D. Smith, *Religion and Politics in Burma* (Princeton: Princeton University Press, 1965), pp. 296–97.

6. S. Tambiah, *World Conqueror and World Renouncer* (Cambridge: Cambridge University Press, 1976), p. 266.

7. J. Mulder, *Monks, Merit and Motivation,* Special Report Series no. 1 (DeKalb: Center for Southeast Asian Studies, Northern Illinois University, 1969), pp. 34–36.

8. Tambiah, *World Conqueror, pp. 267–68.*

9. *Islam in Indonesia Today* (Jakarta: Dewan Kemakmuran Masjid Indonesia, n.d.), p. 62.

10. J. Carroll, *Changing Patterns of Social Structure in the Philippines* (Quezon City: Ateneo de Manila University Press, 1968), pp. 37 and 142.

11. R. Butwell and F. R. von der Mehden, "The 1960 Elections in Burma," *Pacific Affairs* 33(1960): 144–57.

12. C. Caldarola, "Thailand: A Sacred Society in Modern Garb," in *Religion and Societies: Asia and the Middle East,* ed. C. Caldarola (Boston: Mouton, 1982), pp. 371–406.

13. F. R. von der Mehden, "Islam in Public Life in Malaysia," Asia Society (in press).

14. *New Straits Times,* 30 September 1982, and personal interviews with PAS members, 1981 and 1982.

15. E. Rosenthal, *Islam in the Modern Nation State (Cambridge: Cambridge University Press, 1965), pp. 291–92.*

16. G. Means, "Malaysia: Islam in a Plural Society," in *Religion and Societies,* ed. C. Caldarola, pp. 471–72.

17. J. Howell, "Indonesia: Searching for Consensus," in *Religion and Societies,* ed. C. Caldorola, pp. 497–548.

Bibliography

Agoncillo, T. *Revolt of the Masses*. Quezon City: University of the Philippines, 1956.

Ahmad, K. *Studies in Islamic Economics*. Jeddah: International Centre for Research in Islamic Economics, King Abdul Aziz University, 1980.

Alatas, S. *Modernization and Social Change*. Sydney: Angus and Robertson, 1972.

_____ . *The Myth of the Lazy Native*. London: Frank Cass, 1977.

Alfian. "Islamic Modernism in Indonesian Politics: The Muhammadijah during the Dutch Colonial Period (1912–1942)." Ph.D. Dissertation. Madison: University of Wisconsin, 1969.

Ali, S. *Malay Peasant Society and Leadership*. Kuala Lumpur: Oxford University Press, 1975.

Almond, G., and Coleman, J., eds. *Politics of the Developing Areas*. Princeton: Princeton University Press, 1960.

Almond, G., and Powell, G. *Comparative Politics: A Developmental Approach*. Boston: Little Brown, 1966.

Alonso, I., et al. *The Catholic Church in the Philippines Today*. Manila: Historical Conservation Society, 1968.

Amyot, J. *Village Ayutthaya*. Bangkok: Chulalongkorn University, 1976.

Anthropological Studies in Theravada Buddhism, Cultural Report Series no. 13, Southeast Asian Studies. New Haven: Yale University, 1966.

Apter, D. *The Politics of Modernization*. Chicago: University of Chicago Press, 1966.

Asian Social Institute Research Department. *The Church and Development in the Philippines*. Manila: mimeo, 1975.

Attir, M., Holzner, B., and Suda, Z., eds. *Directions of Change*. Boulder: Westview, 1981.

Balkhin, Thray Sithu U. *What Buddhism Is*. Rangoon: Department of Religious Affairs, 1977.

Banerji, S. "Burma: Coup and Aftermath." *Far Eastern Economic Review* 12 April 1962:97–101.

Bellah, R. "Religious Aspects of Modernization in Turkey and Japan." *American Journal of Sociology* 64(1958):1–5.

————. "Reflections on the Protestant Ethic Analogy in Asia." *The Journal of Social Issues* 19(1963):52–60.

————, ed. *Religion and Progress in Modern Asia.* New York: Free Press, 1965.

Bendix, R. "Tradition and Modernity Reconsidered." *Comparative Studies in History and Society* 9(1967):292–346.

Bernstein, M. "Modernization Theory and the Sociological Study of Development." *Journal of Developmental Studies* 7(1971):141–60.

Bill, J., and Hardgrave, R. *Comparative Politics.* Columbus, Ohio: Merrill, 1973.

Bishop, I. Bird. *The Golden Cheronese.* New York: Putnam, 1883.

Black, C. *The Dynamics of Modernization.* New York: Harper and Row, 1966.

Boland, B. *The Struggle of Islam in Modern Indonesia.* The Hague: Nijhoff, 1971.

Boulding, K. *The Impact of the Social Sciences.* New Brunswick: Rutgers University Press, 1966.

Bouman, H. *Enige Beschowing Over De Ontwikkeling Van Het Indonesiah Nationalisme Op Sumatras Westkust.* Groningen: Wolters, 1949.

Bowring, J. *A Visit to the Philippine Islands.* London: Smith, Elder, 1859.

Brown, J. *The Dutch East.* London: Kegan, Paul, Trench, Truber, 1914.

Burma. *Report of the Committee to Consider and Report Upon Buddhist Pupils in Vernacular Lay Schools Under Buddhist Management.* Rangoon: Government Printing Office, 1931.

Burma. *Pyidawtha Conference.* Rangoon: Ministry of Information, 1952.

Burma. *Pyidawtha.* Rangoon: Economic and Social Board of New Burma, 1954.

Bury, J. *The Idea of Progress.* New York: Dover, 1932.

Butwell, R. *U Nu of Burma.* Stanford: Stanford University Press, 1963.

Butwell, R., and von der Mehden, F. "The 1960 Elections in Burma." *Pacific Affairs.* 33(1960):144–57.

Caldarola, C., ed. *Religion and Societies: Asia and the Middle East.* Boston: Mouton, 1982.

Campbell, J. G. D. *Siam in the Twentieth Century.* London: Edward Arnold, 1902.

Caporale, R. and Grumelli, A., eds. *The Culture of Unbelief.* Berkeley: University of California Press, 1971.

Carroll, J. *Changing Patterns of Social Structure in the Philippines.* Quezon City: Ateneo de Manila University Press, 1968.

Carus, P. *The Gospel of the Buddha.* Chicago: Open Court, 1909.

Castles, L. *Religion, Politics and Economic Behavior in Java: The Kudus Cigarette Industry.* Cultural Report Series no. 15. Southeast Asian Studies. New Haven: Yale University, 1967.

Chee, T. "Sociological Aspects of Religious Reform in Malaya." *Review of Southeast Asian Studies* 1(1971).

————. *Malays and Modernization.* Singapore: University of Singapore Press, 1977.

Clifford, H. *In Court and Kampong.* London: Richards Press, 1897.

Conze, E. *Buddhism: Its Essence and Development.* New York: Philosophical Library, 1951.

Concepcion, M., and Smith, P. "The Demographic Situation in the Philippines: An Assessment in 1977." East-West Population Institute, no. 44, 1977.

Coote, P. "Malay Psychology." *Asiatic Review* 19(1923):285–88.

Crandall, J. R. "Social Customs of Malays." *Sociology and Social Research* 12 (1928):567–72.

Crawfurd, J. *Journal of an Embassy from the Governor General of India to the Courts of Siam and Cochin China Exhibiting a View of the Actual State of Those Kingdoms.* London: Henry Golburn, 1828.

Cuyugan, R., and Bonifacio, M. "Rural Philippines Communities: A Case Study of the Impact of Industrialization." Discussion Paper 69. Kyoto: Center for Southeast Asian Studies, Kyoto University, 1973.

Dautremer, J. *Burma Under British Rule.* London: Fisher Unwin, 1916.

Day, C. *The Dutch in Java.* London: Oxford University Press, 1966.

Desai, A., ed. *Essays on Modernization of Underdeveloped Societies.* New York: Humanities Press, 1972.

Deutsch, K. "Social Mobilization and Political Development," *American Political Science Review.* 55(1961):493–514.

Durkheim, E. *The Elementary Forms of Religious Life.* London: Allen and Unwin, 1915.

Eisenstadt, S. *From Generation to Generation.* London: Routledge and Paul, 1956.

––––––. *Modernization: Protest and Change.* Englewood Cliffs: Prentice-Hall, 1966

––––––. *Tradition, Change and Modernity.* New York: Wiley, 1973.

Espiritu, S., and Hunt, C. *Social Foundations of Community Development.* Manila: Garcia, 1964.

Finkle, J., and Gable, R., eds. *Political Development and Social Change.* New York: Wiley, 1966.

Foreman, J. *The Philippine Islands.* London: Sampson Low, Marston & Company, 1892.

Furnivall, J. S. *Colonial Policy and Practice.* London: Cambridge University Press, 1948.

––––––. *Netherlands India.* London: Cambridge University Press, 1941.

Geertz, C. *The Religion of Java.* Glencoe: Free Press, 1960.

––––––. *Islam Observed.* New Haven: Yale University Press, 1968.

Goldthorpe, J. *The Sociology of the Third World.* Cambridge: Cambridge University Press, 1975.

Gorer, G. *Bali and Angkor.* London: Michael Joseph, 1936.

Gunther, J. *Inside Asia.* New York: Harpers, 1939.

Gusfield, J. "Tradition and Modernity: Misplaced Polarities in the Study of Social Change." *American Journal of Sociology* 72(1967):351–62.

Hainsworth, G. *Village-Level Modernization in Southeast Asia.* Vancouver: University of British Columbia Press, 1982.

Hall, A. D. *The Philippines.* New York: Street & Smith, 1898.

Hall, H. Fielding. *A People at School.* London: Macmillan, 1913.

––––––. *Soul of a People.* London: Macmillan, 1932.

Hardee, J. "Rationality and Advancing Standards and Levels of Living—A Theoretical Model of Socio-Cultural Change." *Philosophical Society Review* 5(1964):54–69.

Harris, W. *East for Pleasure*. London: Edward Arnold, 1929.

Hauser, P. "Some Cultural and Personal Characteristics of the Less Developed Areas." *Human Organization* 18(1959):78–84.

Higgott, T. *Political Development Theory*. London: Croom Helm, 1983.

HRAF. *Area Handbook of the Philippines*. New Haven: HRAF, 1956.

Huntington, S. *Political Order in Changing Societies*. New Haven: Yale University Press, 1968.

————. "The Change to Change: Modernization, Development and Politics." *Comparative Politics* 3(1971):283–322.

Inkeles, A., and Smith, D. *Becoming Modern: Individual Change in Six Developing Countries*. Cambridge: Harvard University Press, 1974.

Ireland, A. *The Far Eastern Tropics*. London: Archibald Constable, 1915.

Isaacs, H. *Scratches on our Minds*. New York: John Day, 1958.

Islam in Indonesia Today. Jakarta: Dewan Kemakmuran Masjid Indonesia, n.d.

Jacobs, N. *Modernization Without Development*. New York: Praeger, 1971.

Jameelah, M. *Islam and Modernism*. Lahore: M. Yusuf Khan, 1966.

Jaspan, M. *Traditional Medical Theory in Southeast Asia*. Hull: University of Hull, 1969.

Jay, R. *Javanese Villages*. Cambridge: MIT Press, 1969.

Johns, A. "The Novel as a Guide to Indonesian Social History." *Bijdragen Tot De Taal-, Land- En Volkenkunde* 115(1959):232–48.

Kahin, G. *Nationalism and Revolution in Indonesia*. Ithaca: Cornell University Press, 1952.

Kampf, Z. *On Modernism: The Prospects for Literature and Freedom*. Cambridge: MIT Press, 1967.

Kaufman, H. *Bangkhaud: A Community Study in Thailand*. Rutland: C. Tuttle, 1977.

Keyes, C. "Buddhism and National Integration in Thailand." *Journal of Asian Studies* 30(1971):551–67.

————. *The Golden Peninsula*. New York: Macmillan, 1977.

Kingshill, K. *Ku Daeng-The Red Tomb*. Bangkok: Suriyaban, 1976.

Kuchiba, M., Tsubouchi, Y., and Maeda, N., eds. *Three Malay Villages: A Sociology of Paddy Growers in West Malaysia*. Honolulu: University of Hawaii Press, 1979.

Ladd, E. and Lipset, S. *The Divided Academy*. New York: McGraw Hill, 1978.

Landon, K. *Siam in Transition*. Chicago: University of Chicago Press, 1939.

LaPalombara, J., ed. *Bureaucracy and Political Development*. Princeton: Princeton University Press, 1963.

LaPalombara, J., and Weiner, M., eds. *Political Parties and Political Development*. Princeton: Princeton University Press, 1966.

Leach, E., ed. "Dialectics in Practical Religion." *Cambridge Papers in Social Anthropology*. London: Cambridge University Press, 1968.

Lerner, D. *The Passing of Traditional Society*. New York: Free Press, 1958.

————. "Modernization: Social Aspects." *International Encyclopedia of the Social Sciences*, edited by D. Sills, vol. 10, pp. 386–95. New York: Macmillan & Free Press, 1968.

LeRoy, J. *The Americans in the Philippines*. Boston: Houghton Mifflin, 1914.

Lester, R. *Theravada Buddhism in Southeast Asia*. Ann Arbor: University of Michigan Press, 1973.

Levy, M. *Modernization and the Structures of Society*. Princeton: Princeton University Press, 1966.

Leys, C., ed. *Politics and Change in Developing Countries*. Cambridge: Cambridge University Press, 1969.

Liang, D. *The Development of Philippine Political Parties*. Hong Kong: South China Morning Post, 1939.

Ling, T. "Buddhist Factors in Population Growth and Control." *Population Studies* 23(1969):53–60.

Loomer, B. "Religion and the Mind of the University." In *Liberal Learning and Religion, edited by A. Wilder*. New York: Harpers, 1951.

Lorimer, F. *Culture and Human Fertility*. Paris: UNESCO, 1954.

Mabry, B. "Peasant Economic Behavior in Thailand." *Journal of Southeast Asian Studies* 10(1979):400–19.

Macridis, R., and B. Brown, Eds. *Comparative Politics: Notes and Readings*. 4th ed. Homewood, Illinois: Dorsey, 1972.

Makhzani, B. "Gombak: A Malay Village East of Kuala Lumpur." CSEAS Discussion Paper no. 77, Kyoto, 1974.

Malcolm, G. A. *The Government of the Philippine Islands*. Rochester, N.Y.: Lawyers Cooperative Publishing Co., 1916.

————. *Commonwealth of the Philippines*. New York: Appleton, Century Crofts, 1936.

Maung Maung. *Burma and General Ne Win*. New York: Asia, 1969.

McClelland, D. *The Achieving Society*. Princeton: Van Nostrand, 1961.

Mende, T. *South-East Asia Between Two Worlds*. London: Turnstile Press, 1955.

Mendelson, E. "Religion and Authority in Modern Burma." *The World Today* (1960):110–18.

————. *Sangha and State in Burma*. Edited by J. Ferguson. Ithaca: Cornell University Press, 1975.

Miles, D. *Cutlass and Crescent Moon*. Sydney: Center for Asian Studies, University of Sydney, 1976.

Moerman, M. *Agricultural Change and Peasant Choice in a Thai Village*. Berkeley: University of California Press, 1968.

Morfit, M. "Panchasila: The Indonesian State Ideology According to the New Order Government." *Asian Survey* 21(1981):838–51.

Mulder, J. *Monks, Merit and Motivation*, Northern Illinois University. Special Report Series no. 1. Dekalb: Center for Southeast Asian Studies, 1969.

Nagata, J. "Muslim Entrepreneurs and the Second Malaysia Plan: Some Socio-economic Considerations." *Asia Research Bulletin* (August 1972):1139–42.

————. *The Reflowering of Malaysian Islam*. Vancouver: University of British Columbia Press, 1984.

Nash, M. *The Golden Road to Modernity*. New York: Wiley, 1965.

Neuman, S., and Singman, S. "The Southeast Asia Specialist: A Preliminary Report." *The American Behavioral Scientist* 5(1962):9–14.

Nguyen Van Khoi. "A Study of the Impact of Christian Missionaries on Education in Thailand, 1662–1910." Ph.D. dissertation, St. Louis University, 1972.

Nisbet, J. *Burma Under British Rule—and Before*. London: Archibald Constable, 1901.

Nisbet, R. *Social Change and History*. New York: Oxford University Press, 1969.

Noer, D. *The Modernist Muslim Movement in Indonesia 1900–1942*. Singapore: Oxford University Press, 1973.

_____ . *Administration of Islam in Indonesia*, Monograph Series no. 58. Ithaca: Cornell Modern Indonesia Project, 1978.

Northrop, F., and Livingston, H. *Cross-Cultural Understanding: Epistemology in Anthropology*. New York: Harper and Row, 1964.

Organski, A. *Stages of Political Development*. New York: Knopf, 1965.

Orr, K., Billah, M., and Lazarusli, B. "Education for this Life or for the Life to Come." *Indonesia* 23(1977).

Orwell, G. *Burmese Days*. London: Gollancz, 1935.

Packenham, R. *Liberal America and the Third World*. Princeton: Princeton University Press, 1973.

Pal, A., and Polson, R. *Rural Peoples' Response to Change: Dumaquete Trade Area, Philippines*. Quezon City: New Day, 1973.

Palmer, M. *Dilemmas of Political Development*. Itasca, Illinois: Peacock, 1973.

Parkinson, B. "Non-Economic Factors in the Retardation of the Rural Malays." *Modern Asian Studies* 1(1967):31–46.

Peacock, J. *Muslim Puritans: Reformist Psychology in Southeast Asian Islam*. Berkeley: University of California Press, 1978.

Pedersen, P. *Batak Blood and Protestant Soul*. Grand Rapids: Eerdmans, 1970.

Penders, C. *The Life and Times of Sukarno*. London: Sidgwick and Jackson, 1974.

Phillips, H. *Thai Peasant Personality*. Berkeley: University of California Press, 1965.

Po, San C. *Burma and the Karens*. London: Elliot Stock, 1928.

Potts, M., and Selman, P. *Society and Fertility*. Estover, Plymouth: MacDonald and Evans, 1979.

Pratt, J. *The Pilgrimage of Buddhism*. New York: Macmillan, 1928.

Purser, W. "Burma in Transition." *International Review of Missions* 17(1928):655–62.

Pye, L. *Aspects of Political Development*. Boston: Little, Brown, 1966.

Pye, L., and Verba, S., eds. *Political Culture and Political Development*. Princeton: Princeton University Press, 1965.

Raffles, S. *Memoir of the Life and Service of Sir Stamford Raffles*. London: John Duncan, 1835.

Raffles, T. *The History of Java*. London: Oxford University Press, 1965 (originally 1817).

Rahman, T. A. *Looking Back*. Kuala Lumpur: Pustaka Anatara, 1977.

Rivera, G., and McMillan, R. *An Economic and Social Survey of Rural Households of Central Luzon*. Manila: United States Operations Mission, 1954.

Rosenthal, E. *Islam in the Modern Nation State*. Cambridge: Cambridge University Press, 1965.

Rostow, W. *Politics and the Stages of Growth.* Cambridge: Cambridge University Press, 1971.

Rudolph, L. and S. *The Modernity of Tradition: Political Development in India.* Chicago: University of Chicago Press, 1967.

Russell, C., and Rodriguez, E. *The Hero of the Philippines.* New York: Century, 1923.

Rustow, D. *A World of Nations: Problems of Political Modernization.* Washington: Brookings, 1967.

Rustow, D., and Ward, R., eds. *Political Modernization in Japan and Turkey.* Princeton: Princeton University Press, 1964.

Ryan, B. "Institutional Factors in Sinhalese Fertility." *Milbank Memorial Fund Quarterly* 30(1952):359–81.

Said, E. *Orientalism.* New York: Pantheon, 1978.

Sardesai, D. and B. *Theses and Dissertations on Southeast Asia.* Ag Zug Switzerland: Interim Documentation Company, 1970.

Scarritt, J. *Political Development and Cultural Change Theory.* Beverly Hills: Sage, 1972.

Schecter, J. *The New Face of Buddha.* New York: Coward-McCann, 1967.

Scott, Sir J. G. (Shway Yoe). *The Burman.* London: Macmillan, 1896.

Seybold, C. H. "Malay People are Different." *Asia.* 37(1937):514–16.

―――― . "Nature's Gentlemen." *Asia* 37(1937):449–51.

Sharp, L. et al., eds. *Siamese Rice Village.* Bangkok: Cornell Research Center, 1953.

Shiner, L. "The Concept of Secularization in Empirical Research." *Scientific Study of Religion* 6(1967):207–20.

Siddique, S. "Some Malay Ideas on Modernization, Islam and Adat." Master's Thesis, University of Singapore, 1972.

―――― . "Moulding the Muslim Mind." *Asiaweek* 20, March 1981.

Smith, D. *Religion and Politics in Burma.* Princeton: Princeton University Press, 1965.

―――― . *Religion and Political Development.* Boston: Little, Brown, 1970.

Smith, H. *The Religions of Man.* New York: Harper and Brothers, 1958.

Smyth, H. W. *Five Years in Siam.* London: John Murray, 1898.

Snodgrass, D. *Inequality and Economic Development in Malaysia.* Kuala Lumpur: Oxford University Press, 1980.

Spiro, M. "Buddhism and Economic Action in Burma." *American Anthropologist* 68(1966):1163–73.

―――― . *Buddhism and Society: A Great Tradition and Its Burmese Vicissitudes.* New York: Harper and Row, 1970.

SSRC. *Crises and Sequences in Political Development.* Princeton: Princeton University Press, 1971.

Stark, R., and Glock, C. *American Piety: The Nature of Religious Commitment.* Berkeley: University of California Press, 1968.

Story, F. *Buddhism Answers the Marxists' Challenge.* Rangoon: Burma Buddhist World Mission, n.d.

Suksamran, S. *Political Buddhism in Southeast Asia.* London: Hurst, 1977.

―――― . *Buddhism and Politics in Thailand: A Study of Socio-Political Change and Political Activism of the Thai Sangha.* Singapore: Institute of Southeast Asian Studies, 1982.

Swearer, D. *Buddhism and Society in Southeast Asia.* Chambersburg, Pa.: Anima Books, 1981.

Swettenham, F. *The Real Malay.* London: John Lane, 1907.

———. *British Malaya.* London: Allen and Unwin, 1908.

———. *Malay Sketches.* London: John Lane, 1913.

Tambiah, S. *World Conqueror and World Renouncer.* Cambridge: Cambridge University Press, 1976.

Terwiel, B. *Monks and Magic,* Scandinavian Institute of Asian Studies Monograph Series no. 24, Copenhagen, 1975.

Thittila, U. "The Meaning of Buddhism." *Atlantic* 201(1958):142–45.

Thomas, M. *Social Strata in Indonesia: A Study of West Java Villages.* Jakarta: V. Antarkarya, 1975.

Thomas, R. "Attitudes Toward Birth Control for Bandung." *Indonesia* 4(1967).

Tin Aung. "The Burmese Struggle for Independence." *New Burma Weekly.* 3 January 1959.

Tinker, H. *The Union of Burma.* 4th Ed. London: Oxford University Press, 1967.

Trager, F. *Building a Welfare State in Burma, 1948–1956.* New York: Institute of Pacific Relations, 1958.

Tun Pe, U. "Christian Missions in Burma." *Burma Speaks.* Rangoon: Government Printing Office, 1950.

Underwood, K. *The Church, the University and Social Policy.* Middletown: Wesleyan University Press, 1969.

United States. *Reports of the Philippines Commmission.* Washington: Government Printing Office, 1900.

Van der Kroef, J. "The Colonial Novel in Indonesia." *Comparative Literature* 10(1958):215–31.

Van Mook, H. *The Stakes of Democracy in Southeast Asia.* New York: Norton, 1950.

Vella, W. *Chaiyo!* Honolulu: University of Hawaii Press, 1978.

von der Mehden, F. "Burma's Religious Campaign Against Communism." *Pacific Affairs* 33(1960):290–99.

———. *Religion and Nationalism in Southeast Asia.* Madison: University of Wisconsin Press, 1963.

———. "Religion and Politics in Malaya." *Asian Survey* 3(1963):609–15.

———. "Islam in Public Life in Malaysia." Asia Society, in press.

Vredenbregt, J. "The Haddj." *Bijdragen Tot De Taal-Land-En Volkenkunde* 118 (1962):91–154.

Vu Quoc Thuc, ed. *Social Research and Problems of Rural Development.* Brussels: UNESCO, 1963.

Walcott, A. *Java and Her Neighbors.* London: Putnam's Sons, 1914.

Walinsky, L. *Economic Development in Burma 1951–1960.* New York: Twentieth Century Fund, 1962.

Weber, M. *The Protestant Ethic and the Spirit of Capitalism.* London: Unwin, 1930.

Weinberg, H. *Manifest Destiny.* Baltimore: Johns Hopkins Press, 1935.

Weiner, M., ed. *Modernization: The Dynamics of Growth.* New York: Basic Books, 1966.

Wells, K. *Thai Buddhism: Its Rites and Practices*. Bangkok: The Christian Bookstore, 1960.

Wheeler, L. R. *The Modern Malay*. London: Allen and Unwin, 1928.

Wichmann, A. "Burma: Agriculture, Population and Buddhism." *American Journal of Economics and Sociology* 24(1965):71–83.

Wilder, W. "Islam, Other Factors and Malay Backwardness: Comments on an Argument." *Modern Asian Studies* 2(1968):155–64.

Wilson, P. *A Malay Village and Malaysia*. New Haven: HRAF, 1967.

Winzeler, R. "Malay Religious Society and Politics in Kelantan." Ph.D. dissertation, University of Chicago, 1970.

Worcester, Dean C. *The Philippines: Past and Present*. New York: Macmillan, 1914.

Wright, A., and Reid, T. *The Malay Peninsula*. London: Fisher Unwin, 1912

Young, E. *The Kingdom of the Yellow Robe*. London: Archibald Constable, 1907.

Younghusband, G. J. *The Philippines*. London: Macmillan, 1899.

Zaehner, R., ed. *The Concise Encyclopedia of Living Faiths*. New York: Hawthorne, 1959.

Zahn, J. *Religion and the Face of America*. Berkeley: University of California Extension, 1959.

Index

RELIGION AND MODERNIZATION IN SOUTHEAST ASIA

was composed in 10-point Harris Fototronic TxT Palatino and leaded 2 points
by Skillful Means Press;
printed sheet-fed offset on 50-pount, acid free Glatfelter B-31 Natural,
Smyth sewn and bound over 80-point binder's boards in Holliston Roxite B,
also adhesive bound with paper covers
by Thomson-Shore, Inc.;
with paper covers printed in 2 colors
by Thomson-Shore, Inc.;
and published by

SYRACUSE UNIVERSITY PRESS
SYRACUSE, NEW YORK 13244-5160